50 HIKES
IN THE ADIRONDACK
MOUNTAINS

50 HIKES
IN THE ADIRONDACK
MOUNTAINS

FIRST EDITION

Bill Ingersoll

THE COUNTRYMAN PRESS

A division of W. W. Norton & Company

Independent Publishers Since 1923

AN INVITATION TO THE READER

Over time trails can be rerouted and signs and landmarks altered. If you find that changes have occurred on the routes described in this book, please let us know so that correction s may be made in future editions. The author and publisher also welcome other comments and suggestions. Address all correspondence to:

Editor, 50 Hikes Series
The Countryman Press
500 Fifth Avenue
New York, NY 10110

All photographs by the author
Maps by Michael Borop (sitesatlas.com)
Map data provided by The New York State Department of Environmental Conservation

For information about permission to reproduce selections from this book, write to Permissions, The Countryman Press, 500 Fifth Avenue, New York, NY 10110

For information about special discounts for bulk purchases, please contact W. W. Norton Special Sales at specialsales@wwnorton.com or 800-233-4830

Manufacturing by Versa Press
Series book design by Chris Welch
Production manager: Gwen Cullen

The Countryman Press
www.countrymanpress.com

A division of W. W. Norton & Company, Inc.
500 Fifth Avenue, New York, NY 10110
www.wwnorton.com

978-1-68268-303-3 (pbk.)

10 9 8 7 6 5 4 3 2 1

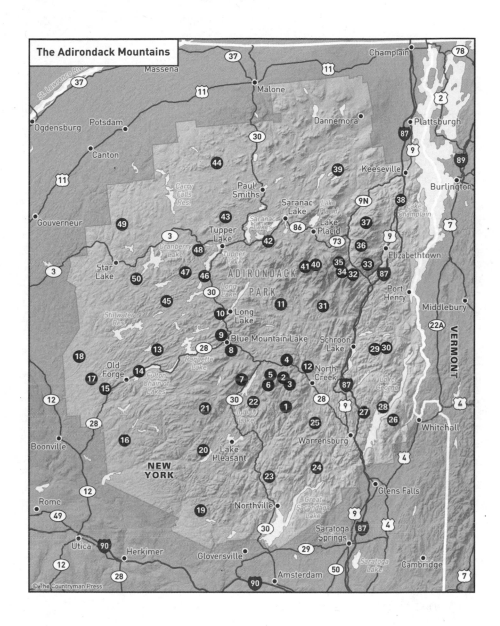

Contents

Hikes at a Glance

Hike	Region	Nearest Town	Distance (miles)	Mountain Vista
1. Siamese Ponds via the East Branch Sacandaga River	Central Adirondacks	Bakers Mills	12	
2. Peaked Mountain via Thirteenth Lake	Central Adirondacks	North Creek	7	✓
3. Botheration Pond Loop	Central Adirondacks	North Creek	7.1	✓
4. OK Slip Falls	Central Adirondacks	Indian Lake	6.4	
5. John and Clear Pond Loop	Central Adirondacks	Indian Lake	5.2	
6. Chimney Mountain	Central Adirondacks	Indian Lake	2.2	✓
7. Snowy Mountain	Central Adirondacks	Indian Lake	7.6	✓
8. Cascade and Stephens Ponds	Central Adirondacks	Blue Mountain Lake	7.4	
9. Castle Rock	Central Adirondacks	Blue Mountain Lake	3.5	✓
10. Owls Head Mountain	Central Adirondacks	Long Lake	6.2	✓
11. Great Camp Santanoni	Central Adirondacks	Newcomb	8.8	
12. Moxham Mountain	Central Adirondacks	Minerva	5.2	✓
13. Constable Pond, Chub Lake, Queer Lake Loop	Southwestern Adirondacks	Eagle Bay	8.5	
14. Bald Mountain	Southwestern Adirondacks	Eagle Bay	1.8	✓
15. Middle Settlement Lake	Southwestern Adirondacks	Old Forge	6.7	
16. Twin Lakes and November Falls	Southwestern Adirondacks	Forestport	6.4	
17. Pine Lake	Southwestern Adirondacks	Brantingham Lake	5.6	
18. Gleasmans Falls	Southwestern Adirondacks	Lowville	8	
19. North Creek Lakes	Southern Adirondacks	Caroga Lake	10.3	
20. T Lake	Southern Adirondacks	Piseco	6.6	✓
21. West Canada Lake Loop	Southern Adirondacks	Speculator	20.5	
22. Long Pond	Southern Adirondacks	Speculator	7.2	
23. Murphy, Middle, and Bennett Lakes	Southern Adirondacks	Wells	6.7	
24. Hadley Mountain	Southern Adirondacks	Hadley	3.2	✓

Lean-to	Fire Tower	Waterfall	Historic Site	Back-packing	Families	Notes
✓				✓		Wilderness hike along a river to a remote pond
				✓		Beautiful shoreline hike leads to a stunning mountain vista
			✓	✓		Four-season loop with multiple side trip options
		✓			✓	Hike to an overlook of an iconic waterfall
✓			✓	✓	✓	Short loop hike through historic site and past two ponds
					✓	Short, moderate climb to interesting geological feature
	✓					Strenuous hike to the highest peak south of Newcomb
✓		✓		✓		Two lean-tos and a small cascade
					✓	Highly attractive view from a small, rocky summit
	✓					Fire tower summit with great views of the western region
✓			✓	✓	✓	Historic Great Camp on the shore of a backcountry lake
					✓	Multiple views from a single climb
✓				✓		Loop hike connecting four wilderness lakes
	✓				✓	Great hike for children
✓			✓	✓		Classic hike to a scenic lean-to
		✓	✓	✓		Visit a former source of water for the state's canal system
✓				✓		Peaceful pond in an often-overlooked area
		✓			✓	Walk along a wild river and its rugged gorge
				✓		Explore a little-known area with prime backpacking potential
✓		✓		✓		Hike to a remote pond and one of the tallest waterfalls
✓			✓	✓		A favorite backpacking loop in the West Canada headwaters
				✓	✓	Gentle hike to a pond with great swimming
✓			✓	✓	✓	Great introduction to backpacking
	✓				✓	Classic fire tower hike

Hike	Region	Nearest Town	Distance (miles)	Mountain Vista
25. Crane Mountain	Southern Adirondacks	Johnsburg	3.6	✓
26. Sleeping Beauty	Southeastern Adirondacks	Lake George	4.3	✓
27. Cat and Thomas Mountains	Southeastern Adirondacks	Lake George	7.4	✓
28. Tongue Mountain Loop	Southeastern Adirondacks	Lake George	12.8	✓
29. Pharaoh Lake Wilderness Loop	Southeastern Adirondacks	Ticonderoga	13.5	
30. Treadway Mountain	Southeastern Adirondacks	Ticonderoga	7.6	✓
31. Boreas Ponds	Northeastern Adirondacks	North Hudson	7	✓
32. Dix Mountain via the Boquet River	Northeastern Adirondacks	Keene Valley	13.8	✓
33. Giant and Rocky Peak Ridge Traverse	Northeastern Adirondacks	Keene Valley	10.5	✓
34. Pyramid and Gothics Loop	Northeastern Adirondacks	Keene Valley	12.7	✓
35. Lower Wolf Jaw via Bennies Brook Slide	Northeastern Adirondacks	Keene Valley	11.1	✓
36. Hurricane Mountain	Northeastern Adirondacks	Keene	6.4	✓
37. Jay Range	Northeastern Adirondacks	Jay	8.2	✓
38. Poke-O-Moonshine Mountain	Northeastern Adirondacks	Keeseville	3.6	✓
39. Silver Lake Mountains	Northeastern Adirondacks	Ausable Forks	1.8	✓
40. Avalanche Pass and the MacIntyre Range	Northern Adirondacks	Lake Placid	11.7	✓
41. Indian Pass	Northern Adirondacks	Lake Placid	10	
42. Ampersand Mountain	Northern Adirondacks	Saranac Lake	5.2	✓
43. Floodwood Mountain	Northern Adirondacks	Paul Smiths	3.4	✓
44. Azure Mountain	Northern Adirondacks	Paul Smiths	1.8	✓
45. Lake Lila and Frederica Mountain	Western Adirondacks	Tupper Lake	9.2	✓
46. Winding Falls Loop	Western Adirondacks	Tupper Lake	6.6	
47. Hitchins Pond Overlook	Western Adirondacks	Tupper Lake	6.8	✓
48. Mount Arab	Western Adirondacks	Tupper Lake	2	✓
49. Grass River Waterfalls	Western Adirondacks	Cranberry Lake	4.8	
50. High Falls Loop	Western Adirondacks	Wanakena	16.3	

Lean-to	Fire Tower	Waterfall	Historic Site	Back-packing	Families	Notes
			✓	✓		"The High Peak of the Southern Adirondacks"
			✓	✓	✓	Charming little mountain with a fairy tale name
					✓	Loop hike over two scenic mountains
✓				✓		One of the best ridge hikes in the Adirondacks
✓		✓	✓	✓		Backpacking loop to nine ponds
✓				✓	✓	Outstanding views from a summit of quartz
			✓	✓		Explore a new addition to the High Peaks Wilderness
✓				✓		Follow a river to a magnificent peak
				✓		Outstanding ridgeline hike with 9,400 feet in elevation change
		✓				Rugged and highly scenic hike in the High Peaks
✓		✓		✓		Climb a "trail" created in 2011 by a hurricane
	✓					Bare summit with 360-degree views
						Traverse a ridgeline with expansive views
✓	✓			✓	✓	Great views of the Adirondacks and Green Mountains
					✓	Excellent short hike with photogenic views
✓		✓		✓		Exceptional loop through rugged terrain
✓		✓	✓	✓		Point-to-point hike past enormous cliffs
						Short but steep climb to view of the Saranac Lakes
					✓	Attractive little mountain near the Fish Creek Ponds
	✓				✓	Short fire tower hike in a secluded part of the park
✓			✓	✓	✓	Hike or canoe to a small mountain with a great view
		✓		✓		Outstanding spring hike along a new trail loop
			✓	✓	✓	Hike through a large bog to a scenic rock ridge
	✓				✓	Easy fire tower hike for all
		✓	✓		✓	Eight short walks to large waterfalls
✓		✓		✓		Explore the wilds of the Oswegatchie River

Preface

I t's hard to believe that I have been in the guidebook business for nearly twenty years. I began as a young, inexperienced hiker in 1997, fresh out of college and completely blown away by this concept called "wilderness." I made a couple embarrassing mistakes before I realized that some of the information I needed—specifically, where to go and the best way to get there—had been collated for me and published in book form. I read all of Barbara McMartin's guides, and in 2000 I became one of her assistants. The first book with my name on the cover came out in 2001, and there have been many more since then.

Being a guidebook writer has given me the pretext I needed to systematically explore every region of the 6-million-acre Adirondack Park. Granted, I probably would've found the motivation to do that anyway, but the books have challenged me to become the most knowledgeable person I can be—and they have provided an outlet for sharing that knowledge with others.

You can search online for information on a hike, and the collective wisdom of the Internet will inundate you with a virtual mountain of trip reports and photo blogs.

ON THE TRAIL TO PEAKED MOUNTAIN

But the act of flipping through the pages of a printed book will provide you with answers to questions you never knew you should ask. While looking up a reference to, say, Indian Pass, you may also accidentally learn about Long Pond, a completely different adventure in a part of the park you've never visited before. Suddenly you're planning two adventures instead of one.

For me, writing 50 *Hikes in the Adirondack Mountains* was an opportunity to revisit dozens of old friends: the West Canada Lakes, Crane Mountain, Gothics, Winding Falls, and more than forty other places that I have come to know well over the years. Looking back at the list of the fifty hikes, I see only four that were completely new discoveries for me—that is, trails I had never hiked before. I'll leave what those four were to your imagination.

By writing this book, I am giving you the inside scoop on some of my favorite places. I'd hate very much to return and find them trashed by careless and thoughtless people. These are my friends, spots I've come to love, and I am entrusting them to your care. Treat them with the respect they deserve.

The process of revisiting these friends (and getting acquainted with some new ones) has been fun. In this book you'll see photos of two of my canine companions: Lexie, who lived to be a sixteen-year-old adventure dog; and Bella, the young pit bull I adopted in 2017 to share my travels. I was also joined on the trail by my good friend Greg Smith, as well as by members of my Adirondack Wilderness Explorers meetup group: Gary Kapps, Kalie Wolmering, Ed Hart, Sherrie Bishop, Jeffrey Levitt, Craig McGowan, and many others. Janelle Hoh joined me on a number of adventures while I was scouting routes for this book, and her companionship and trail knowledge has proven to be especially welcome.

It is my hope that these fifty hikes become more than just scenic destinations for you. May you also come to regard them as friends, taking a special interest in their future.

Introduction

In your hands is a guide to fifty hikes in New York's Adirondack Park. It is not a ranking of the fifty best hikes, or a listing of my fifty favorite hikes, or a guide to the fifty biggest mountains, or anything of that nature. This book is not a catalog of superlatives but a menu of ideas, intended to introduce you to a wide variety of adventures distributed throughout this wilderness park.

This is a book about the largest state park in America—one that is larger than many national parks. At six million acres in size, the Adirondack Park covers an area as large as several states, with natural environments including quaking bogs, pristine lakes, and alpine summits. This is a lived-in park, with dozens of hamlets and thousands of year-round residents. It is a place to reconnect with nature, climb a mountain, paddle to an island, backpack without crossing a road for a weekend or a week, and discover hidden places that few people choose to see.

About half of this park is privately owned land, a category including everything from family camps to working farms to microbreweries to ski resorts to industrial timberlands. This is a place where people have been living and working for generations, with a year-round population of about 130,000 people. In this respect, the Adirondack Park differs greatly from most parks of its size.

The other half is the state-owned Forest Preserve, public land with some of the strongest legal protections anywhere. The preserve was created by statute in 1885 in response to cut-and-run logging practices that were threatening to denude much of the landscape. At the time, it was common practice for many loggers to acquire small tracts of land, harvest the merchantable timber, and then move on without paying the property taxes. In fact, much of the land that constituted the original Forest Preserve had been these logged-over lots acquired at tax sales.

The Adirondack Park itself was established in 1892 after years of study. The original park boundary, traditionally called the "Blue Line," included a much smaller area at the time. It encircled what is now the southwestern quadrant of the Adirondack region, where human settlement had barely made a dent in the forest. This region had been popularized in the years after the Civil War as a wilderness retreat, where vacationers could hire a guide and travel the backcountry waterways for weeks at a time. The Blue Line would be expanded several times in the twentieth century, reaching its current size in 1972.

Despite the establishment of the preserve and the park, there was still concern in the late nineteenth century that lumber interests might gain access to the protected state lands. In 1894, the voters of the state took this protection even further when they approved Article VII, Section 7 in a referendum. This amendment to the state's Constitution declared that the "lands of the State, now owned or hereafter acquired, constituting the Forest Preserve as now fixed by law, shall be forever kept as wild forest lands. They shall not be leased, sold,

LONG POND AND ITS BACKDROP OF ROCK

or exchanged, or be taken by any corporation, public, or private, nor should the timber thereon be sold, removed, or destroyed." This "forever wild clause" has since been renumbered Article XIV, but it is still enthusiastically supported by the citizens of the state.

Today the Forest Preserve is roughly 3 million acres in size, with parcels scattered throughout the park. Some of these parcels are just small, isolated lots, but there are also vast roadless regions. These include twenty areas protected as wilderness, in accordance with Adirondack Park Agency guidelines modeled after the 1964 Wilderness Act. Five of these areas are far larger than any federal wilderness in the northeastern United States, and this high level of protection is one thing that distinguishes the Adirondacks from its neighboring mountain ranges.

So what are the Adirondack Mountains? The region is an area of geological uplift in the northern portion of New York State, created by an unknown force that has caused the earth to bulge upward like a giant bubble. This uplift has exposed layers of metamorphic rocks that are a billion years old—resulting in a relatively new mountain range made with truly ancient building materials.

Because of this uplift, the Adirondacks are one of the world's few round mountain ranges, radiating rivers in every direction. Ecologically speaking, the region has strong ties to the northern Appalachians in nearby New England, making the Adirondacks an integral part of the multi-state Northern Forest. Geologically, however, the Adirondacks are separate from the Appalachians, which are a linear mountain range formed by tectonic actions.

Native Americans were no strangers to the Adirondacks. They hunted and trapped in the interior, and they knew its waterways well. When white settlers began penetrating the region in the 1790s, they were often following old "Indian trails" in the absence of established roads. A few of the river valleys were suitable for farming, and it did not take long for people to discover pockets of iron and graphite in the eastern foothills. Therefore, there are several sections of the Adirondack Park with long and rich human histories.

But in between these pockets of civilization were vast stretches of forest. In some cases the forests were cleared for farming, or to fuel blast furnaces and iron forges. Early logging operations were small in scale, with numerous mills taking advantage of local resources. These mills often produced a specific product in addition to lumber, such as clothespins, broom handles, barrels, or veneer wood for furniture and musical instruments. Later, there was a brief period of time when tanneries flourished, taking advantage of a chemical found naturally in hemlock bark.

Logging was conducted on larger scales within the watersheds of the Hudson and Ausable Rivers. Wealthy lumbermen constructed mills large enough to support the mass production of lumber and pulp, strategically located at Glens Falls and Ausable Forks. This made it possible to harvest spruce logs at distant points in the Adirondack wilderness and transport them by river. It's been many decades since loggers conducted the last log drives, but this practice remains a key component of the regional identity.

Much of the Forest Preserve was assembled from the former holdings of these large corporations, including the J. & J. Rogers Co., based in Ausable

Forks, which at one point operated in what is now the High Peaks region; and International Paper and Finch, Pruyn & Co., both of which still operate paper mills in Glens Falls. The process of adding to the preserve is ongoing, with several potential acquisitions still in the queue.

This has resulted in a lot of turf to explore, and the fifty hikes described in this book barely scratch the surface of what is possible. The Adirondack Forest Preserve is a wild place, with deep wilderness recesses that are miles from the nearest road, as well as a long list of destinations so easily accessible that you can visit them in the space between breakfast and lunch. This guidebook includes examples of both extremes, as well as a healthy sampling of what lies between.

The selection of hikes is also intended to take you through a medley of natural features. Of course, there are all the mountain summits, from the forested domes with their solitary rock ledges to the peaks scarred by fire and culminating in the alpine summits, with their fragile communities of rare plants. But the Adirondacks are more than just a mountain range, and so this guide will lead you to the rivers, the wetlands, and the lakes and ponds that characterize the region. Expect to encounter old growth forests in addition to the younger stands on the recent acquisitions.

Several of the trails included herein are hardly secrets; they are swarmed by dozens or even hundreds of people on any summer weekend. Other routes are hardly known at all. But this is all part of the paradox of the Adirondack Park: it is a pocket of wilderness in one of the most heavily populated corners of North America, within a short drive of millions of people. You are invited to explore it

and come to know it—and in so doing, we hope that you will come to cherish it and help protect it for future generations.

HOW TO USE THIS GUIDEBOOK

This book is intended to be an introduction to the outdoors, providing basic information on where to find a variety of choice hikes suitable for a range of skill levels. Most of the routes are based on marked and maintained trails, with these exceptions: trails that were still in construction as of this writing, a handful of unmarked trails that should be well enough used that anyone can find them with just a little bit of guidance, and one or two off-trail bushwhacks to nearby features not accessed by the main trail.

Each hike description is summarized with the following data points:

Total distance: This is the total walking distance of the hike, expressed in miles, measured from the point you set off from the trailhead to the point you return. So if the trail leads to a pond 3 miles in the woods, the total distance of the hike is 6 miles. I personally measured all of these trails with a hand-held GPS (global positioning system) device, so the data I provide here is independent of any other source. Don't be surprised if the distances noted in this book differ from trail signs or other published sources.

Hiking time: This is intended to be the minimal hiking time required to complete a hike, *not* including time to stop and take lots of pictures or eat a big lunch on the summit. The figures provided here are based on an average walking speed of 2 miles per hour—slower on steep slopes, but faster when walking on a well-built roadway with no obstacles. Obviously, the time each person spends on a trail is going to vary greatly, but hopefully the estimates provided here will offer a useful gauge.

Elevation change and vertical rise: Two terms are used, depending on the hike. "Vertical rise" refers to the net elevation gain when climbing a mountain, from its foot to the top. But since many of the trails in this book aren't that straightforward, topographically speaking, a substitute measurement is often provided. "Elevation change" refers to the total amount of climbing and descending on a trail, and it is invoked when a particular trail is notoriously hilly in both directions. Often I use the term "rolling terrain" to describe the elevation change, and in these cases, I mean that the trail is generally hilly but lacks any major inclines worth measuring.

Trailhead GPS coordinates: These are latitude and longitude coordinates for the trailhead parking areas, which some readers might find useful in lieu of driving directions, especially in this age of smartphones and dashboard GPS navigation systems. I strongly recommend that you read the narrative driving directions anyway, because some of the roads leading to these hikes are only seasonally maintained, and a small number might not be suitable for all vehicles.

In addition, each route includes driving directions to the trailheads, labeled **Getting There**. I tried to keep these as straightforward as possible, beginning from main highways or well-known landmarks; some prior knowledge of the location of the park's major hamlets will be useful. Many of the trailheads are located in remote areas, and I have tried to mention all of the special hazards you might encounter along the way (i.e., roads that aren't plowed in the winter,

those that might require high ground clearance, and so forth).

TERMS OF ART

As a writer, I'm not a big fan of jargon, so I try my best to limit my usage of it. Nevertheless, hiking does come with its own set of "terms of art," unique expressions that are almost unavoidable when writing a guidebook such as this. Here is a brief glossary of some of the terms used in this guidebook:

Access road. This is a catchall term that could mean one of two things: (1) a public right-of-way to a remote trailhead parking area, or (2) a private right-of-way across state land.

Bushwhack. An off-trail hike through the woods, in which the hiker navigates his or her own way to a destination. The ability to bushwhack opens a whole new set of possibilities for hikers eager to explore new places, but this is not intended to be a bushwhacking guidebook. Only a small number of bushwhacks are described herein, mostly as suggestions to augment certain trail-based hikes by seeking out a nearby destination hidden in the woods.

Cairn. A stack of rocks used to mark a trail across an open summit.

Campground. As used in this guidebook, *campground* refers to a developed area intended for mass recreation, with available running water and other amenities. A fee is charged for the use of its facilities.

Campsite. As used in this guidebook, *campsite* refers to a primitive, backcountry camping area. Most come with a little more than a fire ring and room for up to three tents; some of the more posh sites might even feature a picnic table and a privy. Most campsites are free to use and available on a first-come basis.

A site is **designated** if it bears a yellow disk indicating it has been approved by DEC. Campsites that lack this disk could be legally suspect.

Canoe carry. A marked trail leading from one waterway to another (called a *portage* in some other regions).

Col. This is the low spot on a ridge-line between two summits. Many mountains in the Adirondacks have multiple summits, so the word "col" is a useful way to describe the gap as you hike from one knob to the next.

Conservation easement. Private land on which public rights have been acquired by the state.

Department of Environmental Conservation (DEC). This is the state agency in charge of the day-to-day management of the Adirondack Forest Preserve.

Fall line. The route that running water typically takes, straight down a slope. When an older style hiking trail climbs the fall line, the slope is usually steep and there is almost always water erosion present.

Fire tower. This is a steel structure constructed circa 1917–1920 as a fire observation station. Although many were removed in the 1970s, quite a few still remain. Fire towers are no longer used to spot fires, but most are still maintained for public recreational access. On some mountains, there are no views except from the fire tower.

Height of land. For a trail that rises over part of a mountain before going down the other side, this term refers to the highest point on the trail.

Herd path. Alternate term for an *unmarked trail*, as defined below. The term "herd path" typically refers to a trail that seems to have been created accidentally by people hiking the same route over and over. Often these are side

DESIGNATED CAMPSITE AT PHARAOH LAKE

trails leading to an interesting view. Some longer herd paths may be faint and vaguely defined.

High Peaks. The forty-six mountains first climbed by Bob Marshall, George Marshall, and Herb Clark. At the time all of the mountains were believed to be greater than 4,000 feet in elevation, although later surveys proved that four were actually shorter. Most people aspiring to become "46ers" still abide by the traditional list.

Inlet. A stream flowing into a lake or pond.

Jug-handle loop. A side trail that detours off the main route, visits a side

LEAN-TO AT SAMPSON LAKE

encounter old routes built by lumbermen. Early logging roads were little more than wagon trails—narrow and primitive. Many modern hiking trails can trace their origins to logging roads of this nature. In later decades, as the logging industry became more mechanized, the roads became more heavy duty; these newer-style roads are wider and may even have a gravel surface. By describing a trail as "an old logging road," I am saying that it is a bit wider and straighter than a typical footpath, while at the same time providing insight into the trail's origin.

Marked trail. Official state trails in the Adirondacks are marked with colored plastic disks and yellow-on-brown wooden signs. Other organizations may also mark trails for public use on their property. The distinction being made here is that a marked trail is intended to be self-evident, so that even novice hikers may find their way.

Outlet. The stream that flows out of a lake or pond.

Plantation. A stand of trees planted by hand in the early twentieth century. The trees are not always in even rows, but they are always of a uniform age and they consist of only a handful of species: white pine, red pine, Scotch pine, or Norway spruce. Early conservationists would create these plantations when they were eager to reforest an old clearing of some kind, often an abandoned farm.

Point-to-point hike. A route that begins at one trailhead and ends at another. Also called a "through hike."

Puncheon. A small wooden bridge over a patch of mud, constructed with planks or with a log split lengthwise in two. Also called "bog bridging."

Scree wall. A row of small rocks placed by stewards on the alpine

destination, and then returns to the main trail at another point. On a map, such a side trail resembles the handle on a jug.

Lean-to. This is a three-sided log shelter common in the Adirondacks; the modern structure is a modification of the temporary shelters constructed by nineteenth-century guides. Lean-tos are available for camping on a first-come basis, typically with a capacity of about six people. Etiquette requires that you make room for latecomers. Lean-tos are favored by many backpackers because they are often easier to find than campsites.

Logging road. Because much of the public land in the Adirondacks was at one time logged, hikers frequently

summits of some of the High Peaks to protect fragile vegetation. They indicate the edge of the hiking path, so do not step across them.

Skid trail. This term refers to a route cut through the forest by giant logging equipment. There are several machines that might create a skid trail, including tractors called skidders—some known for their tank-like treads, and others for their large, knobby tires. Unlike a logging road, no engineering or forethought is involved in the creation of a skid trail; they merely mark the path the tractor happened to take. A skid trail is identified by its twin ruts, which are often deep—and because of this deepness, the route is evident long after the logging operations have moved on. Where a hiking trail intersects a skid trail, you need to pay close attention to the trail signs and markers to avoid making a wrong turn.

Slide. A scar on a steep mountainside, tracing the path of an old landslide. Slides are most prevalent in the High Peaks region; a few make good hiking routes.

Snowmobile trail. A marked trail intended for snowmobile use in the winter but available for hiking in the summer. The implication is that a snowmobile trail is apt to be wider than a typical hiking trail and probably less desirable for hiking in the winter. Snowmobiles are not permitted in wilderness areas.

Stillwater. A section of a stream or river with no rapids of any kind.

Unmarked trail. Not all Adirondack trails have markers and signs. Some are traditional routes that have been used for years by people familiar with the area. However, they are less suitable for novices, and you need to pay closer attention to your surroundings while following one. Furthermore, these routes may not be maintained as frequently as an official trail. Unmarked trails are prominent elements in Hikes 37, 46, and 49, among others.

Vly. A Dutch word reflecting the settlement history of the Mohawk Valley and the southern Adirondacks. Sometimes pronounced "fly," it can refer to any wetland, marsh, beaver meadow, or random opening in the woods.

Wild Forest. One of the two primary classifications for state land in the Adirondacks, accounting for more than half of the Forest Preserve. Snowmobiles, fire towers, access roads, and mountain bikes may be allowed here, unlike the areas classified as wilderness.

Wilderness. One of the two primary classifications for state land in the Adirondacks, this one modeled after the 1964 Wilderness Act. Mechanized forms of access are prohibited, ensuring a more natural experience. There are currently twenty wilderness areas in the Adirondacks, totaling 1.2 million acres.

ENJOYING THE OUTDOORS

Generally speaking, the Adirondacks are a benign wilderness, and the majority of people who venture into the woods make it out safely; the accidents and fatalities that do occur always seem to stem from preventable causes. No guidebook can thoroughly prepare anyone for the rigors of wilderness recreation, but what follows are some key points that all visitors to the Adirondacks should know.

BITING FLIES

Every year the entire region is beset by a deluge of biting insects. The first batches appear by May and the last may

HIKING BENNIES BROOK SLIDE

not completely disappear until after Labor Day, the height of the season usually falling between Memorial Day and Independence Day. Black flies are small gnats that like to overwhelm you with their numbers, mosquitoes appear as individuals or in swarms, and deer flies would like nothing more than to burrow into your hair.

These are the three most common species, but there are others that appear on a more limited basis. "No-see-ums" tend to dwell near shorelines and come out at dusk. They are so named because they are very small, and you tend to feel their bite before you see them flying about you. Stable flies are a Labor Day special; they look like common house flies but love to bite your ankles.

All of these insects are an annoying part of the Adirondack experience but they should not discourage you from enjoying your outdoor plans. People employ different strategies for dealing with them, from the use of repellents to wearing long-sleeved clothing. A cool, breezy day is often the best time for a hike during bug season, as this helps keep the populations in check.

DEER TICKS

Unfortunately, ticks are becoming an increasing concern in the Adirondacks. Historically, these tiny arachnids were not associated with the backcountry, but they are slowly gaining territory. Deer ticks are particularly problematic because they are vectors for Lyme disease, making them a threat to human health, and not just a nuisance like black flies and mosquitoes.

To guard against ticks, you may want to consider wearing long clothing treated with permethrin, followed by a check of your body after the completion of the hike. Fortunately, the tall grassy environments favored by ticks are not a frequent staple along most Adirondack trails, but the threat they pose is real. From personal experience, I can confirm that ticks are indeed present in the woods.

BLACK BEARS

Few denizens of the woods cause as much concern as bears. Certainly, you should never confront a black bear directly, but in my experience encounters are rare. The primary risk is not in meeting one on the trail, but in your campsite. For this reason many people hang their food and toiletries in a "bear bag" every night. To be effective, a good bear hang keeps the bag out of reach from the ground. Remember that bears are excellent climbers, so the food should also be well away from the trunk of the tree.

Bear encounters have been a long-standing issue in the High Peaks Wilderness, so in this one region the Department of Environmental Conservation requires the use of bear canisters. These are durable containers that a bear can knock around but can't break open, available for lease or purchase at gear stores around the High Peaks region. Though bulky, canisters are the simplest solution for anyone concerned with protecting their food from bears, regardless of which section of the park you're visiting.

HIKING WITH DOGS

The Adirondack Forest Preserve is generally very dog-friendly. The only place with a firm leash requirement is the High Peaks Wilderness, and the only hike in this book where dogs are prohibited outright is the Pyramid and Gothics Loop (Hike #34). In most other cases, dogs appreciate a good day on the trail as much as you do.

As someone who has been hiking with dogs for years, I can offer this advice:

Carry a leash, regardless of whether the regulations say you need one or not. This will be beneficial when you encounter other dogs on the trail or people with dog phobias. No matter how well-behaved your dog is, he or she may still trigger a negative reaction in others. Not all dogs are cut out to be independent hikers anyway; some, in fact, have an incurable desire to run.

Porcupines can be found just about anywhere and at any time. These critters are slow-moving and very easy to catch, and so some dogs never seem to learn to leave them alone. Removing quills from a dog's face is not that easy.

Mountain summits can be very hot and dry in the summer, so always remember to bring extra water and a packable bowl.

The presence of dogs can be stressful for wildlife, so non-hunting dogs should never be encouraged to chase any of the animals you may encounter in your travels.

HIKING IN WINTER

Hiking is a four-season activity in the Adirondacks, and many of the trails in this book are suitable for snowshoeing as well as summer hiking. Cold-weather hiking does require more preparation, however, because winter can be an unforgiving season. Mistakes at this time of year have the potential to be very costly.

The main snow season varies from

year to year, but generally speaking it lasts from December through the end of March. During these months there are often several feet of accumulation in the woods, ranging in quality from soft and powdery to hard and crusty. Some trails are used so frequently that you can almost expect to find a good track to follow; other trails, not so much. Some trails are inaccessible in winter because the access roads aren't plowed.

The preferred means of getting around the woods on foot is with snowshoes, at least for the purposes of this guidebook. (Not to knock cross-country skiing, but a good ski trail has its own set of criteria, distinct from the criteria for a good hiking trail.) This should be common sense, but it bears repeating more often than you'd expect: snowshoes are a practical requirement whenever the snow is 8 or more inches deep, even on well-used trails. Without snowshoes,

you risk damaging the trail with post-holes, when your feet sink through the surface. Postholing is tiring for the person who does it, and it is aggravating for everyone afterward who walks in the wake of destruction.

Winter also comes with two very long shoulder seasons at each end, when ice is apt to be more prevalent than snow. In this case traction is the larger concern, since a fall on an icy slope could have catastrophic consequences. There are a number of crampon-like devices available at outdoor retailers now to assist in these conditions; they stretch over your hiking boots and provide small spikes that bite into the ice. They do not make you invincible, but you do feel a lot steadier on your feet.

Regardless of the amount of snow and ice, a winter hike will assuredly be cold. Layered, non-cotton clothing is the key to keeping warm and dry. The idea

DOGS LIKE HIKING IN THE ADIRONDACKS TOO!

is to add or subtract layers as necessary, so that you are not sweating while you are in motion or chilled while you are at rest. Cotton clothing is a big *faux pas* in winter, because it never dries once it gets wet, thus setting you up for a bad case of hypothermia.

SAFE AND RESPONSIBLE WILDERNESS RECREATION

Remember, by setting off into the backcountry, you are entering a rugged area where cell coverage is apt to be limited and help may not be just a phone call away. A little bit of preparation therefore goes a long way. Below are some basic tips that are easy to follow and will better your chances of having a safe and enjoyable journey.

Always let someone know where you are going. Provide your hiking itinerary and your expected return time with someone reliable—and particularly someone who will notice if you don't make it home. In the event you are overdue from a hike, that person should be prepared to call the Forest Ranger Dispatch at 518 891 0235.

Carry a map and compass. This may sound old-school, but it works. Mindlessly following a trail is a fine strategy until you miss a turn and have to troubleshoot where you went wrong. Maps and compasses require no battery and will not die on you. By investing the personal effort to know and understand your route, it is easier to determine your location and get back to where you want to be.

Always carry water with you, or bring along the means to purify water from streams and lakes. The presence of *Giardia* makes most backcountry water sources suspect.

Never wear cotton clothing, including denim. Once it gets wet, cotton is

WINTER ON MOXHAM MOUNTAIN

very slow to dry, and once the weather turns cold nothing will sap your energy like feeling as though you're dressed in a wet washcloth.

Carry a small day pack with insect repellent, sunscreen, lip balm, matches, headlamp, first aid kit, extra snacks, knife, whistle, rain jacket, and a wool sweater, even in summer. Conditions can change quickly in the mountains, so adaptability pays dividends.

When camping, be sure to use only established sites and build a campfire using only dead and down wood. Green wood doesn't burn, and no one wants to look at the stumps. Much of the top layer of soil in an Adirondack forest is duff, which is made of decomposed plant matter. Duff is combustible, and once it is ignited by a poorly located campfire, it may smolder for days, leaving a large pit in the campsite and killing the roots of any trees in its path. There is one really good way to prevent a duff fire, and that is to thoroughly douse your campfire before you leave.

Practice low-impact hiking and camping techniques, meaning that the next person to come along shouldn't have to clean up after you or count the many ways you left your mark. You came in search of a fresh, unblemished landscape, so allow others to have that pleasure, too. Visit Leave No Trace at www .LNT.org for more information.

If you are unsure of your abilities in the wilderness, then join a group! In the Internet Age, there is no shortage of ways to seek out hiking clubs and meetup groups that suit your interest. I am the organizer for a group called the Adirondack Wilderness Explorers, and one of my finest pleasures is introducing people to new places. There are many other trip leaders out there in addition to me, and they would love to have you along, too.

MAP LEGEND

———	Described trail		═══	Interstate highway
- - - -	Important trail		═══	Secondary highway
◄———	Hike direction arrow		———	Minor highway, road, street
———	Perennial stream		- - - -	Unpaved road, trail
- - - - -	Intermittent stream		+—+—+	Railroad
———	Major contour line		—··—	International border
········	Minor contour line		--·--··	State border
�	National/state park, wilderness		**P**	Parking area
[ ]	National/state forest, wildlife refuge		🚶	Trailhead
▯	Perennial body of water		•	City, town
[ ]	Intermittent body of water		⋙	Overlook, scenic view
~~	Swamp, marsh		Λ	Campground, campsite
			⋔	Shelter
▯	Wooded area		×	Mountain peak
			▪	Place of interest

I.

CENTRAL ADIRONDACKS

Siamese Ponds via the East Branch Sacandaga River

TOTAL DISTANCE: 12 miles round-trip

HIKING TIME: 6 hours

ELEVATION CHANGE: 2,400 feet

TRAILHEAD GPS COORDINATES: N43° 35' 25.1" W74° 05' 24.3"

It is hard to imagine a better wilderness hike. This route follows an old wagon road over the shoulder of Eleventh Mountain and down into a secluded portion of the East Branch Sacandaga River's valley. After following the river for several miles, the trail crosses it on a suspension bridge and ascends into the hills toward its final destination, the not-so-twin ponds at the heart of the Siamese Ponds Wilderness. The combination of all these elements makes this an extremely satisfying adventure for anyone ready to tackle the longish miles.

The Siamese Ponds are among the remotest locations in the Adirondack Park, but compared to other remote areas, this one is reasonably accessible, due to the direct nature of the trail. Today this is a route for hiking and skiing, but it was originally built in the nineteenth century as a wagon road connecting the lost settlement of Oregon with Old Farm Clearing at Thirteenth Lake.

Some settlement occurred in these hills, such as at Curtis Clearing to the south of the river, but this has always been a land inhospitable to human cultivation. Lumbermen were active here through the 1880s, building dams on the East Branch and its tributaries in an effort to control the water levels for their spring log drives. The state began acquiring this land in the 1890s, and today all signs of past human occupancy are few and far between. Modern maps still list the locations of the old lumber shanties, but these "clearings" have now all filled in with new forest growth.

The hike along the river to the ponds can be done as a day hike, but it excels as a backpacking route. There is a popular lean-to located at one end of the suspension bridge, and several choice tent sites scattered all around the larger of the two ponds. Most of the latter

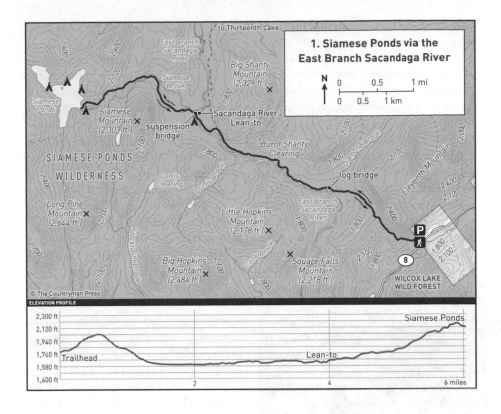

ELEVATION PROFILE

require bushwhacking off the trail to find, however.

GETTING THERE

The Eleventh Mountain Trailhead is located on NY 8 about 3.7 miles southwest of the hamlet of Bakers Mills, or 13.5 miles from the junction with NY 30 near Wells. There is a large parking area marked by a typical yellow-on-brown DEC sign, and the slopes of Eleventh Mountain loom nearby.

THE HIKE

The aspen grove near the start of the trail will not impress, but as you follow the blue-marked foot trail westward from the parking area, you are soon immersed in a more rugged environment, with the rocky slopes of Eleventh Mountain to your right. The old road begins to climb, and at times the modern trail veers off the original route to find a less eroded way up the shoulder of the mountain. Observant hikers may notice that there are several old roadbeds leading up this slope; this climb would have been a hard pull for the old teamsters, and apparently it was preferable to build a new road whenever the previous one became too rough to use.

This initial climb lasts 0.6 mile and brings you to a shoulder of Eleventh Mountain 250 feet above the trailhead. Dense pockets of nettles line the ·trail here. The trail traverses this high ground briefly before making its long, 410-foot descent into the river valley, where you can no longer hear the traffic sounds of NY 8. Tall hardwoods shade the mountainside, but here in the valley you walk through a mixed forest that also includes balsam fir, red spruce, and hemlock. Make a note of this descent, because at the end of your hike, as you make your way back to your car, this will be one of the longest and most tiring climbs on the entire hike.

At 1.6 miles you reach the log bridge over Diamond Brook. The East Branch Sacandaga River is a short distance downstream, but thick brush makes it hard to see here. The trail cuts a corner through the floodplain of the brook,

passing a scenic wetland on the right with a view of Diamond Mountain.

Soon you reenter the woods, with one of the best sections of the hike about to begin. For much of the next 2.4 miles, the old road is located deliciously close to the river. The East Branch Sacandaga is a wild river, almost entirely state-owned and spanned by only one highway bridge—happily, many miles downstream from here. The river is not particularly wide or deep, but in this unspoiled valley it is most certainly a master of its own fate. As it bends, often so does the trail, and only occasionally are you out of sight of the water.

You reach the site of Burnt Shanty Clearing at 2.8 miles, although this site is now so thickly forested that it is easy to miss. Gone, too, is the old side trail that once led down to a ford across the river, providing access to the abandoned farm sites at Curtis Clearing. At 3.5 miles, you reach a fork; the way right was once the direct trail to Old Farm Clearing, but DEC has stopped maintaining that route and now all traffic bears left.

So far, you have been following the river upstream as it guides the trail northwest, into the heart of the forest. At 3.9 miles it makes a distinct turn to the north, and here you encounter the suspension bridge and its neighboring lean-to. This is a popular and well-used campsite, favored for its views of the river. The shelter is showing its age, and access to the water entails a steep step down the bank. If privacy is your preference, you will find none here—not because it is typically crowded with other campers, but because the trail passes so close.

From the lean-to, the blue-marked foot trail continues north through the river valley toward Thirteenth Lake. To get to the Siamese Ponds, you need

EAST BRANCH SACANDAGA RIVER

EXPLORING THE LOWER SIAMESE POND

to cross the suspension bridge (also showing its age, but still safe) and follow what is now a trail with yellow markers. Instead of the river, Siamese Brook is now your guide. This trail follows the stream less closely, but 1 mile from the bridge (4.9 miles overall), you get a good look at it as you walk across it on whatever stones or logs happen to be available. The brook is small, but it is big enough to cause wet feet if you are not surefooted enough.

It is a 2.1-mile, 530-foot climb up to the Siamese Ponds from the lean-to, still following one of the old wagon roads. Some clarification is required, however. There are two ponds on this mountainous shelf, and maps refer to them collectively as the Siamese Ponds. The name is likely a vague reference to a pair of famous conjoined twins from the nineteenth century, but these ponds are neither twins nor currently conjoined. The marked trail leads you to a small beach near the outlet of the larger, lower pond; no trail leads to the upper pond.

Even if you never stray from the marked trail, the view from the beach is quite rewarding. There is a large campsite nearby, and another, somewhat more hidden site just off the trail, about 0.1 mile before its end. Despite the remoteness of the Siamese Ponds, more than a few people have made their way here over the years, so the remote off-trail corners of the lower pond might not be as pristine as you'd expect. There are five or six primitive campsites all around its shores, some of them perched on attractive ledges—and several with litter issues. It's a shame, because a place this remote and beautiful deserves so much better.

The hike back out to NY 8 is just as pleasant as the hike in . . . except that the climb back over Eleventh Mountain is apt to seem to like a cruel joke at the end of a long day.

Peaked Mountain via Thirteenth Lake

TOTAL DISTANCE: 7 miles round-trip

HIKING TIME: 3.5 hours

VERTICAL RISE: 1,250 feet

TRAILHEAD GPS COORDINATES: N43° 43' 07.1" W74° 07' 05.6"

There is no question how 2,919-foot Peaked Mountain got its name. Nor is there any question that this is among the finest hikes in the Adirondacks. Not only is this small, rocky mountain an outstanding destination, but the trail leading to the summit is an exceptional adventure.

Peaked Mountain lies at the northern end of the Siamese Ponds Wilderness, and it is one of that area's most iconic landmarks. The mountain is visible from multiple locations, but the views as you hike toward the mountain are just as photogenic as are the vistas seen from the summit itself. The 3.5-mile route begins on the rugged shores of Thirteenth Lake, climbs along Peaked Mountain Brook, and weaves around a chain of scenic beaver meadows. After a brief respite at Peaked Mountain Pond, the hike culminates with a steep 0.6-mile scramble to the summit. There are very few dull moments.

If the mountain's name seems self-evident, most first-time visitors are stumped by the origins of the name Thirteenth Lake. Did the first twelve lakes dry up? Did a superstitious trapper discover it on a particular Friday? Actually, the logic behind the name is buried in the history of the Adirondack Park. The first surveyors in the region were not here to map the terrain but to identify the boundaries of the old colonial-era land grants. One of the largest was the Totten and Crossfield Purchase, which included a vast swath of Adirondack territory. It was subdivided into fifty townships, and each was assigned a number instead of a name. Thus Thirteenth Lake got its name because it was the largest lake in Township 13.

This is an excellent hike in all four seasons. In the winter it is a challenging snowshoe hike, and in late September

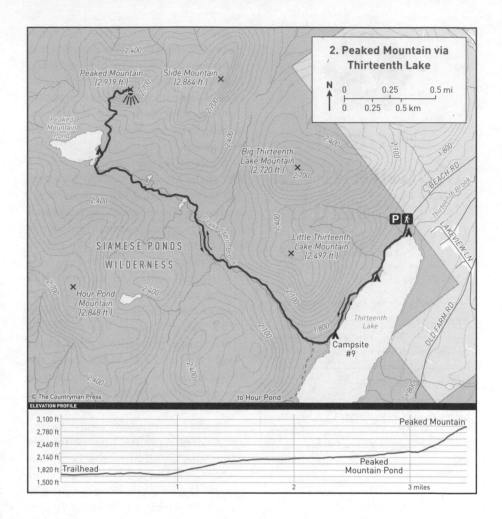

the fall foliage can be quite spectacular. Summer hikers enjoy the swimming opportunities at Thirteenth Lake and Peaked Mountain Pond. The biggest challenges occur during early spring and some winter thaws, when Peaked Mountain Brook becomes a wild little torrent that may be difficult to cross.

GETTING THERE

Follow NY 28 to the hamlet of North River, located on the banks of the Hudson River near the Hamilton-Warren county line. Turn southwest onto Thirteenth Lake Road, where a brown DEC sign indicates you can find access to the Siamese Ponds Wilderness. The road winds and climbs through Christian Hill and alongside Thirteenth Brook, passing the entrance to the Barton garnet mine on Ruby Mountain. At 3.3 miles, turn right onto Beach Road, which dead-ends 0.6 mile later at the trailhead parking area.

THE HIKE

In the summer, the Beach Road trailhead is often bustling with activity.

Thirteenth Lake is a mere 400 feet away down a hardened path, with four walk-in campsites between the parking area and the shoreline. It is easy to carry a canoe or kayak down the access path to the nearest sandy beach, which is also a popular swimming area. It is a very communal setting, especially in warm weather; during the colder months, the wind blowing off the lake makes this a less attractive campsite.

To find Peaked Mountain, proceed down the gravel path to the trail register, which features a map of the regional trail system. The beach path forks left, and the hiking trail forks right. Just after passing a picnic area, the trail narrows into a proper footpath and begins to follow Thirteenth Lake's rugged western shoreline, where there are several rock ledges with attractive views of the lake. Colorful columbine blossoms may be spotted in season. The lake is 2 miles long and almost entirely state-owned,

A BRILLIANT FALL DAY AT THIRTEENTH LAKE

PEAKED MOUNTAIN POND FROM THE SUMMIT

of a dedicated place to land at the spot where the hiking trail turns inland. The closest potential landing site is at Campsite #9, but if other paddlers are using that site, there may be no room for day hikers to stash their boats as well.

Just after passing Site #9, the trail leaves the lake and arrives at the side of Peaked Mountain Brook. At 1 mile, there is a junction with the trail to Hour Pond, another fine backpacking destination. The trail to Peaked Mountain now begins to climb alongside its namesake brook, which will be your constant companion for this second phase of the hike. There is a massive rock between the trail and the brook at 1.2 miles, and at 1.6 miles you reach the first of four unbridged stream crossings. For most of the year you can step across the stream without getting wet by using the available rocks, but this may not always be possible.

After climbing nearly 400 feet up from the lake, the trail passes the first of three large wetlands. At 2 miles you reach the second stream crossing and then continue around the north side of the second wetland. Here you will find a handsome view of Hour Pond Mountain. Beaver flooding has altered the location of the third crossing at the head of this wetland, so pay close attention to the trail markers.

The third wetland is the most interesting of all, partly because of the huge, mossy boulders beside the trail, but

except for a private beach on the opposite shoreline. Garnet Hill Lodge can be seen high above the lake.

This first mile of the hike would be worthwhile even if it didn't lead to a mountain. There are two designated campsites along the way, although neither offers much privacy; a third site has been closed for rehabilitation. Alternatively, you could skip this part by paddling the lake. If there is any drawback to the water route, though, it's the lack

mostly because of the tremendous views of Peaked Mountain as it looms above the valley. Its face seems to be nearly all rock, promising fun times ahead.

At 2.8 miles you reach the southeast corner of Peaked Mountain Pond, where a rock ledge offers yet another good view of the mountain. This is a favored stopping point, especially for day hikers. The trail makes the fourth and final stream crossing here at the outlet, and then it continues through the woods east of the pond. Watch for a side trail at 2.9 miles; it leads left to the best campsite on the pond.

The trail continues past the northeast corner of the pond and finally reaches the foot of the mountain. At this point, you've had several good looks at your destination, and you've seen just how steep it is. Therefore, it should come as no surprise that this final half-mile ascent is no picnic. The trail avoids the rugged rock face that you saw earlier, circling around to tackle the more moderate western slopes instead, but the nature of the mountain prevents this from being an easy climb. There are a few ledges where you may need to use your hands, as well as several eroded sections that may require remedial trail work in the future. The climb is short, however, and within minutes you find yourself in the spruce-filled forests of the upper slopes.

All of the toil becomes worthwhile when you reach the summit, 3.5 miles from the trailhead and 1,250 vertical feet above it. A short distance down the other side, an inviting ledge of open rock offers plenty of places to sit, rest, and enjoy the wilderness vista. The pond below is the focal point of the landscape, which also includes the slopes of Hour Pond Mountain in front of Bullhead and Puffer. Distant Gore Mountain can be identified by its abandoned garnet mine and summit towers, and a peripheral ledge even offers a glimpse of the High Peaks to the north. The chain of beaver meadows in the valley in front of you points the way to the one small corner of Thirteenth Lake visible from the mountain; the rest of the lake is hidden by foothills.

Returning to the trailhead along this same route is just as enjoyable. There are two good swimming spots if you want to cool off on a hot summer day. The first is at the campsite on Peaked Mountain Pond, and the better option is at the beach on Thirteenth Lake closest to the trailhead. Be on the lookout for leeches, which inhabit all of the ponds in the Siamese Ponds Wilderness, but don't let them be a deterrent.

3

Botheration Pond Loop

TOTAL DISTANCE: 7.1-mile loop with 3.6 miles in optional side trips

HIKING TIME: 3.5 hours (side trips not included)

ELEVATION CHANGE: rolling terrain

TRAILHEAD GPS COORDINATES: N43° 42' 16.8" W74° 07' 03.0"

This loop was created in 2004 for cross-country skiing, and indeed it is an excellent winter trail. However, the Botheration Pond Loop also deserves more credit as a summer hiking destination, because no matter the season, this is a scenic area with a colorful human history.

Although now an integral part of the Siamese Ponds Wilderness, the Botheration Pond area was sandwiched between two active garnet mines in the early twentieth century: the Barton Mine on Gore Mountain and the Hooper Mine in the hills above Thirteenth Lake. A portion of the Botheration Pond Loop was once the most direct route between the two mines.

Frank C. Hooper closed his mine in 1928, but one log building from his industrial complex survives as Garnet Hill Lodge. Barton remains active in the area; the company is currently mining a pocket of garnets on Ruby Mountain northeast of Thirteenth Lake. Garnets remain common in the rocks of this area, but none are considered gem quality. Rather, they are used in the manufacture of abrasive products. When you encounter these dark red crystals on your hike, feel free to examine them, but remember it is illegal to extract minerals from state land. Leave what you find for others to discover.

Despite its industrial past, though, the area really is quite attractive. The 7.1-mile loop guides you through the heart of the so-called "garnet hills," and it can easily be hiked in a day. However, to make the most of a visit, you should really consider exploring some of the lateral trails that lead to some extraordinary features a short distance off the main loop: Balm of Gilead Mountain, The Vly, Elizabeth Point, and even the old Hooper mine itself.

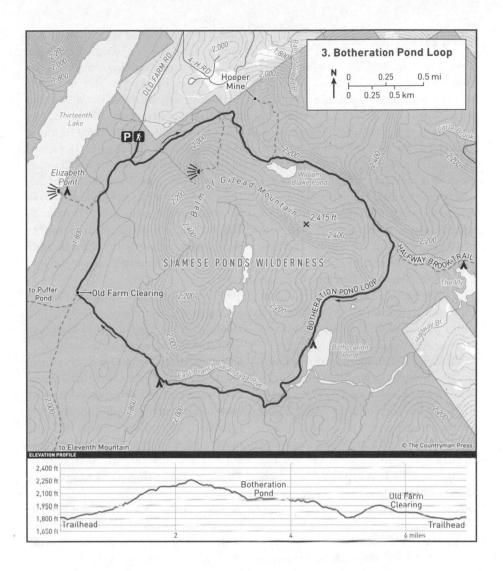

3. Botheration Pond Loop

ELEVATION PROFILE

Small campsites can be found at Botheration Pond, The Vly, and the East Branch Sacandaga River. A larger campsite—with the best swimming option—is located at Elizabeth Point.

GETTING THERE

Follow NY 28 to the hamlet of North River, located on the banks of the Hudson River near the Hamilton-Warren county line. Turn southwest onto Thirteenth Lake Road, where a brown DEC sign indicates you can find access to the Siamese Ponds Wilderness. The road winds and climbs through Christian Hill and alongside Thirteenth Brook, passing the entrance to the Barton garnet mine on Ruby Mountain. Follow it for 4 miles to the Old Farm Road junction, which forks right and leads in 0.7 mile to the trailhead parking area.

THE HIKE

This hike begins on the wide, well-used trail to Old Farm Clearing. The road was a town highway as recently as 1987, when it was closed to motor vehicles. It leads south from the parking area, arriving at the trail register in 0.2 mile. To begin the loop in the recommended clockwise direction, bear left off the old road onto the marked foot trail.

For the next 0.7 mile you hike in a northeasterly direction past the foot of Balm of Gilead Mountain; the side trail to the summit of that small hill, described below, turns right 0.9 mile from the trailhead. Continuing on the loop, you reach another junction at 1 mile, where a left turn would lead to Garnet Hill Lodge.

Bearing right, the loop trail climbs gently alongside a small stream for 0.5 mile to its source: a small pond nestled among the surrounding hills. Topographic maps give it no name, but it is well known as William Blake Pond, and it once provided water to the Hooper complex at the foot of the hill. A short side trail leads to a scenic spot at the outlet.

The loop trail makes an arc to the north of the pond, passing the unmarked side trail to the site of Hooper's mine, one of the optional side trips recommended below. Keep right, passing the far end of the pond and climbing up a steep slope (a vexing obstacle for skiers) to a marshy wetland with views of Gore Mountain. The trail hugs the northern edge of the wetland, squeezed by a steep mountainside on your north. You pass through a small notch in the hills and then descend to the next trail junction at 2.6 miles, where the Halfway Brook Trail leads left toward The Vly.

Turn right, following the sign for Botheration Pond. The trail keeps to high ground above a chain of wetlands before descending toward the larger marsh that marks the north end of Botheration Pond. The pond is small and shallow, but it is remarkable for two things. First, this is the official source of the East Branch Sacandaga River, one of the defining features of the Siamese Ponds Wilderness. Second is the pleasing view of Gore Mountain, best enjoyed from the southern shoreline. The pond's charms can be appreciated from the tiny designated campsite found 1 mile from the last junction and 3.6 miles total into your hike.

The trail continues along the western shore, eventually leading to the outlet where the river begins. This is an interesting site, because the modern footbridge is built on top of the remains of an old dam built by lumbermen. You now turn westward, following an old logging road on a traverse of a cool, north-facing hillside. The trail descends, and at 5 miles you reach the river again, somewhat larger now but still just a creek. The log bridge that used to span the East Branch here is gone, and DEC has decided not to replace it; the river is shallow, with ample bedrock to step on. A pleasant campsite can be found on the far bank.

The trail now guides you northwest up a series of small hills, most of which are a hoot on skis (when heading in the opposite direction). The transition from native mixed forest to a plantation of Norway spruce is sudden and hard to miss; this is the outer edge of Old Farm Clearing. The trail follows a narrow alleyway cut through the thick underbrush of balsam fir on a gentle descent to a major trail junction at 5.9 miles.

Old Farm Clearing was once exactly what its name says it was. An 1858 map of Warren County identifies this as an "Indian Settlement," and it later served as a farm that supplied the lumber camps of Township 13. Henry A. Maxam operated his Thirteenth Lake House here in the 1890s, catering to a clientele of sportsmen. The state acquired most of Township 13 for the Forest Preserve in 1899, and conservationists later planted the Norway spruce trees as a means of reforesting the old clearing. Foundations from Maxam's inn can still be found just a short distance from the trail junction, for those who take the time to prowl through the brushy growth.

The trail leading south from Old Farm Clearing leads through the heart of the wilderness to Eleventh Mountain, with connections to Puffer Pond and the Siamese Ponds. To complete the loop, you need to turn north and right. You pass the foundations of a barn on the left and soon pass out of the spruce plantation. At 6.5 miles, the side trail to Elizabeth Point leads left, downhill, to a scenic promontory on Thirteenth Lake. The old road continues north, returning you to the trail register at 6.9 miles and then the trailhead parking area at 7.1 miles.

GORE MOUNTAIN AND THE VLY

SIDE TRIPS

As stated above, one of the things that make the Botheration Pond Loop so interesting is the wealth of attractive features that can be reached so easily by indulging in optional side trips. None are requirements, of course, but they will enrich your understanding and enjoyment of this storied region. The flip side is that these do add some significant miles and elevation change to the day.

1. **Balm of Gilead Mountain.** This marked foot trail leads to a scenic ledge overlooking Thirteenth Lake and the interior of the Siamese Ponds Wilderness. It is 0.5 mile long and ascends 430 feet. The odd name refers to a sterile variety of the balsam poplar tree, known for its fragrance; but if any of these trees remain on the mountain today, it is not immediately evident from the trail. Taken by itself, Balm of Gilead is an outstanding little mountain, suitable for families and very photogenic, especially in the morning when the sun is still to the east.

2. **Hooper Garnet Mine.** Although much of Frank C. Hooper's property is now part of the Garnet Hill Lodge complex, the mine itself is located on

state land. Most Adirondack garnet mines were open pit excavations, and this one was no exception. No signs or trail markers point the way, but unmarked trails do lead to it. One such trail leads north from the Botheration Pond Loop near the outlet of William Blake Pond; it is 0.5 mile long and intersects another trail from the lodge near the entrance to the pit. The mine site is essentially a large quarry, naturally reforested by young cedar trees. It is safe to explore, and garnets can still be found in abundance—keep in mind that it is illegal to collect minerals on state land. The mine operations were well documented, with many photographs archived at the Adirondack Experience museum in Blue Mountain Lake.

3. **The Vly.** The word "vly" (sometimes pronounced "fly") is a regional term handed down from the early Dutch settlers of the Mohawk Valley, and it is still commonly used to describe the ubiquitous open wetlands and beaver meadows of the southern Adirondacks. This particular vly is a shallow pond, noteworthy for its photogenic views of Gore Mountain. A scenic little campsite at the west end of The Vly is just 0.5 mile from the loop trail, and it can be reached by following the Halfway Brook Trail east from the junction 2.6 miles from the trailhead. Just after crossing a small footbridge, look for the side trail leading right to the campsite. A rock on the shoreline is studded with garnets.

4. **Elizabeth Point.** This is a scenic promontory on Thirteenth Lake with a popular (read: often occupied in the summer) campsite. It is recommended as a side trip because the best swimming opportunities on the Botheration Pond Loop are found here. A small sign marks the beginning of the path, which is 0.3 mile long with a 140-foot descent. If you follow the loop in a clockwise direction as described above, the Elizabeth Point trail occurs just 0.6 mile before you return to the trailhead.

OK Slip Falls

TOTAL DISTANCE: 6.4 miles round-trip

HIKING TIME: 3.25 hours

ELEVATION CHANGE: rolling terrain

TRAILHEAD GPS COORDINATES: N43° 46' 20.0" W74° 07' 44.8"

It may surprise you to know that one of the Adirondack Park's most iconic landmarks has only been part of the Forest Preserve since 2013. Before that, it was owned by the Finch Pruyn logging company and closed to the general public for more than a century. Since its acquisition, the OK Slip Tract has become a popular hiking destination. Now managed as part of the Hudson Gorge Wilderness, its star attraction is OK Slip Falls, an extraordinary waterfall located a short distance south of the Hudson River.

The state's purchase of OK Slip Falls was a major news story at the time, and many grandiose claims were made about its superlative features. Some of those claims may still persist, because who wouldn't want to hike to the tallest waterfall in the state? Some descriptions of the waterfall say it is 200 to 250 feet tall, which would be remarkable if true—that would make OK Slip taller than Niagara.

While it is an impressive cascade, a close scrutiny of the contours on USGS topographic maps reveals that OK Slip is only about 100 feet tall—less than half as tall as Roaring Brook Falls in Saint Huberts. But it is still a remarkable sight!

There are also some tall tales in circulation about the source of the name, including on educational placards located at the trailhead parking area. The "slip" is a reference to an old logging sluice. From the early days of Adirondack logging in the nineteenth century to the middle of the twentieth century, the preferred method for transporting logs to the great sawmills at Glens Falls was to float them down the Hudson River. The slip would have been a clever device in which logs harvested in the mountains above the Hudson Gorge were shot down to the river on

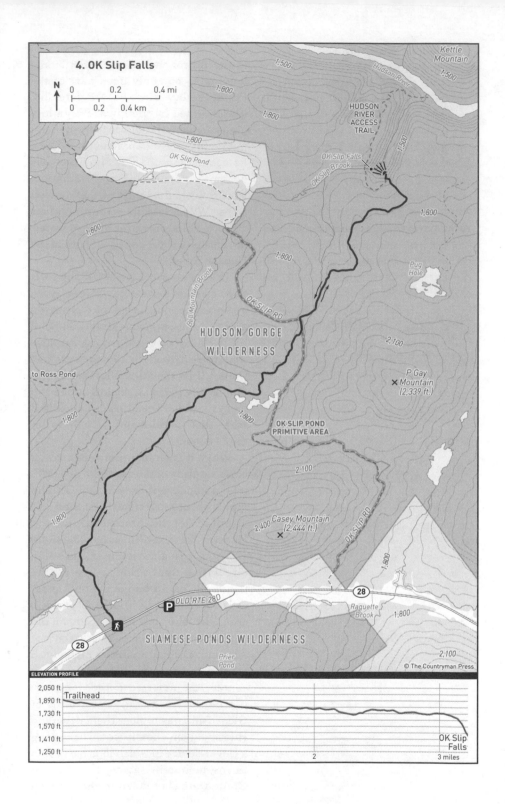

4. OK Slip Falls

N

| 0 | 0.2 | 0.4 mi |
| 0 | 0.2 | 0.4 km |

Kettle
Mountain

1,500

Hudson River

1,500

HUDSON
RIVER
ACCESS
TRAIL

1,800

OK Slip Falls

1,500

OK Slip Brook

1,800

OK Slip Pond

1,800

Pug
Hole

Bell Mountain Brook

OK SLIP RD

1,800

HUDSON GORGE

WILDERNESS

2,100

to Ross Pond

P Gay
Mountain
(2,339 ft.)

1,800

OK SLIP POND
PRIMITIVE AREA

1,800

2,100

Casey Mountain
(2,444 ft.)

2,400

OK SLIP RD

1,800

28

P OLD RTE 28D

Raguette
Brook

1,800

28

SIAMESE PONDS WILDERNESS

Prier
Pond

2,100

© The Countryman Press

ELEVATION PROFILE

2,050 ft	Trailhead		
1,890 ft			
1,730 ft			
1,570 ft			
1,410 ft			OK Slip
1,250 ft			Falls
	1	2	3 miles

a plume of water—sort of like a modern waterslide.

The popular story takes a detour into speculation when it comes to the "OK" part of the name. Supposedly, lumbermen called out those letters as a verbal warning to anyone below before the logs went a-sliding. This is a cute story, but it discounts an 1890 newspaper article I once found describing a river-driving fatality "at a place between 'O. K. slip' and 'P. K. slip,' in the fourteenth township." The presence of a PK Slip a short distance downstream from OK Slip suggests that the letters were more likely someone's initials.

Note that modern maps still identify a place called P Gay Mountain on the gorge's south rim; if you say "P.K." and "P Gay" aloud, they sound almost identical. It would have been easy for an old-time surveyor to hear one name but record the other in his notes, and I suspect several Adirondack place names were thus corrupted. There is another summit a few miles away called Pete Gay Mountain. Therefore, I have to wonder: was Pete Gay a lumber jobber with a log sluice in the Hudson Gorge? And by any chance, did he have a brother named Oliver?

Admittedly, this is all conjecture on my part, and further research is warranted. Whatever or whoever "OK" was, the name OK Slip was also applied to the brook, the waterfall, and a nearby pond.

GETTING THERE

The trailhead parking area can be found on NY 28, 7.8 miles east of the intersection with NY 30 in Indian Lake, at a fork with an unnamed side road. You will need to walk westward along the shoulder of the highway for 0.2 mile to find the sign for the start of the trail.

THE HIKE

The trail to OK Slip Falls shares a common trailhead with the route to Ross, Whortleberry, and Big Bad Luck ponds. Begin by walking 0.2 mile west along the shoulder to the brown sign marking the start of the trail. Follow it down from the highway and north through a short muddy area, intercepting an old road within minutes. Bear right and follow the marked foot trail for 0.7 mile, over a small hill to a junction where the blue-marked trail to OK Slip bears right.

What follows is a 1.4-mile section of newly constructed trail leading northeast from the older section of state land into the newer tract purchased from Finch Pruyn. As a credit to the former owner, the boundary between the two properties is not clear; it is all a wild forest with intermixed hardwood and hemlock stands. The trail threads a course between small hills and wetlands, making for a pleasant walk.

At 2.1 miles, or about 1 hour from the start, you reach a prominent gravel road. This is the access right-of-way for the youth camp at OK Slip Pond, which is now a private inholding surrounded by state land. The pond is to the left, but there is no public access to it. You could, however, follow the road to the right back toward NY 28 (a distance of 1.9 miles). The most remarkable feature in that direction is the mineshaft south of P Gay Mountain—the remains of an old garnet operation. As you might expect, the location of the shaft is intentionally hard to find.

The trail to OK Slip Falls turns briefly left on the road, and then it veers right again, less than 200 feet later back into the woods. You are now on an older trail that follows a former tote road. Despite the logging history, the forest is quite

OK SLIP FALLS AS SEEN FROM THE OVERLOOK

nice, aesthetically not much different from lands that have been part of
the Forest Preserve for many years—
suggesting that Finch Pruyn had not
logged this area in a long while. Parts
of the trail are muddy, but overall it is
an enjoyable hike with a subtle downhill
grade.

You descend more noticeably as
you near the falls, entering the spruce-
hemlock stand that covers the slope on
the east side of the OK Slip gorge. At
3.2 miles you reach a junction, where
a sign points right to the overlook 100
feet away. This is the best view you will
find of OK Slip Falls from a marked trail.
The cascade is about 450 feet away and
slightly below you, roaring over a wall of
dark rock into the rugged valley below.
Your viewing point is a small ledge surrounded by conifers; it will do for now,
but the opening will surely grow in over
the course of time as many feet come to
see the falls.

SIDE TRIP: THE HUDSON RIVER

Returning to the trail junction, the route
to the left is a 0.9-mile spur that wraps
around the falls to the mouth of OK Slip
Brook. Although the walk to the OK Slip
Falls overlook is undulating but not too
hilly, this continuing walk to the Hudson
River entails a steep descent of 350 feet
into the bottom of the gorge . . . which
becomes a steep 350-foot ascent on the
return. It is an attractive walk into an
historic river driving area (now domi-
nated by commercial rafting ventures),
but it does not lead directly to any further views of the falls, unless you search
for them off-trail. The marked trail ends
at the river directly below Kettle Mountain, 4.1 miles from the trailhead. There
is a small sandy beach here as well as
a campfire ring, although the site is too
small, root-filled, and sandy to be a good
campsite.

5

John and Clear Pond Loop

TOTAL DISTANCE: 5.2-mile loop	

HIKING TIME: 3 hours

VERTICAL RISE: 275 feet

TRAILHEAD GPS COORDINATES: N43° 44' 05.6" W74° 13' 04.5" (eastern); N43° 43' 54.8" W74° 13' 13.5" (western)

In 1897 the state acquired a 24,000-acre tract southeast of Indian Lake for the Forest Preserve. Known as Township 15, it extended from Lake Francis at its northern corner all the way south to Kings Flow. Peaked Mountain and the hamlet of Sabael also fell within its boundaries. It had been owned by the Glens Falls logging company Finch Pruyn, and the sale included nearly the entire township. However, it soon became obvious there was a problem: over the years, the company had already sold off numerous farm lots to local residents, and these previous sales had not been deducted from the state's purchase.

This created an awkward situation in which the state and the occupants held conflicting titles for the land. Surveys to determine correct property lines only made the situation more complicated. Therefore the state set up a special court in 1914 to resolve the conflict. Any resident who could produce evidence that he or she had purchased their lot before the state's acquisition was granted clear title; those parts of Township 15 were no longer claimed by the state. Judging by modern maps, local residents were able to redeem about a third of the tract.

Not everyone was able to satisfy the court's criteria, however; these people were ruled to be squatters on public land. The law does not permit claims of adverse possession against the state, and so these portions of Township 15 were added to the Forest Preserve. All of the buildings were demolished, and the clearings were reforested with plantations of pine and spruce.

Of all these sites, Little Canada is the most notable. A modern foot trail passes through the former settlement, where several cellar holes and one small cemetery still remain. Little Canada occupied a scenic valley on John Pond Brook,

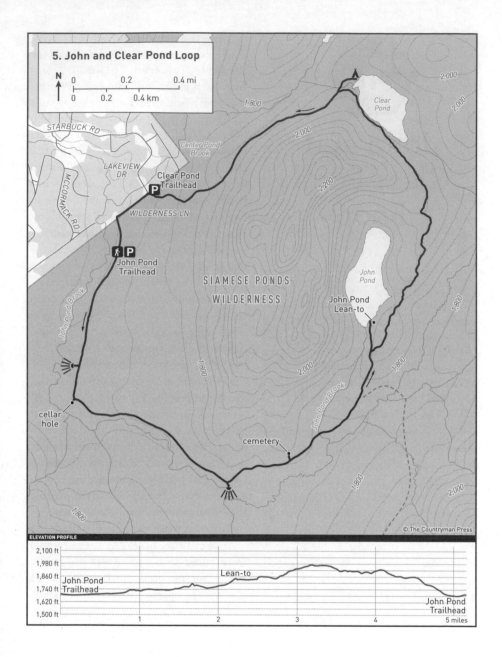

5. John and Clear Pond Loop

ELEVATION PROFILE

located at the foot of Bullhead Mountain. Its boundaries can still be identified by the hard edges of the planted forest, especially when viewed from one of the nearby summits.

Today, John Pond and its valley are the setting of a relatively short and easy hike. The lean-to near the pond's outlet provides views of the rocky ridge snuggling against the western shore, and the trail follows the course of the road that once led through the Little Canada settlement. And if these features weren't enticement enough to explore this corner of the Siamese Ponds Wilderness, in 2017 the state completed a new link trail connecting John Pond with nearby Clear Pond; what had previously been two dead-end trails now make part of a scenic 5.2-mile loop.

Enjoy this outing as either a half-day hike or as a short backpacking trip. The lean-to site at John Pond is a fine place to spend an evening, as are the small tent sites at the north end of Clear Pond. It is a favorite route in winter as well, especially the John Pond half of the loop, which is frequented by skiers. The only obstacle—and it's a minor one—is the unbridged stream crossing about 0.5 mile south of the lean-to.

GETTING THERE

The loop trail begins from a pair of trailheads located on Wilderness Lane, southeast of Indian Lake. From NY 30 about 0.5 mile south of the intersection with NY 28, turn southeast onto Big Brook Road, also marked as County Route 4. This is a twisting country road, with a scenic causeway across the width of Lake Abanakee at 1.4 miles. At 3.4 miles turn left onto Starbuck Road, which leads to Wilderness Lane 1 mile later. The eastern trailhead for Clear Pond is located at this intersection. Turn right to find the John Pond trailhead at the end of the road; signs point left to a driveway leading to the parking area

BIRD'S-EYE VIEW OF JOHN POND AND ITS MOUNTAINOUS NEIGHBORHOOD

WINTER CAMPFIRE AT JOHN POND

on state land, a total of 4.6 miles from NY 30.

THE HIKE

The yellow-marked loop trail is equally enjoyable regardless of whether you hike it in a clockwise or counterclockwise direction. Because the John Pond end has a dedicated parking area, let's begin there. The trail leads south from the trailhead, level and nearly straight as an arrow. This part of the trail was open to vehicles as recently as 1987, but now it is a designated foot trail. It is not the most exciting route, but it has the advantage of being easy. One moment of excitement comes at 0.4 mile, where you dip through an open wetland; a short side trail leads right at 0.5 mile to a view of John Pond Brook. At 0.7 mile, the loop trail makes a sharp turn left. Continuing straight toward the brook on a faint herd path brings you to the first of the Little Canada foundations.

Turning eastward on the loop trail, you encounter a small rise as you parallel the course of John Pond Brook. You'll enjoy the scenic view of Bullhead Mountain across the valley at 1.4 miles, where the trail bumps up against the edge of a large wetland on the brook. Bullhead is not a particularly tall mountain, but it is quite long, and therefore its profile seems massive. It is essentially a long ridge running north–south, with a prominent peak anchoring its southern end near Puffer Pond. This will not be your only view of Bullhead Mountain today, and once you learn to identify its signature profile, you can easily spot it from many other mountains throughout the central Adirondacks.

You encounter yet another side trail at 1.7 miles. This one leads north for 120 feet to a small cemetery—Little Canada's most poignant site. Here you will find the graves of Elizabeth Amelia King and Peter Savarie, two half-siblings who died in 1897 from diphtheria. Today their resting place is located deep within a forest of white pine.

Continuing northeast on the loop trail, you reach the crossing of John Pond Brook at 1.9 miles, where only visitors during a winter thaw or the early spring runoff will be stymied in their efforts to reach John Pond. Everyone else should be able to step across this small stream without much concern.

At 2 miles, you reach a junction with a blue-marked trail leading south along the foot of Bullhead to Puffer Pond. Just before this intersection, and within sight of it, look for a cellar hole off to the right.

A subtle ascent leads up to the south end of John Pond at 2.4 miles. A moment before you reach the pond, the yellow-marked loop trail bears right, but for now you should stay on the old road as it leads the final 0.1 mile to the John Pond Lean-to. A plantation of red pine surrounds this site, which offers views of the rocky ridgeline to the west. That small mountain has no official name, nor does it have a trail—but its bald ledges and knobs offers some outstanding vistas of the pond and the surrounding wilderness landscape. Experienced hikers may be tempted to leave the loop trail and seek out its secrets. Most people refer to the mountain as John Pond Ridge.

To continue the loop hike, you will need to backtrack south from the lean-to to the point where the new loop trail turns northeast. This connector trail is well constructed, although it passes so far east of John Pond that you will have no further views of it. Instead of the shoreline, it favors the high ground, slowly working its way up the flanks of John Pond Ridge. The valley to your right was also an extension of Little Canada, as evidenced by the plantation of Norway spruce that now grows there. Your only encounter with that part of the settlement occurs after you crest the height-of-land between John and Clear

Ponds and begin the slow descent into the next watershed; a handful of those Norway spruce trees have taken root here on the hillside.

Clear Pond lacks the close-up mountain views that John is known for, and when you first see the pond at 3.6 miles, you may find the view somewhat underwhelming. The trail passes very close to the southwestern shoreline, leading inland to a trail junction at 3.8 miles. Left leads back to Wilderness Lane, but first you really should explore the red-marked spur to the right. This trail leads across the rocky outlet stream with its nearby cattail marsh, then it hooks through the woods to a scenic shoreline ledge with a fine view down the length of the pond to Bullhead Mountain. A herd path continues around the shoreline to Clear's best campsites.

Returning back across the outlet, the yellow-marked loop trail climbs briefly away from the pond before making a slow descent southwest, back to the junction of Wilderness Lane and Starbuck Road. You reach this trailhead 4.9 miles into your adventure. If you have a car spotted here, then your hike is over. However, if you parked at the John Pond trailhead, then you will need to turn left onto Wilderness Lane and keep walking for a few minutes more; the distance between the two endpoints is a mere 0.3 mile by road.

6

Chimney Mountain

TOTAL DISTANCE: 2.2 miles round-trip

HIKING TIME: 1.5 hours

VERTICAL RISE: 860 feet

TRAILHEAD GPS COORDINATES: N43° 41' 16.8" W74° 13' 48.7"

There are hundreds of mountains in the Adirondack Park, but Chimney Mountain near Indian Lake stands out as one of the most geologically unusual. The eponymous chimney is a pillar of metamorphic rock standing conspicuously on the summit, the remnant of an intrusion into a softer sedimentary layer of rock that has long since eroded away. It is common to see isolated boulders parked on top of mountains throughout the region; these are called glacial erratics, transported by a slow-moving river of ice during the last ice age and deposited as debris when the glacier melted. But chimneys such as this are a spur of bedrock sticking up into the air, and these are very rare.

Chimney Mountain has been a popular hiking destination since at least the 1920s, when local resident Charles S. Carroll opened a former farmhouse on Kings Flow as the Chimney Mountain House. This was a hotel that catered to what was then the new breed of motoring tourist, at a time when automobile ownership was first becoming widespread. He cut the first trail to the summit, which the Glens Falls Chapter of the Adirondack Mountain Club marked with yellow disks a few years later.

The original hotel is long gone, and for a few years the site served as a Boy Scout camp. Today the Carroll property is managed as a colony of vacation rentals known as the Cabins at Chimney Mountain. It sits at the north end of Kings Flow, a scenic reservoir created during the lumbering days, now used for recreation. Because the landowner controls the dam and the northern half of the flow, access is limited to the guests of the cabin.

Fortunately, the tradition of public access to Chimney Mountain across the private property continues to this

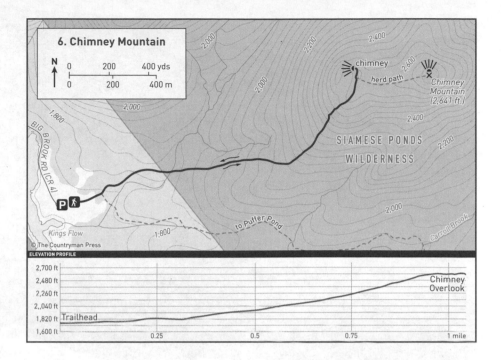

6. Chimney Mountain

N
0   200   400 yds
0   200   400 m

chimney
herd path
Chimney
Mountain
(2,641 ft.)

SIAMESE PONDS
WILDERNESS

BIG BROOK RD (CR 4)

Kings Flow

to Puffer Pond

Carroll Brook

© The Countryman Press

ELEVATION PROFILE

2,700 ft
2,480 ft
2,260 ft
2,,040 ft
1,820 ft — Trailhead
1,600 ft

Chimney
Overlook

0.25   0.5   0.75   1 mile

day. The only concession is that hikers are asked to pay a modest daily fee of $2 per car. Kings Flow is a strategic gateway into the Siamese Ponds Wilderness, with connecting trails to Puffer Pond and beyond. But certainly, most day hikers come here to see Chimney Mountain.

This is a short trail, steep in places but otherwise well suited for families and novice hikers. Experts love this mountain too, because of all the additional features found on the summit—particularly the caves that permeate the rift valley at the foot of the chimney. These caves are known for their tight spaces, and several require climbing gear. Because of these technical difficulties, and the fact that some of the caves serve as bat hibernacula, this book does not describe the location of any of the cave entrances.

GETTING THERE

The Kings Flow trailhead is located 8 miles south of the hamlet of Indian Lake. From NY 30 about 0.5 mile south of the intersection with NY 28, turn southeast onto Big Brook Road, also marked as County Route 4. This is a twisting country road, with a scenic causeway across the width of Lake Abanakee at 1.4 miles. Big Brook Road makes a hard right turn at 5.4 miles, but otherwise stay with it all the way past the end of the pavement and the Kings Flow dam to the public parking area at the center of the Cabins at Chimney Mountain campus. The landowner charges a daily fee of $2 per car for parking, which can be deposited into a lockbox attached to a nearby signpost.

PUFFER MOUNTAIN AS SEEN FROM CHIMNEY'S TRUE SUMMIT

THE HIKE

The trail to Chimney Mountain is as basic as they come—short and to the point. The hiking trails to Puffer and Chimney start to the east of the parking area, at the far end of a large clearing. There is a trailhead register at the edge of the forest, and then the two trails go their separate ways. The Chimney Mountain trail is to the left; it enters the woods, crosses a pair of streams within the first 0.3 mile, and then it begins to climb. From there it is a steady, sometimes steep ascent to the mountain's western summit. Just below the top, a herd path leads across

Not so the mountain, though! The chimney stands about thirty-five feet above the end of the trail, on the edge of the mountain. You can see across the rift valley and the west rim to the mountains between Kings Flow and Indian Lake—Crotched Pond Mountain and Kunjamuk Mountain in particular—with the massive Snowy Mountain Range on the western horizon. Blue Mountain's distinctive profile is easily identified to the northwest. John Pond Ridge, the rocky backdrop to Hike 5, figures prominently in the middle distance.

The rift valley sprawls out below you, and its origin tells much about the natural history of the mountain. According to geologists, the massive rock that constitutes the western end of Chimney Mountain was undercut by erosion—and like any building with a bad foundation, it began to lean away. The resulting gap filled with fractured rock, creating the rift and its plethora of caves.

Completing the hike is a simple matter of returning to Kings Flow via the marked trail. However, the adventurous and curious hiker may enjoy a brief and scenic side trip before leaving the mountain. Chimney's true summit lies a short distance to the east, and it features a large bald area with fine views of Kings Flow. A herd path leads to it, beginning on the state trail just before the steep ledge leading up to the chimney. It descends past a designated campsite, and then leads for 0.2 mile and 150 vertical feet to the summit. There are no signs and markers, so you need to be self-reliant to find it. The initial views include the distant High Peaks to the north, as well as the massive forested slopes of Bullhead and Puffer mountains. With some searching, you should be able to find a photogenic view down the valley toward the man-made flow.

a small gully to the western rim of the mountain's rift valley, where additional views can be found. The marked trail, though, continues to the eastern rim, where the chimney is located, 1.1 miles from the parking area and 860 vertical feet above it. Except for one short ledge where a bit of scrambling is required, the hike is unremarkable.

7

Snowy Mountain

TOTAL DISTANCE: 7.6 miles round-trip

HIKING TIME: 4 hours

VERTICAL RISE: 2,090 feet

TRAILHEAD GPS COORDINATES: N43° 42′ 04.1″ W74° 20′ 05.5″

At 3,899 feet in elevation, the summit of Snowy Mountain falls tantalizingly close to the 4,000-foot "High Peak" threshold. By a quirk of history, Snowy is actually taller than several of the traditionally recognized High Peaks, each of which were originally thought to be 4,000 feet high but later revealed to be much shorter—a factoid that many climbers are quick to point out. Regardless of its park-wide ranking, though, this is the highest mountain south of those peaks, and one of the park's most distinguishable landmarks. Once you learn to identify its knobby profile, you can easily pick it out from many distant viewpoints.

The mountain has gone by several names during its history; Snowy was the option endorsed by the famed nineteenth-century surveyor Verplanck Colvin, and the one that has appeared on topographic maps ever since. Certainly, the name is apt. It presides over a fourteen-mile range that includes several other massive summits, most of them unknown to the hiking public due to the absence of trails. The forests here are grand; the portion of the mountain that lies within the Forest Preserve was acquired by the state in 1897. No lumbering has occurred since then, and very little probably occurred before.

There never would have been a trail on Snowy had the old Conservation Commission, a precursor to today's DEC, not erected a fire observation tower here in 1917. This was one of dozens of steel fire towers built in the aftermath of a series of devastating fires that occurred in the early twentieth century. The materials for many of the towers, including Snowy, were hauled to the summits by teams of horses or oxen. Most had a cabin nearby where an observer lived for three seasons every year. The most critical times

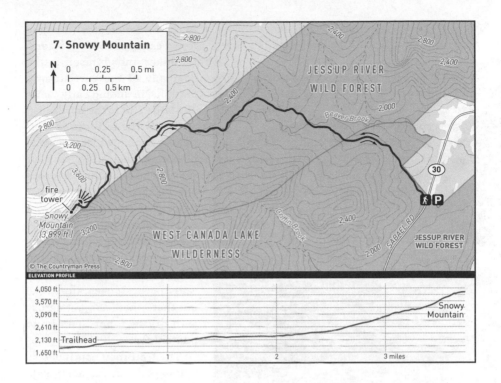

7. Snowy Mountain

N

0   0.25   0.5 mi

0   0.25   0.5 km

JESSUP RIVER
WILD FOREST

Beaver Brook

fire
tower

Snowy
Mountain
(3,899 ft.)

WEST CANADA LAKE
WILDERNESS

Griffin Brook

SABAEL RD.

JESSUP RIVER
WILD FOREST

© The Countryman Press

ELEVATION PROFILE

4,050 ft
3,570 ft
3,090 ft
2,610 ft
2,130 ft Trailhead
1,650 ft

Snowy
Mountain

1   2   3 miles

of the year for spotting fires were spring and fall, when the woods were dry and there were many leaves on the ground. Phone lines connected the mountains to the outside world.

The Snowy Mountain tower has not been manned since 1971, but in 2001 it was refurbished and reopened for recreational use. Not everyone will appreciate the climb up the rickety wooden steps to a cab that tends to rattle in the wind, though. Two ledges on the summit—one located right on the trail, another hidden along an unmarked herd path—complement each other with ground-level views across the wild valleys on each side of the range.

This is a long, steep, and tiring climb—well above average in all three of those categories compared to other fire tower hikes. The challenge is part of the appeal, though, and it is certainly no hindrance to the mountain's popularity. On

any given weekend throughout the year, especially when the weather is good, you can bank on the likelihood that someone is out there climbing Snowy. On summer weekends, those people number in the dozens.

GETTING THERE

The Snowy Mountain trailhead is easy to find, located on NY 30 some 17 miles north of Speculator and 7 miles south of Indian Lake. On a clear day, there are good views of the mountain from either direction along the highway. The parking area is located on the east side of the highway, and the trail begins on the west.

THE HIKE

Unlike many fire tower hikes, this one begins with a long approach to the foot

VIEW OF INDIAN LAKE FROM SNOWY MOUNTAIN

In the colder months when the forest canopy is bare of leaves, the hiker finds himself in the company of the surrounding foothills, including early views of a large cliff to the north.

Slowly the trail draws near Beaver Brook, which you may hear in a deep gully to your right. At 1.2 miles the trail drops and reaches a crossing of that brook, the first of several adventurous moments on this hike. There is no bridge, just a series of large rocks that you can step or hop across, depending on the water levels. It generally works out that hikers can get across with dry feet, but there is no guarantee.

The trail then continues as before, now on the north side of the valley. If you are alert to your surroundings, you might steal some glimpses of Snowy's summit from the flanks of one of the knolls, getting closer but still quite high above you. At 1.5 miles you encounter the next notable stream crossing, this one on a log bridge next to a wild little wetland.

of the mountain through a wild valley, and it ends with a tremendously steep climax. Although not a dawn-to-dusk affair, it is a significant effort—not unlike an adventure in the High Peaks, to which Snowy is often compared.

Beginning across the highway from the parking area, the trail climbs a short bank to the register box and then begins a rolling traverse through the valley of Beaver Brook. In the summer, this is an uneventful trek through deep woods, over the knolls and through the gullies.

For such an oft-used trail, everything up to this point is generally well maintained. Eventually, though, the terrain starts to resist human efforts to keep a dry, erosion-free trail. You first notice this at about 1.9 miles, when the trail and Beaver Brook come in much closer contact with each other. There are several more stream crossings in quick succession, none as wide as the first, but the likelihood for mud is now higher.

The last stream crossing is followed immediately by a rock staircase up a steep bank. The trail work is impressive, but it ends too soon; there is some significant erosion above this spot, and much of the remaining climb is steep. Your vertical progress is marked by changes in the forest: the hemlocks of the lower elevations give way to red spruce, and beech trees give way to birches. The woods become distinctly more coniferous, and after a brief traverse you reach the bottom of a chain of glades that guide you along most of the remaining climb to the summit. The way is exceedingly steep, with several ledges to negotiate just before reaching the open ledge where the observer's cabin once stood, 3.7 miles from the trailhead.

And what a reward! This large grassy clearing is now the favored stopping point for hikers, with a view of Indian Lake, a broad swath of the Siamese Ponds Wilderness, and the distant High Peaks. The lake was so close when you started this hike, but now it is several miles distant.

This is not the end of the trail, though. The markers continue southwest into the woods for about 0.1 mile more to the foot of the fire tower, which you cannot see until you are practically underneath it.

The view from the top extends the view to a far greater range than the ledge at the cabin site, including the Cedar River headwater region to the west of the mountain and the vast region of the West Canada Lake Wilderness and Moose River Plains Wild Forest. Wakely Mountain, another favorite fire tower summit, stands prominently to the northwest.

While you are on the summit, do yourself a favor and keep an eye out for the herd path leading to the small open ledge on the west side of the mountain. This spot overlooks the outstanding wild region to the west; although you don't see the river itself, much of that forest contains the headwaters of the Cedar River. For those who choose not to climb the tower, this ledge and the one at the cabin site are more-than-adequate substitutions.

Descending the mountain may take as much time as the ascent, especially on the steeper upper slopes, where steady footing is important. Then comes the 2-mile hike through the Beaver Brook watershed, where you have the chance to see anew some of the forest details you might have missed on the hike in.

Cascade and Stephens Ponds

TOTAL DISTANCE: 7.4 miles end-to-end

HIKING TIME: 3.5 hours

VERTICAL RISE: 400 feet

TRAILHEAD GPS COORDINATES: N43° 50' 53.4" W74° 25' 26.1" (western); N43° 50' 31.2" W74° 23' 10.9" (eastern)

When I first visited Cascade Pond years ago, I was amused by an entry in the lean-to journal. A visitor to the Adirondacks from New York City had been staying at the nearby campground on Lake Durant and hiked this loop trail through the Blue Ridge Wilderness. This was likely his first time in the Adirondacks, because the beauty of Cascade Pond caught him off guard. He remarked that he had come here expecting to find a "mud hole," not a stunning little lake with a mountainous backdrop.

Ever since then, I've always tried to visualize just what that anonymous hiker must have imagined he would see—perhaps a puddle of water in the woods filled with tadpoles, with water cascading into it over a mossy log?

There are several bodies of water in the Adirondacks with the name Cascade, but I admit this one is my personal favorite. It sits in a scenic basin just a few miles outside of Blue Mountain Lake, making it a good option when I crave a wilderness setting but don't have the time for a longer getaway. Sometimes I continue to nearby Stephens Pond, and sometimes I don't. The old lean-to where I found that journal entry is gone, but it is still the prettiest waypoint along the shoreline. The view from the rock ledges toward distant Blue Ridge is photogenic, and the small cascade on the pond's outlet is always a charmer.

There are several trails converging on Cascade Pond, but to make the most of a visit you really should do the point-to-point hike described here, starting at the western trailhead and ending at the campground. This loop takes you past the pond toward Stephens, which is also attractive. There are lean-tos at each body of water, both of which are good options to consider for first-time back-packers. If camping is not your thing, no

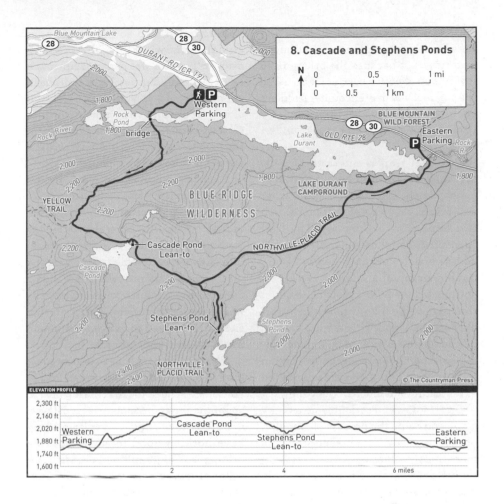

8. Cascade and Stephens Ponds

ELEVATION PROFILE

worries; this is a great day hike, available for exploration all year round.

GETTING THERE

The western trailhead is located on a gravel driveway on Durant Road, south of Blue Mountain Lake. This narrow lane begins 0.2 mile west of the eastern intersection of Durant Road and NY 28 and 30, next to a cemetery. The driveway passes the trailhead and reaches a point where boats may be launched on Lake Durant. It is not plowed in winter, but the extra distance you have to walk to the trail is nominal.

The eastern end of the trail begins at the well-marked parking area on NY 28 and 30 between Indian Lake and Blue Mountain Lake, near the Lake Durant Campground and just 2.6 miles from the main intersection at Blue Mountain Lake. There is ample parking on both sides of the road.

THE HIKE

From the western trailhead near the cemetery, follow the red-marked trail west. In just 0.6 mile, roughly a 15-minute walk, you reach a long, low-lying bridge spanning the channel between Lake

Durant and Rock Pond. Technically both bodies of water are one continuous waterway, but because the bridge is so low, it is an effective barrier for boats. In the summer you may encounter paddlers congregated on this bridge as they try to scoot their canoes and kayaks underneath it.

The foot trail reenters the woods and makes a short climb up and over a steep knoll. The descent on the other side brings you to a small stream, which you hop across right away. The trail then turns to follow this stream on a southwesterly heading, gently climbing higher into the valley. It is a pretty setting, but the unfortunate truth about this part of the hike is that it is miserably wet and muddy. There are several places where the trail splits, with detouring herd paths created by people trying to keep their boots dry. This condition extends through much of the valley.

At 1.7 miles you scramble up a rocky slope and begin the process of climbing out of the valley. This higher ground is more thickly coniferous, in contrast with the verdant hardwoods below. A dark, damp forest of red spruce and balsam fir surrounds Cascade Pond, so as you enter this region of the wilderness you start to feel as if you are getting somewhere—even if the pond is still some distance ahead of you.

There is a prominent T-junction 2.1 miles into the hike. The yellow-marked trail to the right is a relatively recent addition to the local trail network; it leads to the Grassy Pond trailhead on NY 28, and though it is infrequently traveled, it makes an excellent alternative to the trail you just followed from Lake Durant.

But as the signs indicate, the way to Cascade and Stephens Ponds is a left turn. This route was once part of a wagon road, and so the way is a bit straighter and wider than what you have seen so far. The wet spots occur much less frequently. As you head southeast, keep an eye out to your right. The trail slowly approaches the north shore of Cascade Pond, and you may glimpse it through the trees long before you reach the old lean-to site at 2.6 miles.

Even without the lean-to, you should have no problem recognizing this site. It is located a short distance above the cascading outlet, with several rock ledges leading down in steps toward the shoreline. Slender white pine trees frame the view across the pond toward Blue Ridge, a massive mountain occupying the distant heart of the forest. Although this site is now closed to camping, it is still the best lunch spot around.

The replacement lean-to is located on the opposite side of the cove. To find it, you will first need to cross the log bridge spanning the eponymous cascade. If you are prone to vertigo, you will probably have nothing good to say about this bridge; it is high and narrow, with the water dropping noisily below you. Otherwise, it is a scenic spot, with rocks just downstream from the cascade where photographic opportunities may be found. The rock ledges on the upstream side offer more good views of the pond.

The trail is briefly rugged as it navigates the outlet area, but be on the lookout for the lean-to sign pointing the way right. This side trail leads to the current shelter, which is located in a stand of white birch. The shelter itself has no faults, but the site lacks the views of the old spot, and the water access is not as good. It is not uncommon to find small aluminum boats stored here, though.

The continuing red-marked trail leads generally southeast for another 0.8 mile past the lean-to site, coming to

LOOKING TOWARD BLUE RIDGE FROM CASCADE POND

STEPHENS POND

an end at 3.5 miles, at a junction with the blue-marked Northville-Placid Trail. The way left leads to Lake Durant, but before you go that way you will definitely want to see Stephens Pond. So

turn right, following the N-P Trail southbound on a slow descent toward the Stephens Pond Lean-to, 0.6 mile away. This shelter is set back from the water, but trails lead down to scenic spots. From a hiker's perspective, Stephens is less visually dynamic than Cascade, perhaps because there is no huge mountain to serve as a backdrop. Some people who have paddled both ponds, however, insist that Stephens is actually the more intriguing destination.

When you are ready to complete the hike, backtrack up the N-P Trail toward the Cascade Pond junction, then continue northbound (or northeast, to be more accurate) toward the campground. After so many enjoyable miles in the backcountry, the sudden sight of RVs and people when you arrive at DEC's Lake Durant Campground may seem startling. Unless you are camping here yourself, you will need to turn right onto the campground road and follow it past the shower building, toward the dam that creates the lake. Here the N-P Trail crosses the Rock River and leads back to your waiting vehicle on NY 28 and 30, a total of 3.3 miles from the Stephens Pond Lean-to.

9

Castle Rock

TOTAL DISTANCE: 3.5-mile loop with optional side trips

HIKING TIME: 1.5 hours

VERTICAL RISE: 600 feet

TRAILHEAD GPS COORDINATES: N43° 52' 22.3" W74° 27' 03.7"

The Adirondack Park is home to hundreds of mountains, both large and small. The rugged virtues of the largest peaks recommend themselves, because when it comes to mountains, adventurers will always be attracted to superlatives: the biggest, the most rugged, the most famous. And in the central Adirondacks, few mountains are more popular and well trodden than Blue Mountain, the 3,740-foot peak that towers above its namesake lake, smack-dab in the middle of the park. It is hard to look at Blue and not be struck with a desire to climb it.

But the scenic qualities of the smaller mountains should never be underestimated—especially when those lower summits hover close above one of the region's largest lakes. Such is the case with Castle Rock, a small knob of rock standing sentinel above Blue Mountain Lake's northern shoreline. While Blue Mountain is bigger and more popular, I much prefer the photogenic vista from this lower summit. You could not ask for a better bird's eye perspective of the lake than the one found on the summit, even if you were to board a sightseeing plane.

Castle Rock is serviced by a fun loop trail that includes a little bit of everything, including a pond, a "cave," and of course, the summit views. There are steep sections on this trail, but all in all this is a fun family hike, full of adventure.

If your schedule is flexible, be sure to time your arrival on the summit for late afternoon, when the sun has shifted to the west. This is because the summit ledge faces southeast and is therefore most photogenic when you are not looking directly into the sun.

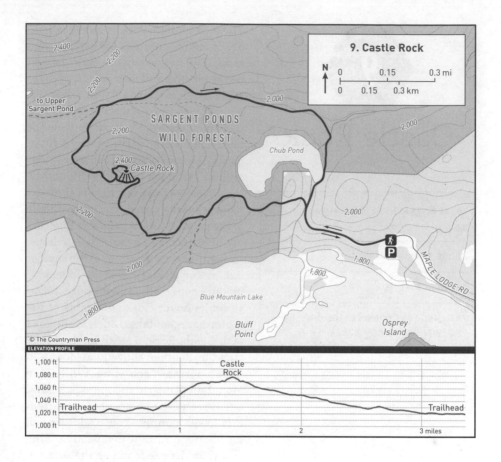

ELEVATION PROFILE

GETTING THERE

The trailhead for Castle Rock is located at the end of Maple Lodge Road, which turns northwest from NY 30 just 0.6 mile north of downtown Blue Mountain Lake. This is a narrow residential road, and the parking area is located on private land next to a small conference center. Be sure to park in the designated public parking area, and keep your pets leashed at least as far as the state land boundary.

THE HIKE

Your hike begins on a private gravel road leading west from the conference center. Don't get accustomed to the wide, easy walking surface, because within minutes the trail markers direct you to turn right onto a poorer logging road. A moment later, at 0.4 mile, you reach a junction. This is where the loop begins; either trail will eventually get you to Castle Rock.

I usually choose to hike this loop in a clockwise circuit, since that is the most direct way to the summit. Turn left, crossing a stream and heading into a wild forest on a narrow foot trail. You pass the southwestern corner of Chub Pond, where you do not have to step far off the trail to get a good look. A moment later, at 0.8 mile, you reach another trail junction. The route to the left leads down to the shore of Blue Mountain Lake and is one of two side trips you might want to consider; this one is only 0.2 mile long, but you do lose about 120 feet in elevation.

The main trail bears right at the junction and begins to climb more aggressively. For the most part the trail is well used and easy to find, although about halfway up the mountain, it makes a hairpin turn to the left that could potentially be confusing. One of the purposes of the bend is to lead you to a peculiar rock overhang beside the trail, a cave of sorts that most hikers stop to explore.

Past the "cave," the trail climbs up to a third junction at 1.4 miles, this one located high on the mountain's shoulder. A left turn here would lead you off the mountain, so turn right toward the summit. This final part of the climb is short, only 0.1 mile long, but it is very steep with several ledges.

When you reach the summit at 1.5 miles, the main ledge overlooking the lake will be on your right. It seems as though every part of Blue Mountain Lake is visible below you, including its assortment of islands. Blue Mountain frames the view on the far left, and beyond the

CASTLE ROCK'S GRAND VIEW OF BLUE MOUNTAIN LAKE

hamlet on the east shore you can see Lake Durant with Gore, Bullhead, and Puffer mountains on the horizon. Blue Ridge is the long mountain dominating the southern horizon. If you search around the summit rocks, you may find a second opening with a view north, but this one is much less far-ranging than the one found at the main ledge.

To complete the loop, you will need to head back down the steep ledges to the last trail junction you encountered. This time bear right and west, and begin descending down the back side of the mountain. This route is less steep, but also less eventful. Although you are leaving the mountain behind, you are still hiking away from your starting point.

The target of this trail segment is a small valley at the northern foot of Castle Rock. Here, 2 miles into the hike, you reach yet another trail junction. The trail to the left is a long, 3.2-mile valley hike leading to a scenic spot on Upper Sargent Pond; it passes through grand forests for nearly that entire distance, and it makes a fine wilderness-style hike for anyone looking to turn a visit to Castle Rock into a full day's outing.

Most people, however, turn right to continue on the loop around the mountain. This trail now heads east on a gentle descent that is sometimes marred by mud. The trail turns south to skirt the eastern edge of Chub Pond, and at 3.1 miles you complete the loop when you return to the junction where you first made your clockwise approach to the summit. Keeping left, you should soon find yourself back on the private road leading back to the conference center.

Owls Head Mountain

TOTAL DISTANCE: 6.2 miles round-trip

HIKING TIME: 4 hours

VERTICAL RISE: 1,100 feet

TRAILHEAD GPS COORDINATES: N43° 57′ 48.4″ W74° 27′ 09.7″

The fire tower on the summit of Owls Head Mountain near Long Lake offers some of the finest views available of the vast western Adirondack wilderness, an area that possesses very few summits of its own. If you want to know that region, sometime it's better to grab a paddle and start planning a canoe trip. But that's what makes the Adirondack Park so outstanding: the broad diversity of its terrain, with an abundance of everything from alpine summits to lowland bogs.

But the strategic location of this particular Owls Head Mountain (several summits in the Adirondacks have similar names) makes it the bridge between the mountainous central region to the east and the lake-studded west, with a sweeping vista from the top of the tower that takes in everything. When you get tired of trying to identify all the peaks in view, turn slightly and give the lakes a try.

The tower was erected in 1919, eleven years after a major forest fire devastated an area northwest of the mountain. For many years it was manned by observers who lived near the summit and maintained a telephone line the entire length of the trail. Eventually the tower was taken out of service, and it fell into disrepair; on my first visit, the stairs were removed and the cab at the top had no floor. In 2004 it was repaired by volunteers and state employees so that hikers can once again climb to the top for the nearly 360° view.

In many ways, this is a historical hike—not because any major events occurred here, but because the experience of climbing Owls Head is probably much as it always has been. The telephone line is down, but most of the poles that supported it remain. Likewise, the observer's cabin was razed in 1979, but the base supports remain.

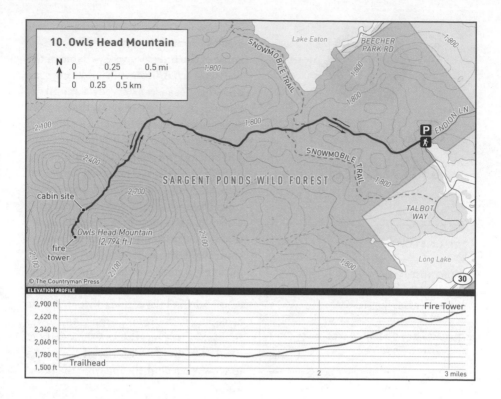

On the other hand, the trail is a prime example of how trails used to be built, with fall lines that have become eroded gullies. The last 0.3 mile of the hike is very steep.

This is a fine year-round hike, although the portions of the trail with running water down the middle will be less pleasant in the non-summer months. Ice may be a major issue on the final summit knob, where the trail ascends a series of steep ledges.

GETTING THERE

The trailhead is located on Endion Road, just outside of the hamlet of Long Lake. From the intersection of NY 30 and NY 28N downtown, follow NY 30 north over the bridge across Long Lake. At 1.3 miles, turn left (south) onto Endion Road. The trailhead is about 1.5 miles ahead, located on the right where the road swings left.

THE HIKE

Following red markers, the foot trail leads southwest. The climbing begins right away, with an ascent of 200 feet in the first 0.4 mile; but then the grade moderates, becoming a gentle hike through a mature forest. If this trail was created as a reaction to the 1908 forest fire that wiped out the hamlet once known as Long Lake West, you'll see no evidence of that fire here; the mixture of tree species and ages is consistent with native forests all across the park. If not true old growth now, it is becoming increasingly harder to tell the difference.

At 0.8 mile you reach a junction with a prominent snowmobile trail connecting Lake Eaton with Long Lake. To reach the mountain, bear left through the hemlock forest and follow this snowmobile track for just 0.2 mile, or no more than six or seven minutes. There the snowmobile trail makes a sharp left turn, but the foot trail to Owls Head keeps right.

Now just a narrow footpath again, the trail begins a gentle ascent parallel to a small stream, rising through a forest of beech, maple, and yellow birch. Beech trees produce edible nuts that attract a variety of wildlife, most notably bears; although many of these beeches are pocked with disease, you may spot claw marks where bruins have climbed to the uppermost limbs. There, they will break off the branches to reach the nuts, creating "nests" high in the treetops.

Things start to get serious as the trail angles more southward and reaches the mountain proper. The trail is moderately steep, but it becomes quite rugged when the red markers lead you into what appears to be more of a streambed than a trail. Through much of the year it really is a stream, with water running straight down the path. This is what is meant when we say a trail follows the "fall line," or the route that running water is naturally inclined to take as it flows directly down a slope. A modern trail would be cut at an angle to the fall line, encouraging water to flow across the trail rather than straight down it.

At 2.7 miles, you encounter a short respite from the climbing, where the trail tops out at 2,600 feet and passes between two of the mountain's peripheral summits. Then a short descent begins, where yet another small stream hijacks the trail for a short distance.

You are now high on a plateau, surrounded by all of the mountain's summit knobs. Here, 2.8 miles from Endion Road, you reach the site of the observer's cabin. The structure itself has long

since been removed, leaving only the concrete pylons upon which it stood. These cabins were modest affairs, providing a comfortable living space for the often solitary fire watchman. The site is now surrounded by a stand of paper birch, notable for its shaggy bark that is white on one side and light bronze on the other.

The main summit looms just ahead, and moments after passing the cabin site you reach the foot of a steep slope. Several rocky ledges stand between you and the fire tower, and although running water may not be a problem, ice certainly will be a problem in winter. Even for summer hikers, some scrambling is required to get you up several of these steps.

You do not see the tower until you are practically underneath it, 3.1 miles from the trailhead. The tower stands at the edge of a large summit clearing, which slopes down to the edge of several natural ledges. Even if there was no tower, the ground-level views would justify the hike. They take in the mountains surrounding the south end of Long Lake, with South Pond located midway between you and Blue Mountain; the

ALONG THE TRAIL TO THE SUMMIT

AT THE TOP OF THE FIRE TOWER

distant mountain just to the left of Blue is Gore Mountain, located an even thirty miles away.

But to appreciate the full view, you must climb to the top of the tower. The view is not completely unobstructed, as some of the nearby trees have now grown to be nearly as tall as the tower. But what you can see is impressive. The High Peaks stand as a massive grouping of mountains to the northeast; Blue Mountain is the most distinctive landmark to the southeast, with a service road zigzagging up its slopes. Portions of Forked and Raquette lakes can be seen to the southwest.

The most enigmatic view lies to the northwest. That is the region of the Adirondack Park better known to paddlers than to hikers, since it features more lakes than it does large mountains. It takes some patient and skilled map-and-compass work to identify the landmarks in that direction, such as Rock Pond in the William C. Whitney Wilderness, or Frederica Mountain near Lake Lila (Hike #45).

On the return hike, the most difficult section will be descending the steep ledges back to the cabin site and then negotiating the potentially wet rocks on the northern slopes. But if you start this hike early enough in the morning, you might be back in Long Lake in time for a late lunch.

Great Camp Santanoni

TOTAL DISTANCE: 8.8 miles round-trip with optional loop

HIKING TIME: 3 hours

ELEVATION CHANGE: rolling terrain

TRAILHEAD GPS COORDINATES: N43° 58' 21.5" W74° 09' 50.6"

During the 1970s, the state acquired four Great Camps and their surrounding estates for inclusion in the Forest Preserve. All four tracts were instrumental in improving public access to outstanding wilderness backcountry, but the presence of the camps—most of which were showing signs of deterioration—presented a constitutional conundrum. And in all four cases, the state took a completely different course of action.

Article XIV of the state Constitution mandates that all forestland owned by the state in the Adirondack Park be forever maintained in a wild state—the so-called "forever wild" clause. There is no provision for buildings. Typically, when the state acquires land with a camp on it, the building is razed or dismantled. But in these four cases, the state had acquired buildings of an unusual historical and architectural significance.

In the case of Nehasane Lodge on Lake Lila in the Nehasane Preserve, the structure was razed so that the site could be brought into full compliance with Article XIV—and would fulfill the conditions of the sale of the property. At Camp Sagamore, near Raquette Lake, a statewide referendum approved a constitutional amendment that allowed a non-profit to purchase the entire camp complex and preserve the buildings. At Topridge, the state disposed of the buildings and surrounding 102 acres by placing them on the auction block without seeking a constitutional amendment. The auction, though technically illegal, went unchallenged, because all agreed it was the most expedient solution to the question of what to do with the Great Camp.

At Camp Santanoni, the state retained ownership of the buildings, although it took a number of years to

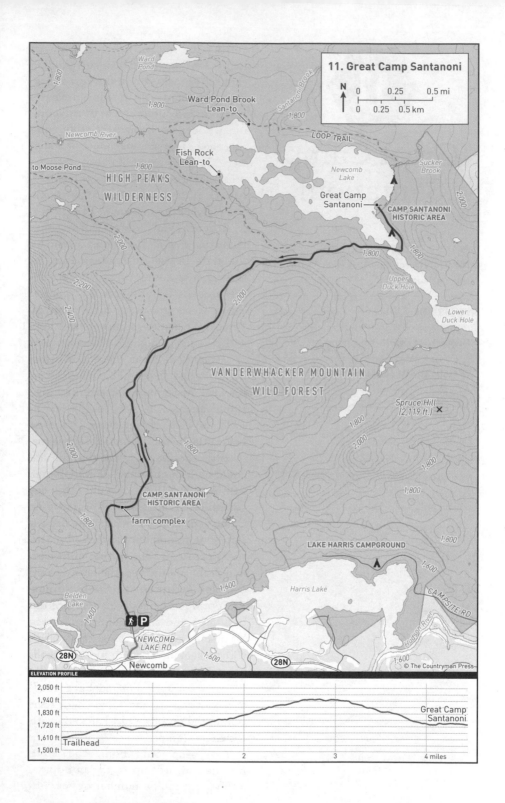

11. Great Camp Santanoni

decide what to do with them. Concerns for protecting the legal sanctity of the Forest Preserve and the historic value of the buildings have created a unique situation here. The camp complex, which is no longer occupied or furnished, is now maintained as a kind of backcountry museum. You can hike, bike, or ski to the camp at any time—or even ride there on a horse-drawn wagon—but public motor vehicle use is not allowed.

Robert Pruyn bought the Santanoni Preserve (pronounced "santa-NO-knee") in 1892 and began construction on the camp soon thereafter. Influenced by Japanese architecture, the main camp was a series of log buildings joined by a continuous verandah and united under a common roof. Outlying buildings included the farm complex and the Gate Lodge. The Pruyn family owned the property for sixty-one years, selling it to the Melvins of Syracuse in 1953. The Melvins owned the preserve until a family tragedy in 1971—the disappearance of an 8-year-old boy, who was never found—disinclined them to remain there. They sold the property to the Adirondack Conservancy the next year, which then transferred it to the state.

The general public is barred from driving the 4.4-mile access road to the camp, but hiking and cross-country skiing are immensely popular. Several times throughout the winter, visitors can enjoy interpretive tours with the staff of the historical group working to preserve the buildings. And since this is a backcountry destination, attractive lean-tos are available nearby along the shore of Newcomb Lake for people who want to extend their visit.

GETTING THERE

Take NY 28N to Newcomb, where, 1.9 miles west of the Hudson River, signs point the way to the Santanoni Preserve. Newcomb Lake Road leads across a narrow bridge to the Gate Lodge complex, where there is a large parking area maintained year-round. The Gate Lodge houses a visitors center that is open in the summer.

THE HIKE

The narrow road leading to the camp is an easy, though long, trail. The miles pass quickly, and the road never seems as long as it really is. Setting off from the trailhead, you reach the farm complex at 0.9 mile, where a distinctive building constructed of fieldstone—the creamery—stands to the left, along with several houses. A barn and silo once stood to the right of the road, but these burned to the ground in 2004 under suspicious circumstances.

At 2.2 miles you reach the horse trail to Moose Pond. The road to the lodge bears right, and the walking is uneventful until it begins to descend toward the lake. This descent is very gentle at first, but soon after passing the red-marked trail that leads around the south shore of Newcomb Lake at 3.6 miles, you encounter the steepest grade on the entire road to the Great Camp. If you are on skis, this is a zippy drop that leads around a turn and levels out within sight of the bridge over Newcomb Lake, 4.1 miles from the start.

The road crosses the bridge and turns north. There are several numbered campsites to the left along the shore. Then you approach the main lodge from behind at 4.4 miles. Some of the buildings are locked, but others are open to explore. Camping in the lodge is prohibited, but picnic tables abound on the long verandah. The reconstructed boathouse lies to the left of the lodge as you face the lake, and an art studio stands apart to the right; this serves as a warming hut during the winter weekend events.

SIDE TRIP: LOOP AROUND THE LAKE

While the opportunity to explore a Great Camp is the obvious draw for most visitors, it is important to point out that this also a great backcountry destination. The best way to enjoy Newcomb Lake on foot is to tackle the 3.9-mile loop that extends all the way around its northern and southern shores. The two lean-tos at the far end of the lake are its best campsites.

The loop trail begins near the studio building, leading northwest toward a series of designated campsites near the lake's eastern shore. At 0.2 mile you reach the reconstructed bathhouse, which faces a cedar-lined beach. A moment later you reach the last of the tent sites, just before the bridge over Sucker Brook.

Unfortunately much of the trail is routed too far back from the shoreline to offer views, but 1.5 miles from Camp Santanoni, just after crossing the log bridge over Santanoni Brook, look for the side trail leading left to the first of the lean-tos. This one, the Ward Pond Brook Lean-to, comes with its own small beach for swimming.

Bear left at the junction with the Moose Pond trail at 2.1 miles and cross the bridge over Newcomb Lake's western inlet. Now paralleling the southern shore, you reach the side trail to the

BLISSFUL TIMES AT THE WARD POND BROOK LEAN-TO

THE RESTORED BATHHOUSE AT GREAT CAMP SANTANONI

southern lean-to at 2.8 miles. This shelter (often called the Fish Rocks Lean-to) is located near a prominent rock on the shoreline, with an outstanding view of Santanoni Peak, the 4,606-foot summit that anchors the southern end of the Santanoni Range.

The remaining portion of the loop trail is uneventful, except for the occasional wetness. At 3.9 miles it rises to a junction with the main trail to the Great Camp. If you turn left it is just 0.8 mile to the camp; the trailhead is 3.6 miles to the right.

12

Moxham Mountain

TOTAL DISTANCE: 5.2 miles round-trip

HIKING TIME: 2 hours

VERTICAL RISE: 900 feet

TRAILHEAD GPS COORDINATES: N43° 46' 13.2" W74° 00' 43.6"

Moxham is a multi-peaked mountain that straddles the Essex-Warren county line. At about 2,441 feet in elevation, it is well off the list of the highest summits in the park—actually, its highest point is just about even with quite a few ponds in the central highlands.

But driving past Moxham Mountain on NY 28N between North Creek and Minerva, its profile is nothing short of monumental. That's because it is the epitome of a homocline, a mountain type that is common throughout the Adirondacks but reaches its most impressive form here. Homoclines have gentle northern slopes and precipitous, often rocky southern faces. But to say that Moxham's southern slope is merely rocky would be an understatement— parts of the mountain are sheer cliffs!

Therefore Moxham is a sight to behold as much as it is a mountain to climb. The easternmost extent of the mountain, called Moxham Point, is an imposing landmark as viewed from NY 28N, like a scale model of one of Yosemite's signature cliffs. The portion of the mountain that the trail visits is the central and highest summit, which is less cliff-like. Nevertheless, it offers unobstructed views of the chain of ponds at its foot. The state's ownership of the mountain is incomplete—the foot of the mountain, for instance, is privately owned—but what the public does have access to is pretty outstanding. This is a favorite hike, worth visiting time and again.

The relatively modest hiking distance, moderate grades, and multiple vistas make this a tempting family hike, an exciting adventure for all ages. The one caveat is the sheer drop-off at the top of the mountain, which is sure to make parents and pet owners nervous.

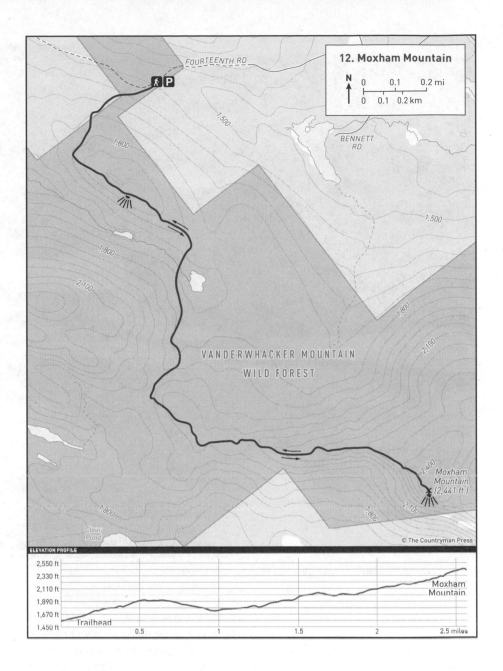

GETTING THERE

Follow NY 28N to the hamlet of Minerva, located in southern Essex County. From the four corners in the middle of town, turn southwest onto Fourteenth Road, so named because it leads into Township 14 of the old Totten and Crossfield Purchase. This dead-end road starts off as a paved county byway but eventually turns to gravel, dropping into the valley at the northern foot of the mountain. The trailhead for Moxham is 2.1 miles from Minerva.

DISTANT PEAKS OF THE SIAMESE PONDS WILDERNESS FROM MOXHAM'S SUMMIT

THE HIKE

The foot trail leads southwest from the parking area, climbing away from Fourteenth Road at an angle. There are three noteworthy views along this trail, and the first comes from a foothill that you summit just 0.6 mile from the start, as little as fifteen minutes into the hike. The trail circles around to the western flank of this small rock knob and ascends to a viewpoint 375 feet above where you parked. This view is not all-encompassing, but it is a good preview of what is ahead, including your first glimpse of the main summit, which is still 1.4 miles away as the crow flies.

You lose about 175 feet as you descend off this knob to the outlet of a small beaver meadow at 1 mile. At this point the trail is angling south toward a draw that ultimately divides two of the mountain's

take pictures—is just a little more than an hour. The trail approaches it from behind, and you can enjoy the sweeping vista from the treeline without the need to proceed any closer to the edge. The open rock is capped by a benchmark affixed to the mountain by a 1942 federal survey, with bolts nearby that once anchored the surveying equipment.

The thrust of the view is southwest, meaning that the best time to experience the mountain is in the morning, especially if you want to come away with good pictures. The chain of beaver meadows and ponds at the foot of the mountain point the way like landing lights on a runway toward the mountains west of the Hudson River. Of these, the remote peaks of the Siamese Ponds Wilderness are the most prominent, especially Bullhead and Puffer. The knobby summit of Snowy Mountain can be easily picked out from the lineup of peaks on the western horizon.

One of the best things about this hike is that when you turn around to head back to your car, you get to experience all of these scenic views a second time.

summit clusters, turning southeast to climb over a 2,034-foot knob on the main ridgeline. Thus begins the most exciting part of the hike, for the climb to Moxham is not just about the final scenic payoff, but about the build-up of excitement as you follow the ridgeline to its highest point. The penultimate view *of* the summit is just as photogenic as the view *from* the summit.

The hiking time to the summit—not counting all the stops along the way to

II.
SOUTHWESTERN ADIRONDACKS

13

Constable Pond, Chub Lake, Queer Lake Loop

TOTAL DISTANCE: 8.5-mile loop

HIKING TIME: 4.5 hours

ELEVATION CHANGE: rolling terrain

TRAILHEAD GPS COORDINATES: N43° 49' 26.0" W74° 50' 14.7"

The Pigeon Lake Wilderness is notable for its thousands of acres of old-growth forests, which have been part of the Forest Preserve since 1897. That was the year that William Seward Webb, a lumberman and railroad builder, settled his lawsuit with the state over the enlargement of Stillwater Reservoir. Webb argued successfully that the extended reach of the lake cut off access to his vast forest tracts, and as compensation the state was forced to acquire those lands. Fortunately for all lovers of the outdoors, most of those lands had never been logged, and this area remains one of the finest examples of old-growth forest in the Adirondacks.

The southern portion of the Pigeon Lake Wilderness features a trail network with multiple looping connections, most of them converging on Queer Lake, so named because of its irregular shape. With several trailheads accessible from the roads between Eagle Bay and Big Moose Lake, this is an area that connects many people with wilderness adventures; the setting is gorgeous, the woods are as good as they come, and the location is easy to reach. It is a place made for weekend adventures.

With so many trail connections, the trip-planning possibilities are numerous, making it hard to recommend just one outing. After much thought, I settled on the 8.5-mile loop at the northern end of the network. This route connects four ponds and is just the right length for a satisfying day hike or a relatively easy weekend backpacking trip. For the latter option, there are two scenic campsites on this loop: a primitive tent site on Chub Lake and a popular lean-to at Queer Lake.

In terms of elevation, none of the four ponds on this loop are much higher than the starting point—but that's not to say

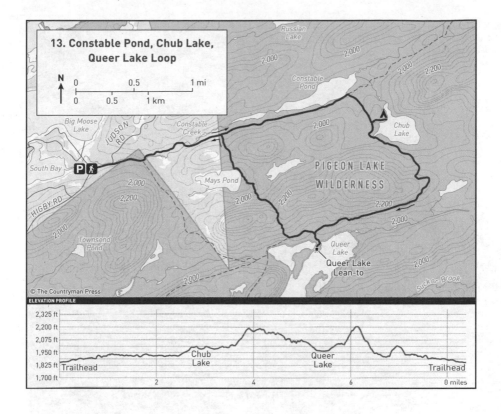

13. Constable Pond, Chub Lake, Queer Lake Loop

this is a level trail. Small hills are located at several points along the way, with the biggest being between Chub and Queer and between Queer and Mays. Additionally, there are a few sections where the trail is prone to perennial muddiness, as well as having a few potentially confusing turns near Constable Creek. But all of the trails are well marked by DEC, and signs point the way at each junction.

GETTING THERE

From NY 28 in Eagle Bay, turn northwest onto Big Moose Road and follow it for 3.8 miles. Here, bear right onto Higby Road and continue for another 1.3 miles to the start of Judson Road, a gated private road on your right. Although there are few signs, this is a popular access point for state land. Leave your car

parked on the shoulder, being careful not to block the driveway.

THE HIKE

The beginning of this loop hike follows a route that leads in and out of private land for the first 1.3 miles; while you are on those private parcels, be sure to stick to the approved trail corridor.

Start by walking past the gate and following Judson Road for 0.2 mile. Here the blue-marked foot trail veers right off the road, following a pretty section of Constable Creek with a stand of white cedar along the banks. The trail register is located just past the first encounter with the state land boundary. At 0.5 mile you reach the first trail junction, where signs may point right toward Queer Lake. This side trail is one of several

QUEER LAKE

redundant routes in the area, and it is not the one I recommend for this outing. Instead, bear left across the bridge over Constable Creek.

This turn puts you back on private property, and for 0.4 mile there is ample signage to remind you of this fact. At 0.9 mile, the trail comes back out on a gravel access road, closed to the public except for foot access. Bear right onto the road, cross the bridge back to the south side of Constable Creek, and look for the signs pointing left where the trail reenters the woods.

Some of the muddiest sections of trail are found between that last road crossing and the state land boundary; this condition has persisted as long as I've been hiking here, and it is a serious detraction from an otherwise outstanding route. The mud is not impassable— there are dry spots where you can step—but it is a shame that nothing has been done to either bridge the wet areas or reroute the trail to drier ground.

You enter state land for good just before reaching the junction with the Mays Pond trail at 1.3 miles. The route to the right will be your return route from Queer Lake later in the day. For now, continue eastward toward Constable Pond, following the narrow footpath through the primeval forest.

The term "old growth" in the Adirondacks does not always mean that the trees are taller than in forests that were logged in the past, although sometimes that may be the case. The distinction is more likely to be seen in the variety of trees that make up the forest, with specimens of each species at every stage of growth and decay, from sapling to mossy log. Instead of sun-loving trees like black cherry, which mostly grow in stands that were disturbed in the past, Adirondack old growth often consists of trees capable of persisting even in deep shade, including yellow birch, sugar maple, red spruce, and hemlock. The girth of the trees is just as telling as their height.

In this case, the mixture of tree species is quite nice. You are following a north-facing slope through the valley of Constable Pond, so look for lots of spruce and hemlock trees intermixed with the hardwoods. Down along the shoreline are tall and graceful white pines. The trail parallels the southern shoreline of Constable Pond, but it is set back from the water for most of the way. If you see an opportunity to go down for a closer look, certainly do so.

The next junction comes 2.5 miles into your hike, where you have the option to continue through the wilderness toward Pigeon Lake or turn toward Chub and Queer. This is the last of the three connecting trails to Queer Lake, so by all means turn right, southeast. This trail climbs gently past a wetland to another junction 0.4 mile later. Here, turn left onto a dead-end side trail leading to Chub Lake's most scenic spot.

Here, 3 miles from Higby Road, you will find an attractive campsite on Chub's northern shore. It has room for several tents, with a fire ring situated on a wide rock ledge with an unobstructed view of the water. Chub Lake is a circular pond with a brook trout fishery. The rock ledge is a fine place to contemplate the mysteries of the wilderness, whether you spend the night here or just stop for a snack break; in warm weather, you may be tempted to swim.

To continue the loop, you'll need to backtrack to the last trail junction and then continue south. There is an adventurous section where the trail crosses a wide inlet stream on a long log bridge. You circle high above the pond's south

CAMPSITE AT CHUB LAKE

and then climbs over a small knoll to reach the lean-to at 5.5 miles.

Queer Lake's lean-to is a popular and scenic camping location. It stands next to a large rock on the shoreline and has good water access, including a tiny sand beach. You are standing at the base of a large peninsula that nearly divides the lake in two, and a herd path leads out to its tip. But there are also signs of over-use here, from litter in the lean-to to the stumps that fill the surrounding woods. It is impressive—and sad—that so many campers over the years have cut down live trees in the mistaken belief that green wood burns well in a campfire. Good firewood is a scarce commodity at this lean-to, so if you decide to camp here, consider foregoing the pleasure of an evening fire.

To complete the loop, you will need to follow the trail back across the isthmus. Look for the side trail leading to Mays Pond, which turns northwest at a junction 0.4 mile from the lean-to. This is the hilliest trail on the loop, with one climb on the way to Mays, and then another after you pass the pond's eastern tip. This section is also not well traveled, and there have been times in the past when it has not been kept in tip-top maintenance. But Mays Pond, which lies half on private land, is an attractive waypoint, and the trail deserves more attention than it gets.

At 7.2 miles the Mays Pond trail returns you to the Constable Creek trail. From here it is a matter of turning left and following what should now be a familiar route through private land, across the muddy section, across the two bridges, and finally back to Judson Road. Once you return to your vehicle, you will have covered 8.5 very eventful miles.

shore before venturing into the hills, where the trail traverses a slope forested mostly with hardwoods. This section between Chub and Queer is not well traveled and may be vague in places.

At a point 2.2 miles from Chub, or 5.3 miles from the trailhead, you arrive at a junction a short distance north of Queer Lake. Even if the signs marking the junction are missing, the trail you are intersecting should be obvious, since it is a primary trail that leads to the lean-to. Bear left, following the lean-to trail as it dips down to cross a narrow isthmus between two parts of the lake

14

Bald Mountain

TOTAL DISTANCE: 1.8 miles round-trip

HIKING TIME: 1 hour

VERTICAL RISE: 400 feet

TRAILHEAD GPS COORDINATES: N43° 44' 44.6" W74° 53' 58.1"

Bald Mountain is a small peak in one of the best-loved corners of the Adirondack Park, with outstanding views of the Fulton Chain of Lakes. As mountains go, this climb is one of the easiest trails out there, and it has introduced more people to the joys of hiking than any other summit in the vicinity. I count myself among those people; when I was a child, my family climbed Bald Mountain numerous times.

The mountain has gone by several names over the years, and even today it is simultaneously referred to as "Bald" and "Rondaxe." The confusion is a product of the steel fire tower that stands on the summit. Because there are multiple Bald Mountains throughout the Adirondacks, including one in Lewis County that also had a fire tower, state foresters named this structure Rondaxe to better distinguish it. Therefore, in a break with the standard format for naming fire towers, this one has a different name than the mountain upon which it stands. The tower has not been manned as a fire observation post in decades, but it is open to the public.

If you are a veteran hiker, you may be put off by the tourist nature of this mountain, because Bald attracts just about anyone with the inclination to seek out a mountain view, regardless of skill or experience. But the popularity of this mountain is justified, and everyone who enjoys the Adirondacks should make a point of visiting this signature peak. The mountain itself does not discriminate.

The trail I used to climb as a kid was an adventurous route up the steep rock face, with cables to assist the ascent. That route, which began on private land, has long since been closed to the general public; but having been introduced to the mountain that way, the current

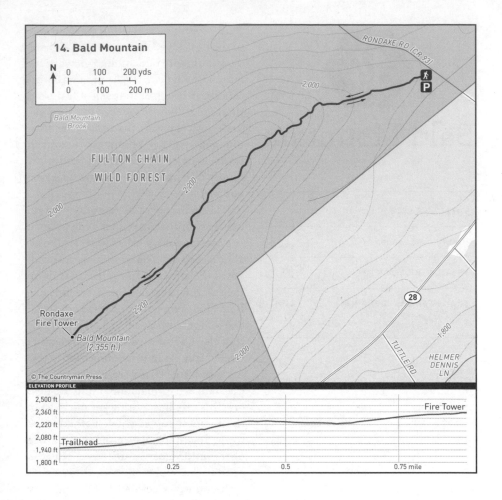

14. Bald Mountain

N

| 0 | 100 | 200 yds |

| 0 | 100 | 200 m |

RONDAXE RD (CR 93)

Bald Mountain Brook

FULTON CHAIN WILD FOREST

2,000

2,200

2,200

Rondaxe Fire Tower

Bald Mountain (2,355 ft.)

© The Countryman Press

28

1,800

TUTTLE RD

HELMER DENNIS LN

ELEVATION PROFILE

2,500 ft				Fire Tower
2,360 ft				
2,220 ft				
2,080 ft	Trailhead			
1,940 ft				
1,800 ft		0.25	0.5	0.75 mile

state-maintained trail seems easy and straightforward to me by comparison. This is not to say that it's boring. This is a short, direct climb, with just enough vertical rise to get the heart pumping. The grades are mostly moderate, and the scenic payoff at the top would be worth far greater effort.

GETTING THERE

Ample signs point the way to Bald Mountain and the Rondaxe Fire Tower from NY 28, roughly 4.5 miles from both Old Forge and Eagle Bay. Turn northwest onto Rondaxe Road and follow it for 0.2 mile to the large public parking area, located on the left.

THE HIKE

Little really needs to be said about the trail, in terms of direction. It heads southwest from the parking area and follows the mountain's spine all the way to the fire tower. The climbing is gentle at first and more moderately steep later on, with lots of exposed bedrock. Some of that rock forms narrow ridges in the trail, like the spines of ossified dinosaurs. The trail is only 0.9 mile long and takes less than thirty minutes to complete.

VIEW OF THE FULTON CHAIN FROM BALD MOUNTAIN

Bald Mountain is not completely bald, but the name "Receding Hairline Mountain" wouldn't be quite as attractive. Certainly, there is a lot of open rock, and plenty of space for everyone to sit and enjoy the view. These ground-level views all face the lower four lakes in the Fulton Chain and the vast expanse of forest beyond. There are no big mountains in the immediate vicinity, but as your eye follows Fourth Lake eastward, the topography becomes distinctly more riotous. Those peaks are too distant for easy identification, but the conical profile of Blue Mountain, located near the center of the Adirondack Park, is recognizable. On the rare clear day, even the distant High Peaks may be visible, but it doesn't take much haze or cloudiness to prevent that from being the case.

If you want a full 360° view, you'll need to climb the fire tower, although you'll probably agree that the most visually stunning portion of the mountain's vista has already been accounted for. The region to the north of Bald/Rondaxe is foothill country, known more for its scattered small ponds than for its rugged peaks, and so your eye will still be drawn back to Third and Fourth Lakes. The circular map in the tower's cab is a replica of the one used by the old fire observers; if they spotted a distant plume of smoke, they could provide a bearing to the nearest district office. The bearings provided from multiple fire towers helped rangers pinpoint the location of the forest fire.

The return hike is just as straightforward as the climb. If by some chance you have the mountain to yourself, it might be tricky locating the place where the hiking trail exits the open summit and reenters the woods. But on most summer weekends, all you really need to do is follow the people ahead of you.

Middle Settlement Lake

TOTAL DISTANCE: 6.7 miles between trailheads

HIKING TIME: 3 hours

ELEVATION CHANGE: rolling terrain, with a steep 130-foot climb at the beginning

TRAILHEAD GPS COORDINATES: N43° 40' 33.7" W75° 03' 08.0" (northern); N43° 39' 20.0" W75° 04' 59.4" (southern)

The source of Middle Settlement Lake's name is tied to the settlement history of the Old Forge region. John Brown of Rhode Island came into possession of a vast swatch of land in northern New York in the 1790s, at a time when the Adirondack region was unknown and unnamed. He hired a crew to build a road into Brown's Tract in an attempt to encourage settlement, but the land was too remote and rocky to host a successful farming village.

Some years later, a son-in-law named Frederick Herreshoff made a second effort to establish a village. This time the bid to attract settlers was not strictly agricultural in nature, because Herreshoff had identified a small deposit of iron ore a short distance from the Moose River. He built a second road to the site and attracted several families to the area, but although it died a slower death, this colony failed too. After a third attempt to establish a farming community on Brown's Tract, the family eventually sold off the property.

Old Forge and Thendara, of course, eventually did become successful communities, but this was accomplished through tourism, not agriculture. But the story of the Brown family's struggles to develop the tract are central to the region's identity; the name Old Forge is itself a reference to Herreshoff's attempt to profit from his iron ore discovery. People have speculated that Middle Settlement Lake was named for another lost Brown settlement in the woods, midway between two other landmarks, but it was probably just derived from Herreshoff's enterprises on the Middle Branch of the Moose River.

This "lake" is really just a small pond, but what a gem it is anyway! The lean-to perched atop a rock ledge on its north shore is a quintessential Adirondack

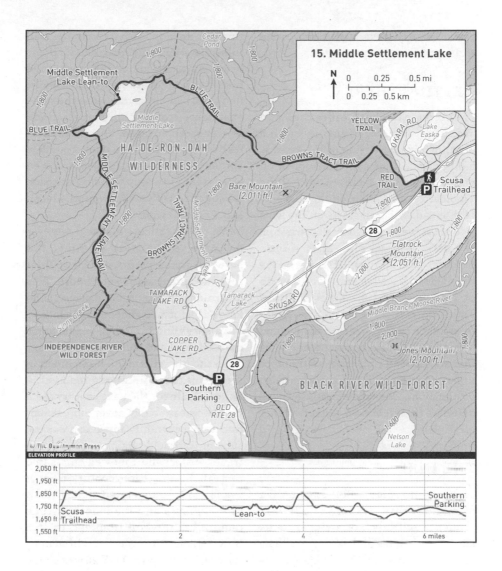

15. Middle Settlement Lake

campsite, the perfect place to observe the nesting loons who haunt this place every summer. With its prominent trailhead on a busy state highway, Middle Settlement Lake is no secret; it is particularly popular with backpackers from the Utica, Syracuse, and Rochester regions. In my experience, though, it is rarely so busy that the lake seems "crowded."

Several trails lead to Middle Settlement Lake, two of them beginning from separate trailheads on NY 28. Most people approach the lake from the northern trailhead, but I have always been partial to both trails. For this reason, I suggest spotting cars at each end and hiking from one trailhead to the other. The resulting route forms a "jug handle" loop through the Ha-de-ron-dah Wilderness, with each half being a little over 3 miles long. The lean-to is occupied nearly every summer weekend, so if your intent is to camp, be sure to bring a tent. There are several primitive camp-sites in addition to the shelter.

GETTING THERE

The northern trailhead, called the Scusa Trailhead on some signs, is located prominently on the side of NY 28. It is a large Department of Transportation parking area just 3 miles south of the Thendara train station, on the east side of the road. The trail starts on the west side of the road, marked by a brown sign.

The southern trailhead is a little harder to find. A brown DEC sign on the west side of NY 28, about 3 miles north of McKeever and 6.7 miles south of Thendara, marks the start of an access road for the Browns Tract Easement and the Ha-de-ron-dah Wilderness. Follow this access road right and continue for 0.5 mile to a small parking area, also on the right. The wilderness trailhead begins as a side road 100 feet further on the left.

THE HIKE

The route to Middle Settlement Lake from the Scusa Trailhead follows a sequence of trails, not a single route. During the course of the day you will be following trails marked with all three primary colors: red, yellow, and blue. There are seven trail junctions along the way, so you will need to pay close addition to the trail signs. Fortunately, the trail signage in Ha-de-ron-dah tends to be quite good.

From the northern parking area on NY 28, cross the road and find the start of the trail, marked by a prom-inent brown sign. This is state land, but private land crowds the beginning of the trail, including a cabin within sight of the register. The proximity of this private land is what forces the trail immediately up a steep rock knoll. If this brisk 130-foot climb at the start of the hike gets you breathing a little heavily, don't feel bad—everybody has the same experience. No other hill on the trail will be this steep or tiring. The red-marked trail levels off after the knoll, rounds a corner of the private property, and then sets off into the deep woods. You reach a T-junction with a yellow-marked trail at 0.6 mile. Turn left.

You will follow this segment for 0.9 mile to the next junction. But between those points, take a look at the trail underneath your boots. This no ordinary footpath, but a piece of Old Forge's history. You happen to be follow-ing a surviving section of Herreshoff's road, constructed in 1811 as the primary access to his settlement. It remained in service as the main wagon road to the Fulton Chain for the next century. As a road, it was probably never more elabo-rate than it currently appears; it was the subject of ridicule by just about every travel writer who followed this same route in the nineteenth century, most of whom made exaggerated claims about its roughness and the length of time required to travel it from end to end. Browns Tract Road was not retired until the original version of NY 28 was paved circa 1911. Parts of it were completely abandoned, but other sections now sur-vive as a wilderness footpath, as you can currently see.

At 1.5 miles you reach the next trail junction, where now you turn right onto a blue-marked trail. This route dips to cross a small stream within sight of a large wetland, and then it climbs up and over a hardwood-forested hill. The next descent takes you into Middle Set-tlement Lake's watershed, where you may notice a steep, rocky knoll looming above the trail; the next junction, located 2.6 miles from the highway, lies at the foot of this cliffy little mountain. Giant blocks of rock fill the valley, standing where they landed after breaking away from the cliff face.

The blue trail ends here, so turn left onto the yellow-marked trail. As you round the corner, Middle Settlement Lake comes immediately into view. Your first task is to cross a muddy inlet at the tip of the lake, but then the trail follows a pleasing course around the northern shore. On your way to the lean-to, you pass two well-used campsites—one designated by DEC, the other a de facto site with no official status. The lean-to itself is 3.1 miles from the trailhead.

The scenic qualities of the lean-to are indisputable; its location atop a rock ledge is the most desirable piece of real estate on Middle Settlement. The water is deep enough for swimming, and you can try your hand at brook trout fishing.

Compared to other Adirondack lakes, though, this one makes a peculiar visual impression due to the scarcity of conifers along its shoreline. This may be a result of a 1903 forest fire that denuded much of what is now Ha-de-ron-dah.

The trail to the southern trailhead continues straight through the lean-to site, still following the north shore. It dips down a steep slope to the pond's outlet stream, which you cross on a long log bridge. Fern-filled glades typify the woods near the south end of Middle Settlement; they are verdant and attractive in the fullness of summer.

Just 0.5 mile from the lean-to, or 3.6 miles overall, the yellow trail bears left at the next intersection. Stay on this trail, circling back around the southwestern tip of the pond for one last view before climbing away over a hill. You descend into the secluded valley of a small stream, then venture cross-country to a second stream at

MIDDLE SETTLEMENT LAKE

HIKING ALONG "COFFEECAN VLY"

pond. On my first visit here I found a rusted Chock Full o' Nuts can hanging from a tree branch by a wire handle; ever since, this place has been "Coffeecan Vly" in my mental map of the area.

The trail climbs away from the beaver pond and works its way south back toward the old Browns Tract Road, which you reach at another trail junction at 5.2 miles. Turn right, still heading south, following the historic roadway for just a short distance. After crossing a rocky stream, you reach a dirt road used by the owners of a camp on nearby Copper Lake. The public hiking trail turns left and piggybacks on this road for 0.4 mile, then bears right back into the woods.

4.6 miles. This one is sure to get your attention, because there is nothing but an assortment of small logs spanning it. Pick one and hope it makes a good bridge.

The trail turns downstream, bringing you to the edge of a pretty beaver meadow. In years past this was a grassy meadow, but when the beavers returned they created an attractive

The last 0.9 mile of trail are not too interesting; much of this distance passes through managed timberland protected by a conservation easement. Pay close attention to the yellow markers, because there are several intersecting logging roads and skid trails. But after about twenty minutes you reach the southern trailhead register box, just a few hundred feet from the parking area and 6.7 miles from your starting point at the Scusa Trailhead.

16

Twin Lakes and November Falls

TOTAL DISTANCE: 6.4 miles round-trip

HIKING TIME: 4 hours

ELEVATION CHANGE: rolling terrain

TRAILHEAD GPS COORDINATES: N43° 28' 21.3" W75° 00' 36.6"

Twin Lakes near the Black River is an eclectic destination, and few people would consider this among their favorite hikes. I freely admit to being one of its fans. I have returned here many times because of its accessibility—the trailhead is not that deep within the Adirondack Park's boundaries—and its ability to transport me into a seldom-visited, remote landscape without the need to travel very far. Although not officially recognized as wilderness, the area possesses all the same intangible values of solitude and unimpaired natural processes as those places that have been formally protected. Other people might see a "plain vanilla" forest and a destination that is not particularly scenic, but to each their own.

The Twin Lakes are a pair of pools dwarfed by the extensive wetlands that surround them; you have to venture out into that wetland just to see the nearest of the two ponds. Fortunately, those wetlands are friendly to human exploration, and you can visit just about any part of the area you want, including the more secluded upper pond, without the risk of sinking into the mire.

It is easier to appreciate the area when you understand its history. In the nineteenth century, state officials were highly interested in the headwaters of the Black River as a source of water for its canal system, including the Erie Canal. They began surveying the region as early as 1849, and during a period that lasted from about 1860 through 1881, several ponds and lakes were converted into small reservoirs.

Twin Lakes was one such reservoir. The dates of this dam are murky, but it likely fell within the same timeframe. All of what is now an open wetland was once submerged in a man-made flow, turning the two little pools into what

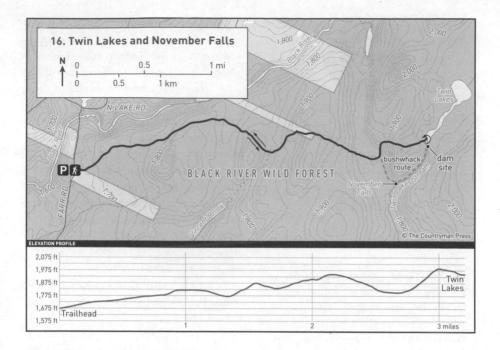

16. Twin Lakes and November Falls

must have been an interesting lake. But the absence of hills surrounding the reservoir meant that the water was no more than nine feet deep; had the dam been any taller, water would have started flowing out at random places.

Many of the so-called "canal lakes" were abandoned after just a few years. Managing a network of small, remote reservoirs turned out to be impractical, and so the focus turned to larger projects in more accessible locations, such as Forestport and Hinckley. A portion of the Twin Lakes dam can still be found on the outlet, and this is one of the features you should seek out when you explore the area.

Other highlights include a pair of waterfalls located a short distance downstream, requiring an off-trail excursion to find. This bushwhack increases the difficulty of the hike, but with some basic directions, the cascades are not too hard to locate.

GETTING THERE

From NY 28 in Forestport, turn east onto Woodhull Road just north of the bridge over the Black River. This leads to Forestport Station in 1.2 miles, where North Lake Road forks left. Follow this road through a residential area and into the wildness of the Black River Wild Forest. At 10.1 miles, you reach an intersection at Reeds Pond, where Farr Road bears right. Follow this gravel byway south across the Black River and up to the Twin Lakes trailhead, located at 0.5 mile on the left.

THE HIKE

What is now the trail to Twin Lakes was once regarded as a jeep trail, although it is hard to imagine wheeled motor vehicles ever using this route without chewing up the unimproved surface. It is still nominally a snowmobile trail, but in reality the primary users are hikers and skiers.

It leads eastward into the hardwood forest, encountering only a few small hills in the first mile. This is not a level trail, though, and as you continue deeper into the backcountry, the hills seem to get bigger and bigger. Small streams and wetlands occupy the low spaces between these hills, adding a bit of visual interest to your hike. At 1.7 miles you encounter a tiny bog that seems to block your path; this is the source of Vincent Brook. You have to step carefully around the muddy pool.

In the course of the next mile, you rise over another hilltop and then begin a descent into a spruce-filled forest. The trail becomes more rugged at this point, with blowdown and wetness being long-standing management issues here. At the bottom of the hill is a large, grassy swale located 2.5 miles from the start. This site has been an even bigger obstacle in recent years, as it is subject to periodic beaver flooding. When the dam is out you can cut through the width of the wetland, crossing the small stream on whatever logs happen to be available. When the beavers convert the meadow into a large pond, you might have to seek out their dam and cross on top of it.

Beyond the meadow, the final 0.6-mile section of the trail is the least used and most rugged of all. It reenters the woods, veers north to follow a small stream, and then climbs steeply up onto the hill where the Twin Lakes are found.

The marked trail ends at 3.1 miles near the outlet. Just before it exits the woods, look for a path to the right leading to the site of the dam. The earthen embankment is still very obvious, and the path leads across the top to the remains of a stone sluiceway. The

DAM RUINS AT THE OUTLET OF THE TWIN LAKES

A NOVEMBER DAY AT NOVEMBER FALLS

campsite located here is the best in the entire Twin Lakes basin.

To see the ponds you will need to venture out into the wetlands. It is easy enough to follow the outlet channel northwest 0.4 mile beyond the end of the trail to the edge of the first Twin Lake; the upper lake is another 0.6 mile deeper into the wetland complex. Only portions of this former lakebed are truly boggy, and by keeping to the dry sections you can find a viable route to the upper pond. There was a campsite there decades ago, but that is now grown in.

The waterfalls are in the opposite direction. Finding them requires some basic navigational skills, first and foremost being the ability to read and understand a topographic map, because you will not be following any trails for a distance of roughly 0.6 mile. If you are unsure about your ability to navigate through a remote and trackless forest, then it is best that you not risk your safety. Bring a friend skilled at wilderness navigation to help you find the way.

Beginning at the dam site, follow Twin Lakes Stream southwest. It is a fun waterway to follow, with several small cascades in addition to the two larger ones. The first that you encounter as you head downstream is Hole-in-the-Wall Falls, where the creek has forced its way around a natural rock barrier. The second and larger cascade is November Falls, located about 0.4 mile below the dam. Here, the stream tumbles about twelve feet over a series of rock ledges, with a tiny campsite on the south bank.

The tricky part of this side trip is finding your way back to the main trail from November Falls. Thick woods surround the cascade, and a large wetland blocks further progress downstream. It is best to follow a northwesterly course over a corner of the nearest hill, heading back down into the valley as soon as the thick underbrush comes to an end. Then you can follow the foot of the hill past the wetland and back to the marked trail in the vicinity of the large beaver meadow. From here, it's a 2.5-mile hike back across the rolling terrain toward your parked car on Farr Road.

17

Pine Lake

TOTAL DISTANCE: 5.6 miles round-trip

HIKING TIME: 2.75 hours

ELEVATION CHANGE: rolling terrain

TRAILHEAD GPS COORDINATES: N43° 43'
31.8" W75° 10' 46.7"

Pine Lake, which lies on the boundary of the Independence River Wild Forest and Ha-de-ron-dah Wilderness, is one of the most pleasant hikes in a region of the Adirondack Park known more for motorized recreation. The trail is a moderately-used snowmobile trail in the winter, but it is also designated as a foot trail. Although hikers are free to use any trail on state land regardless of designation, many of the snowmobile trails in the Brantingham Lake area simply aren't that interesting. This trail, though, is a notable exception.

Your route to Pine Lake follows an old wagon road that dates to at least the 1880s, when it was first mentioned in the popular guidebooks of Edwin R. Wallace. It began at the Botchford Tannery, which was one of three mills operating on Otter Creek at the time. The tannery closed in 1889, and the state acquired the land with bond act money in 1955. Otherwise, not much has changed over the decades.

There is a lean-to at Pine Lake, as well as a handful of nice tent sites. This makes the lake an interesting choice for a weekend backpacking trip. There are also several connecting trails, making Pine Lake not just a scenic destination, but a jumping-off point for deeper explorations as well.

Fair warning: in recent years, there has been a spike in ATV use at Pine Lake. Recreational ATV riding is not permitted on the Forest Preserve, although it is common in the woods near Brantingham Lake. Machines can create deep ruts in the trail surface and make irreparable messes of mud wallows. This ATV usage was a key consideration for including Pine Lake in this guidebook, however, because one of the best things that could happen here is if more hikers ventured into this out-of-the-way region

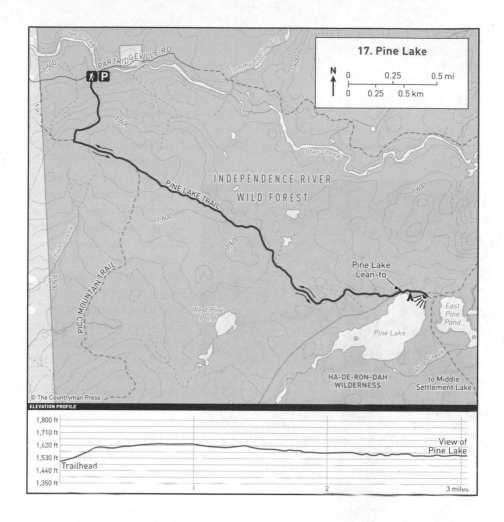

to sample its charms, thus displacing the machines.

GETTING THERE

Finding the Partridgeville Road trailhead east of Brantingham Lake in Lewis County may be more challenging than the hike itself, as it involves a series of byways.

You can reach the Brantingham Lake area from NY 12, which runs north–south between Boonville and Lowville. Turn east from NY 12 at Burdick Crossing Road, between Lyons Falls and Glenfield. Cross the Black River to the intersection with Lyons Falls Road. Turn left and drive 0.7 mile north through the hamlet of Greig to the intersection with Brantingham Road. Turn right and follow it uphill for 3.6 miles to the hamlet of Brantingham, located at the intersection with Partridgeville and Middle roads.

Turn left onto Partridgeville Road as it circles around the north side of Brantingham Lake. At 1.7 miles bear left on a fork, which is the continuation of Partridgeville Road. There are several views of Otter Creek, the principal stream in this area. The trailhead parking area is located on the right, 7.7 miles from Brantingham and just before a bridge over the creek.

THE HIKE

The yellow-marked foot trail leads south from the parking area, bringing you to a register box just before beginning a gentle climb. Small wooden ramps mitigate some muddy spots at the foot of this hill, just past the register. Hemlocks shade the beginning of the trail, but within moments you ascend into a hardwood forest. The ascent in this case is only 100 feet, so you may not even notice it happening.

At 0.5 mile you reach a T-junction with the snowmobile trail, which begins on private land to your right. To reach Pine Lake you must turn left, following this wide and obvious trail southeast. At 0.9 mile you reach a fork, where the main snowmobile trail veers right toward Pico Mountain. The Pine Lake trail keeps left, maintaining the same southeasterly course through the hardwood forest, with its large black cherry and yellow birch trees.

There is a modest descent as you proceed toward Pine Lake, but the elevation change—about eighty vertical feet—is so minor that on any other hike it would not be worth mentioning. Here, however, this vertical drop is the difference between the hardwood forest on the hilltops and the coniferous lowlands. Hemlocks are the first trees you might notice occupying some of the glens that you pass. Red spruce make an appearance, but it is balsam fir that predominates throughout most of the valley. You'll see it

PINE LAKE

edging the small wetlands that you pass, as well as along all of the small streams.

At 2.4 miles, you reach a junction with a red-marked foot trail, which leads right toward Pine Lake's outlet and on toward another trailhead south of Brantingham Lake. Keeping left, your trail dips down a short grade to cross a stream. At this point, the lake's namesake white pines begin to make an appearance, several minutes before you see the lake itself.

Beginning at 2.7 miles, a series of signs beside the trail delineates the western boundary of the Ha-de-ron-dah Wilderness, which envelops the lake but excludes the snowmobile trail. Following the signs right brings you to one potential campsite in 0.1 mile. The snowmobile trail, however, keeps left and skirts the shoreline, leading in just a few minutes to the side trail left to the Pine Lake Lean-to, 2.8 miles from the trailhead.

This is a fine campsite, and since the lean-to was built in 2004, it is still relatively new and in good condition. It stands more than 200 feet from the shore, though, and therefore offers no views of the water.

If you continue following the trail another 0.2 mile east around the end of the lake, you will pass a small campsite near the shore, cross a sandy-bottomed stream, and reach an opening on the shoreline next to a graceful pine tree—perhaps the best view of the lake from the trail.

Just beyond this view, there is a trail junction. The snowmobile trail keeps left and leads northeast toward Big Otter Lake. The blue-marked foot trail on the right leads into the Ha-de-ron-dah Wilderness, passing through the woods between Pine Lake and its neighbor, East Pine Pond. If you are seeking something more pristine than a snowmobile trail, this route will be an interesting option for a side trip. It is a long route, leading in 4.1 miles to the lean-to at Middle Settlement Lake described in Hike 15, but it traverses a glacial landscape rich with small eskers, sprawling wetlands, and stands of black cherry. Highlights along the way include Pine Creek, Middle Branch Creek, and little Lost Lake.

18

Gleasmans Falls

TOTAL DISTANCE: 8 miles between trailheads

HIKING TIME: 4 hours

ELEVATION CHANGE: rolling terrain

TRAILHEAD GPS COORDINATES: N43° 48′ 28.7″ W75° 16′ 35.2″ (western); N43° 46′ 27.4″ W75° 12′ 20.0″ (eastern)

The Independence River got its name when a surveyor marked its location on July 4, 1793. The name is also descriptive of its character, as it is one of the few remaining free-flowing streams running westward off the Adirondack plateau toward the Black River. Much of its course is wild and undeveloped, with a scenic crescendo at the rugged gorge known as Gleasmans Falls.

An excellent trail follows the river as it traverses a section of state land called, appropriately enough, the Independence River Wild Forest. In a section of the western Adirondacks that seems devoted to motorized access and recreation, the presence of this foot trail is a welcome oasis of semi-wilderness. There are private inholdings along the river, and in one case the landowners do use the trail for ATV access to their property, but this limited usage does not detract from the overall attractiveness of the hike.

The direct trail to Gleasmans Falls is an easy route, suitable for all ages, especially if you turn around at the gorge and go no further. This is how most people visit the area, and certainly there are worse ways you could pass a few hours in the Great Outdoors. There are few hills worth mentioning and hardly a drop of mud. On the other hand, you may encounter wildlife in the adjacent wetlands, find some interesting camping opportunities, and discover close-up views of some of the cascades. The round-trip hike to the top of the gorge and back is just 5.6 miles.

But the trail upstream from the gorge is such a fun route that it would be negligence on my part not to point out its existence. Therefore this itinerary incorporates the whole thing, beginning at the western trailhead near Beach Mill Pond and ending 8 miles to the east on

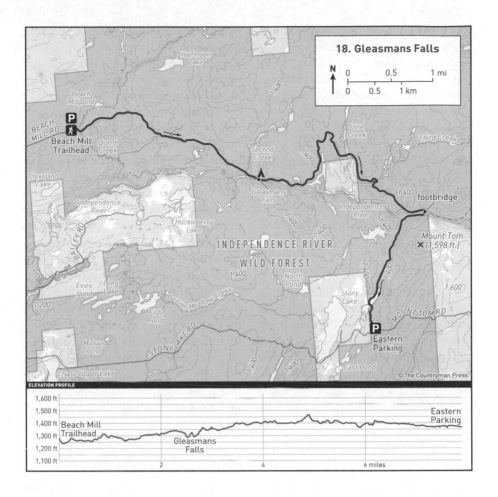

18. Gleasmans Falls

Stony Lake Road. In addition to Gleasmans Falls, you will pass a variety of beaver ponds and a "slot canyon" of sorts on Third Creek. By all standards, this is the finest hike in the Independence River Wild Forest.

GETTING THERE

One of the biggest challenges you will experience on this hike is finding the trailheads, especially if you are unfamiliar with the back roads of Lewis County.

Number Four Road is the main highway between Lowville and Stillwater, and it is the beginning point for these driving directions. At a four-way intersection 9.2 miles east of downtown Lowville, bear right (south) onto Eric Canal Road, which will take you into the woodsy residential area surrounding Chase Lake. Turn left onto McPhilmy Road at 2.5 miles, and left again 0.2 mile further onto Beach Mill Road. This is a narrow gravel lane that continues for a total of 3 miles into state land, and along the way you pass three trails in the Otter Creek Horse Trail system. The western trail to the falls begins at the last clearing, where the road ends.

The eastern trailhead is much more remote. To find it, follow Erie Canal Road

4.4 miles south from Number Four Road. At this point Stony Lake Road leads left, east, passing the north end of Chase Upper Lake at 2 miles. Winter plowing ends at 3.1 miles, and at 5.5 miles you exit state land to pass through a densely settled area at the south end of Stony Lake. State land resumes at 6.4 miles, and immediately after, at 6.5 miles, you reach the trailhead for the Fish Trail and the starting point for the hike to Gleasmans Falls. The public road dead-ends just 0.5 mile later at the end of state land.

THE HIKE

Beginning at the Beach Mill Pond trailhead, the foot trail to Gleasmans Falls leads southwest and downhill to Burnt Creek, just below the site of the former mill pond. The trail enters a mixed forest and leads northeast, approaching an upper portion of Beach Mill Pond. A side trail at 0.7 mile leads left to a campsite near the edge of the sprawling wetland.

Several small hills lie between the mill pond site and the next wetland at 1.3 miles, where I was once able to see a snapping turtle lurking in the shallow water beside the trail. Beaver flooding at this location could easily encroach on the trail, forcing you to improvise a detour.

You do not get your first look at the Independence River until 2.5 miles into the hike, after you drop steeply down to Second Creek. A side path leads right to a campsite next to the river. The trail is now close to the Independence River, and at 2.7 miles you reach a third campsite located right on the trail, this one with a rock ledge extending down toward the water. From that ledge, you can view the mouth of the gorge.

The scenic payoff of the hike occurs in the next 0.1 mile, where the trail climbs up to the top of the rock bluff that constitutes the north rim of the Gleasmans Falls gorge. The trail stays high above the fray, leaving it up to you to venture as close to the rim as you dare to see the river below you. In the spring, of course, the water is roiling; in the summer it is still turbulent, but more rocks are exposed. This overlook is 2.8 miles from the Beach Mill trailhead.

There is a way to enter the gorge safely. Look for a cleft in the rock near the downstream end of the gorge, where it is possible to descend with care to a riverside ledge with the most photogenic views of all. The lower the water, the more this ledge will be exposed, but even in spring it may be possible to appreciate the rapids up close. The gorge is rimmed with hardwoods, meaning there is something to see here throughout the growing season: cherry blossoms in early spring, wild azaleas in June, and a lush display of foliage in the fall.

This is the point where most people turn back. However, if you were able to spot a car at the eastern trailhead, then you still have 5.2 miles of fine hiking ahead of you. It begins with a brief detour inland, away from the head of the gorge, and when you return to the river, it is a much gentler stream, with no hint of the turbulence you just witnessed. The woods are semi-open here, with more brush alongside the river than tree cover.

At 3.3 miles the trail turns inland to begin a long detour necessitated by extensive beaver flooding and a large private inholding. The first large flow that you encounter straddles the private land boundary. Because so few people have traveled this trail, the foot tread is often faint. Fortunately, the way is well marked and the woods are quite attractive, with pine-filled forests sitting atop the rocky knolls and hardwoods—all of them vibrantly colored in late September—lining the wetlands.

At its remotest point north of the block of private land, the trail is 0.7 mile from the river. But then it slowly begins to work its way back southwest. At 4.6 miles you reach a large footbridge over Pine Creek, with a beautiful view of its chain of beaver ponds.

Then, at 5.2 miles, you crest a bald rock knob, the beginning of yet another charm of this hike. There are actually two rocky knolls here, both side-by-side with little Third Creek flowing between them. The trail descends this first knoll and then circles around to cross the creek—a feat that could be challenging if the water is high. You have to bushwhack downstream about 200 feet to see the unusual spot where the creek squeezes between the two enormous rock knobs—the closest thing you are likely to see to a slot canyon here in the Adirondacks. The trail then climbs the next knoll and descends steeply down the other side.

Just past this rugged spot, at 5.5 miles, the hiking trail intercepts the ATV right-of-way coming out of the private inholding. You follow the ATV trail for a distance of 0.4 mile, at which point you finally return to the side of the Independence River. There is a ford here where vehicles can cross the river. The foot trail continues upstream to a footbridge at 6.2 miles, which will take you across the river to the final leg of your hike back to Stony Lake Road. The trail that continues alongside the river leads to Panther Pond.

INSIDE THE GORGE AT GLEASMANS FALLS

Cross the bridge and follow the river back downstream to pick up the ATV trail once again. Although the mud wallows are hard to ignore, the experience of hiking this motorized right-of-way is not too horrendous. The trail is especially pretty where it parallels a long beaver meadow northeast of Stony Lake. The shallow ponds in this chain are freckled with lily pads. At 7.6 miles the foot trail turns left off the ATV trail and crosses a bridge between two of the beaver flows. A few minutes later, at 8 miles, you reach the end of the hike at Stony Lake Road.

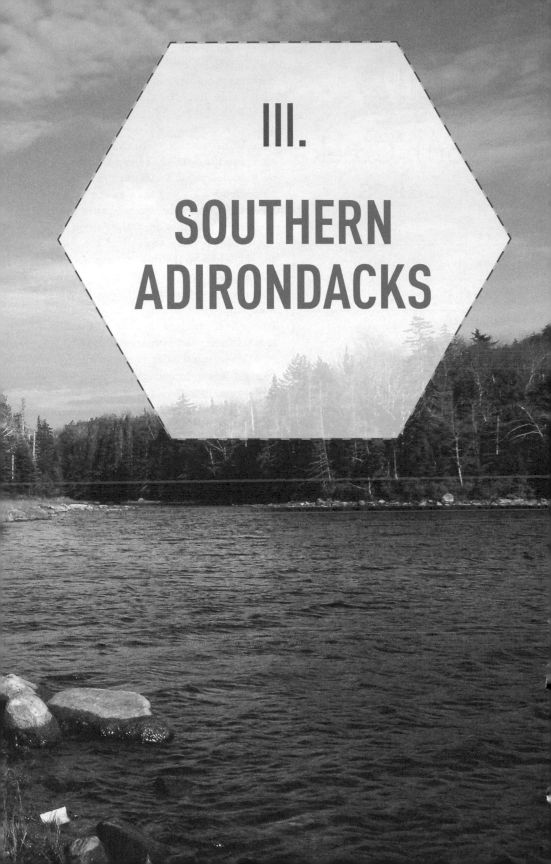

III.

SOUTHERN ADIRONDACKS

North Creek Lakes

TOTAL DISTANCE: 10.3-mile loop

HIKING TIME: 4 hours

ELEVATION CHANGE: rolling terrain

TRAILHEAD GPS COORDINATES: N43° 10' 42.8" W74° 34' 40.9"

In the southernmost region of the Adirondack Park is a cluster of lakes that deserves more attention than it receives. They are encircled by a network of snowmobile and hiking trails offering a rich array of route options. Historically, they were known as the North Creek Lakes, although the name has been forgotten on modern maps. Trails approach this chain from no fewer than seven trailheads, and several choice campsites can be found on their shores. The region is not terribly remote, and in fact it is reasonably close to the densely populated Mohawk Valley.

So why are the North Creek Lakes underappreciated? Part of the problem stems from the fact that the trail system was designed primarily with snowmobiles in mind, with summer hiking being a lesser consideration. Portions are soggier than most hikers would prefer, and in one case the trails can only be connected by striking out across the frozen surface of Spectacle Lake. Some simple modifications and basic trail maintenance could turn this area into one of the Adirondacks' premier destinations; in the meantime, the area doesn't quite live up to its full potential.

Nevertheless, there are a variety of ways you can enjoy this scenic area using the existing trails, despite their faults. The route described here was chosen because it serves as a good introduction for anyone new to the Ferris Lake Wild Forest. It begins at a prominent trailhead on NY 29A, between the communities of Stratford and Caroga Lake, and it creates a cherry-stem loop connecting two of the lakes directly— Long Lake and Third Lake—with two others located a short distance off-trail. There are two good campsites for anyone wishing to spend the weekend here, although the North Creek Lakes are just

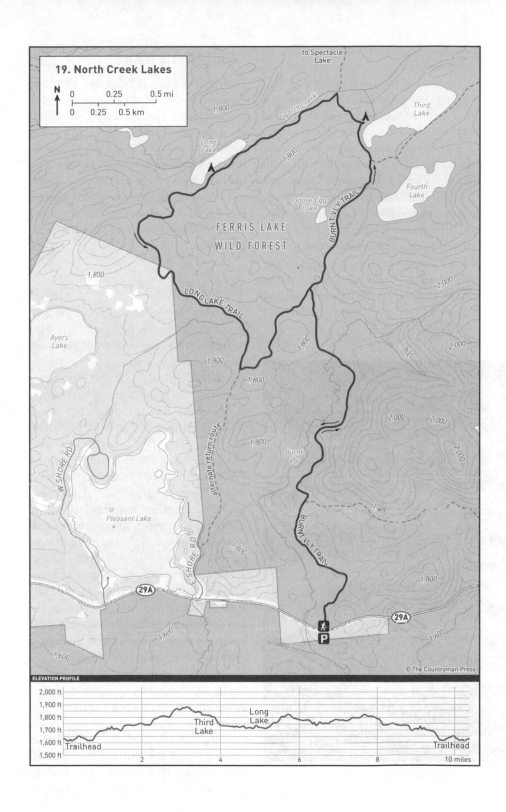

19. North Creek Lakes

N

| 0 | 0.25 | 0.5 mi |
| 0 | 0.25 | 0.5 km |

to Spectacle
Lake

North Creek

1,800

Third
Lake

Long
Lake

1,800

Goose Egg
Lake

Fourth
Lake

FERRIS LAKE
WILD FOREST

BURNT VLY TRAIL

2,000

LONG LAKE TRAIL

1,800

1,800

1,800

Ayers
Lake

1,800

alternate return route

1,800

1,800

2,000

2,000

2,000

1,800

Burnt
Vly

W SHORE RD

Pleasant Lake

BURNT VLY TRAIL

1,800

E SHORE RD

1,800

1,800

29A

1,600

29A

1,600

P

1,600

1,600

© The Countryman Press

ELEVATION PROFILE

2,000 ft					
1,900 ft					
1,800 ft			Long		
1,700 ft		Third	Lake		
1,600 ft	Trailhead	Lake			Trailhead
1,500 ft					

2   4   6   8   10 miles

as enjoyable if your visit is limited to only a single day.

For years I wondered why there was a Third Lake and a Fourth Lake in these woods, but no First or Second. As it turns out, the first entry in the North Creek chain is Waters Millpond, the site of a modest nineteenth-century sawmill, and rocky little Long Lake is the second link. All four waters combine to create North Creek, which for a time was used by lumbermen for floating pulp logs. What are now snowmobile and hiking trails were originally constructed as logging roads, probably used mostly in the winter, judging by the lack of hardened surfaces.

TRANQUILITY AT THIRD LAKE

GETTING THERE

The trailhead is located on NY 29A near Pleasant Lake in Fulton County—not to be confused with the larger Lake Pleasant to the north in Hamilton County. The parking area is 6.1 miles west of Stratford and 3 miles east of Pine Lake. The trail itself starts across the road. Signs mark this as the trailhead for Dexter and Spectacle Lakes, destinations more easily reached by snowmobile from this direction.

THE HIKE

This loop hike follows wide old logging roads for its entire distance. The first segment is a prominent trail that leads north along the series of open wetlands known collectively as Burnt Vly. It is a gentle hiking route, leading to the edge of one of the vlies at 0.7 mile but otherwise keeping a respectful distance. Keep left at the first junction at 1 mile, and at 2.1 miles you cross a bridge over the stream that flows through the vlies.

The loop itself begins at the second trail junction, 2.6 miles from the highway. Bear right, ascending a modest grade to the high ground between Goose Egg and Fourth Lakes, neither of which you can see from the trail. You can descend the slope to your left toward Goose Egg Lake, but the dense forest makes it difficult to approach. If you wish to see Fourth Lake, the better approach is to wait until you reach the next trail junction at 3.5 miles. The trail to the right brings you to the outlet of Fourth Lake, which you can follow to its shore.

Keep left, following the trail that skirts around the western tip of Third Lake. At 3.8 miles, a side trail bears right to the lake's best campsite. The water is shallow here, filled with pickerelweed in the summer and generally not appealing for swimming, but the view down the lake toward West Mountain is very pleasing. If you have time to explore, bushwhack east along the shoreline toward the lake's outlet. There you will find the remains of an old dam and a long series of cascades.

To continue the loop hike, bear northwest from the campsite on the continuing snowmobile trail. It descends into a valley where the ground becomes damp, and then it reaches a trail junction at 4.1 miles that has at times been flooded by beaver activity on North Creek. The way north leads to Spectacle Lake, one of the more intriguing and dynamic bodies of water in the area; but that trail fades away into the lake's surrounding marshes before ever reaching the shoreline, resulting in a disappointing hiking experience.

Therefore, bear left at North Creek for Long Lake. This next part of the trail may remain wet and muddy while you are close to the creek, but things will soon get better. The stream empties into an open wetland, which in turn morphs into Long Lake—a transition that occurs within sight of the trail. Note that "long" in this case describes a distance of only about 0.4 mile between the lake's eastern and western ends, making it actually quite small. But its shorelines are a little rockier than Third, and perhaps a little prettier. The best campsite on this loop is found at 5 miles, on top of one of those rocks.

The loop hike continues southwest along the shoreline, then it snakes its way up a small hill to another trail junction at 6 miles. Bear left, southeast, passing

LONG LAKE CAMPSITE

another large vly and arcing south. At 7 miles you reach another intersection where you have a decision to make. The shortest way back to your car is to head right, south. This trail brings you in 1.2 miles to East Shore Road on Pleasant Lake, with another 1 mile of road walking back to the Burnt Vly trailhead.

On the other hand, you could turn left, following a crossover trail back to the Burnt Vly Trail, where turning right would bring you directly back to your car in 3.3 miles. This option is longer, but it is entirely by trail.

20

T Lake

TOTAL DISTANCE: 6.6 miles round-trip, plus optional side trips

HIKING TIME: 4 hours

ELEVATION CHANGE: 2,700 feet

TRAILHEAD GPS COORDINATES: N43° 25′ 38.2″ W74° 32′ 31.7″

All you have to do is glance at a topographic map and your questions about how T Lake got its name will be answered immediately. This remote body of water occupies the intersection of two fault valleys, forming an inverted letter T high in the hills northwest of Piseco Lake. At 2,470 feet in elevation, it is among the higher lakes in the southern Adirondack region; and with its 3.3-mile-long trail and attractive lean-to, it is a good ambassador for what you can expect to find elsewhere in the lake-studded West Canada Lake Wilderness.

To be sure, this is a hilly trail. The hike begins with a 700-foot initial climb almost as soon as it leaves the parking area, and then it climbs again after passing through the valley of Mill Stream. The total cumulative elevation change by the time you reach the lean-to is about 1,350 feet, making the 3.3-mile distance seem much greater. But this is a trail that takes you past mountains and across streams, so that by the time you've reached your destination, you have the strong sense that you've traveled someplace remote.

Among the reasons I keep returning to T Lake is the potential for exploration this area provides. Although the official hiking trail ends at the lean-to, there are several interesting destinations nearby, most notably T Lake Falls, one of the tallest cascades in the Adirondack Park. Though not a forceful cataract, it is distinctive for its sheer rock face and summit views. The trail to its top was once a marked state trail, but several fatalities led to its abandonment. This is one of Hamilton County's most distinctive landmarks, but it does require some care and caution to explore.

A less hazardous side trip that I've enjoyed multiple times is the short

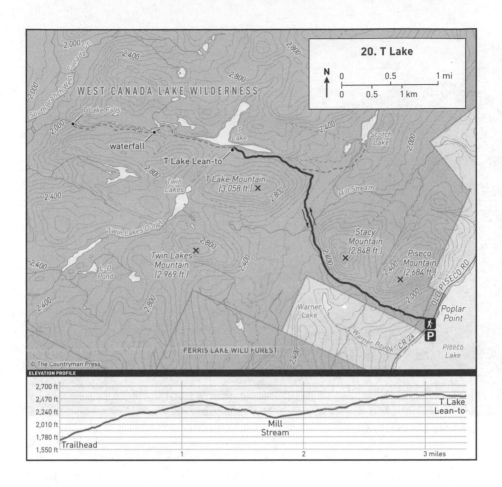

off-trail excursion to Scotch Lake, the seldom-visited sibling to T Lake. An old trail leads in the vicinity of Scotch, but if you want to see water you have to be a little more adventurous.

The trailhead is located on the north shore of Piseco Lake, opposite the former Poplar Point Campground, now a day use area. Despite the lean-to on T Lake, the area seems to see more day hiking than overnight backpacking. And despite the abandonment of the trail to the falls, it seems to remain a popular destination.

GETTING THERE

Follow NY 8 to the hamlet of Piseco, and then turn northwest onto Piseco Road. Follow it for 4 miles past the town hall, post office, and municipal airport, to the T Lake trailhead on the right, located opposite the Poplar Point Day Use Area on the shore of Piseco Lake.

THE HIKE

The blue-marked trail to T Lake wastes no time before beginning the first of its two big climbs; before the ink is dry on your entry in the trailhead register book, you are going up! The climb is never

AT THE SOUTHERN END OF T LAKE

steep, but given the lack of a warm-up period, it is always tiring. Every step takes you farther from civilization, however, and soon you are fully immersed in the wilderness setting.

The purpose of the climb is to get you over the shoulder of Piseco and Stacy Mountains, which stand as protective sentinels between the camp-studded Piseco Lake and the rugged interior forest. From a starting elevation of about 1,700 feet, you climb to the 2,200-foot contour in about 0.7 mile. After a brief pause along the foot of Piseco Mountain, you climb to a height-of-land below Stacy Mountain that is 200 feet higher.

The descent that follows into the Mill Stream watershed has always been my favorite part of the hike. It begins under the rugged ledges of Stacy Mountain and passes a small beaver meadow on the left that didn't exist when I first started hiking here in the late 1990s; what is now a wet opening in the hardwood forest was originally just an anonymous part of that forest. What attracted the beavers to relocate there is a mystery to me, but I've enjoyed watching them transform their new home over the years.

After a 300-foot descent from the shoulder of Stacy Mountain, you reach Mill Stream. This is a relatively wide stream, but I've never seen it impassable to hikers. The trail is annoyingly wet for several hundred feet after the crossing; look for stepping stones and logs concealed by the ground vegetation.

Slowly the trail ascends to higher

ground again, and immediately after a sharp left turn at 2.3 miles, you encounter the steepest slope on the trail: a brief-but-rocky section that begins the final climb toward T Lake. The grade does become more moderate, but it tops out over 2,500 feet in elevation—more than 400 feet above Mill Stream, and even well above the T Lake basin. The trail traverses the lower slope of T Lake Mountain (a former fire tower summit that no longer has many views) and undulates for the better part of a mile before dropping to the old lean-to location near the south shore of T Lake. A sign points uphill to the current lean-to site, and an old herd path leads down the bank to the nearest water access.

SIDE TRIPS

1. **T Lake Falls.** If you are contemplating the side trip to the top of T Lake Falls, there are several important factors to consider before you set off down the old trail.

   First is the fact that several people have died at T Lake Falls, most recently in 1993. The shape of the waterfall is deceitful, because what you will see when you first arrive is a gently sloping rock ledge that tempts you to step out for a better view of the bottom. In reality the mountainside is rounded like a massive upside-down bowl; there is no

UPPER WATERFALL ON T LAKE STREAM

sudden drop-off, but you can venture so far out that you become trapped on the steep rock face, with no easy way down or up. Even if you stay back from the curve, a slip on a patch of ice or slippery rock could be disastrous. Certainly, this is no place for the incautious.

Nor is there is an easy way to the bottom of the falls by keeping inside the forest. You can, with great care, bushwhack through the woods south of the falls, but even here the mountain is just as steep as the waterfall itself.

Because of these difficulties, the former state trail to T Lake Falls is not officially maintained. That means there are no markers or signs to point the way. The foot tread itself is evident and easy to follow for most of the way, but there are several blind turns and steep ledges.

For all of these reasons, this is an adventure for the self-reliant, and therefore only general directions are provided. The trail begins at the old lean-to site and continues westward along the south shore of T Lake. You have frequent views of the outlet, including a large open wetland. Between this first wetland and the next, the creek spills over a small waterfall that would be a worthwhile destination even if there weren't any larger cascades located further up the trail.

The old trail then follows the south side of the next large vly to the point where the mountains close in and the creek begins to spill noisily through a narrow valley. The next opening that you see, approximately 1.6 miles from the lean-to, is T Lake Falls. There is a pleasant little campsite on the north side of the stream. The distant hills across the valley are the Metcalf Range.

2. **Scotch Lake.** This recommended side trip is less dangerous and more solitary; I've seen little evidence on its shores that many people seek out Scotch Lake, even though it is not that hard to reach.

The best way to get there is to follow the old Mill Stream trail to its outlet; this route was part of the original trail to T Lake and the long-gone fire tower on T Lake Mountain. The point where it intersects the modern trail has grown faint, but with a practiced eye it is still evident. Look for it at a point 2.5 miles from Piseco Lake, after making the sharp left turn up the steep, rocky slope. The main trail descends a bit and intersects the old trail; the right turn may be hard to spot, but once you follow it a short distance, it becomes much more evident.

This old trail descends gradually toward Scotch's outlet stream, which you cross at 0.6 mile. It then turns upstream briefly before climbing away to the east, but if you continue following the stream northeast, you'll pass an open vly and then reach the lake itself. Scotch Lake is similar in appearance to T Lake—but without the distinctive shape, of course.

21

West Canada Lake Loop

TOTAL DISTANCE: 20.5-mile loop	
HIKING TIME: 2 to 3 days	
ELEVATION CHANGE: rolling terrain	
TRAILHEAD GPS COORDINATES: N43° 35' 13.7" W74° 29' 07.3"	

What do you think of when you hear the word *wilderness*? Pristine lakes, remote forests, long miles down rugged trails, solitary campsites? This pretty much sums up the West Canada Lake Wilderness, the second-largest protected motorless area in the northeastern United States. This high-elevation plateau of lakes forms the headwaters of three major rivers, and it is home to some of the remotest terrain in New York State.

The dimensions of this wilderness are highly favorable to backpacking. Certainly, some strong hikers could make this circuit through the lakes in a single day, with time to spare. But to savor this region, it is almost mandatory that you bring a backpack and spend at least one night on the trail. All but one of the major lakes have lean-tos, and several have attractive tent sites as well. While you probably won't experience true solitude—this is a moderately popular area, after all—you will feel as though you have put many miles between yourself and civilization.

The West Canada Lake region has always been associated with remoteness, although it has not always been uninhabited. The most famous resident was Louis Seymour, a native of Quebec popularly remembered as "French Louie." For many years he maintained a cabin on West Lake, from which he patrolled his trap lines or guided sportsmen. When he wanted company, he made sojourns to Speculator and Utica. In his later years, he planned to build a larger camp to accommodate his paying guests, but he never got further than the fireplace. That structure, though roughed up a bit by the passage of time, still stands.

Later, French Louie's cabin site became state property, and for many

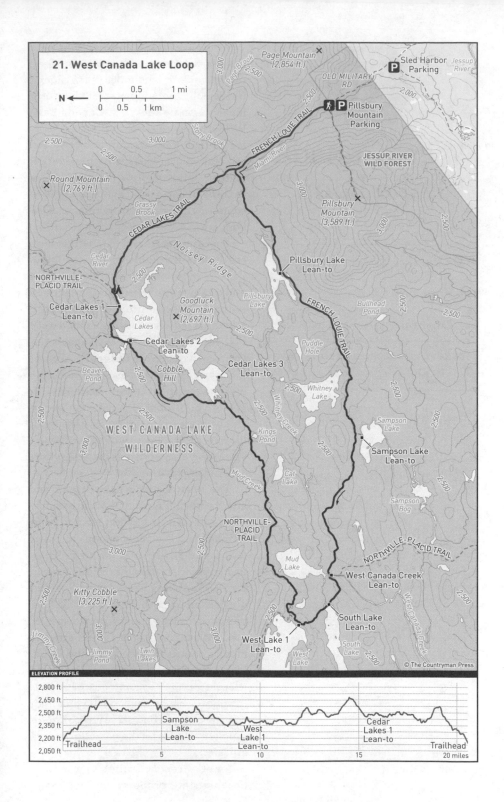

21. West Canada Lake Loop

years the Conservation Department maintained a ranger station there, with a companion site at Cedar Lakes a few miles away. For land-based travelers, the nearest trailhead was many miles away—much farther than it is currently. Therefore many visitors arrived by floatplane. In 1972, when the region was first designated a wilderness area, access by floatplane came to an end, and the ranger cabins were gradually phased out. Today, the only man-made structures you will find are the lean-tos, a few footbridges, and the aging dam at Cedar Lakes.

There are a number of ways to enjoy the West Canada Lake Wilderness, but this 20.5-mile loop is one of the most popular routes. It connects most of the major attractions, and it features some outstanding campsites. The length of the route suggests a two-day, one-night itinerary, but the number of camping options supports a three-day itinerary. I once spent five days here, hauling in an ultralight canoe and savoring just about all of the lakes along the way.

One word of caution: this area can be exceptionally buggy from May through early July. Black flies are especially numerous, followed by mosquitoes. Late summer and fall are the most blissful seasons to visit the West Canadas. Winter is out of the question, since none of the access roads are plowed.

GETTING THERE

Finding the trailhead for this loop hike is nearly as adventurous as the hike itself. This may be one of the most popular entry points for the wilderness interior, but it is located at the end of a rugged gravel road. The final section of the road is very bumpy, but with care, ordinary vehicles can make the journey.

These roads are closed every year from early December to mid-May.

Follow NY 30 for 8.2 miles north of Speculator or 15.6 miles south of Indian Lake, where Perkins Clearing Road begins at an intersection near Mason Lake. Follow this road southwest, passing Mason Lake and several drive-in campsites that are popular in the summer and fall; these are available on a first-come basis. At 3.2 miles turn right onto Old Military Road, which crosses the Miami River 1.2 miles later and reaches a large clearing 4.9 miles from NY 30. This is Sled Harbor, where low-clearance vehicles often park.

The road to the official trailhead, however, turns right just up the next little hill at 5 miles. This is the continuation of Old Military Road. Not too long ago, it was barely passable to cars due to the rocks exposed on the slopes—especially one steep slope found near the beginning that was very eroded. The situation has improved somewhat, although having a high-clearance vehicle still helps. Some people may elect to walk this first 1.2-mile section, which gently ascends 250 feet to the upper parking area. It takes no more than thirty minutes to walk to this point. There is limited parking at the upper trailhead.

THE HIKE

As you set off northwest from the upper parking area, the hike begins gently enough. You are on an extension of the old road, but since it has been barricaded to vehicles, nature has encroached from both sides to narrow the former driving surface into a satisfactory footpath.

After dipping through one washout at 0.8 mile, the climbing begins. Over the course of this 20.5-mile hike, you will encounter numerous small hills, more

PILLSBURY LAKE

an additional 100 feet before making the long descent toward Pillsbury Lake. This trail was also once a road, but it was not as well constructed and is therefore a little rougher today.

At the bottom of the hill you pass through a weedy little clearing, and then the trail passes through a spruce-and-balsam forest with several stream crossings, beaver meadows, and fleeting glimpses of Pillsbury Mountain. To your right are some equally fleeting glimpses of Pillsbury Lake. The side trail to its lean-to bears right at 3.3 miles.

This is the most accessible campsite on the loop, in use on any given summer weekend. A few years ago, the lean-to stood in a shady forest of tall balsam firs with an open understory; the old trees have now died of natural causes, and a dense stand of young trees now crowds the shelter. Nature is an agent of change, for sure. Pillsbury Lake is shallow and not suited for swimming, but it does host a population of loons.

The French Louie Trail continues westward, with additional views of the lake. Then it embarks on a hilly course toward Whitney Lake, which you only glimpse through the trees at about 5.4 miles. Mud pockets are common; indeed, mud is a standard feature of this region, which sees high annual precipitation levels.

At 6.1 miles a side trail leads left to the Sampson Lake Lean-to, about 0.1 mile away. Sampson is an attractive lake, but the lean-to is not in the best location. The best swimming area is on a rocky bit of shoreline about 400 feet to the west of the shelter.

The next section of the French Louie Trail is about as remote as they come. Many weekend backpackers turn back at Sampson Lake, so as you continue west, the trail seems distinctly narrower

than would be worth counting, but one of the biggest begins right here, with an ascent of 420 feet to a notch between Blue Ridge and Pillsbury Mountain. The grade is moderately steep, and it is over in about twenty minutes. The terrain levels off as you enter the notch, and at 1.6 miles you reach the first intersection. Straight ahead leads to Cedar Lakes, and left leads to Pillsbury Lake.

The loop begins here. There is no real advantage or disadvantage in tackling it in one direction or the other, but for simplicity's sake it is described as a clockwise circuit here. So, bearing left at the junction, follow the red-marked French Louie Trail southwest. It dips slightly but then continues climbing and less well-traveled. It takes an hour to reach the next intersection, 8.4 miles from the start. Here you meet the Northville-Placid Trail for the first time, in the coniferous forest near the West Canada Creek. The red-marked French Louie Trail ends here, but the loop hike continues right on the blue-marked N-P Trail.

Right away you reach the large footbridge over the West Canada Creek, within sight of its official beginning as the outlet of Mud Lake. A seldom-used lean-to stands nearby. Just half a mile later, at 8.9 miles, you arrive at South Lake. Signs point left toward its lean-to, one of the most scenic and prized campsites on the entire loop. The shelter stands just a few yards from the water, with sunlight pouring in late in the afternoon. There is a beach of sorts here, although a beaver dam on the lake's outlet keeps much of it underwater. In the summer, you couldn't ask for a finer campsite in terms of scenery, but there is a downside: this is the windward side of the lake, and the shelter faces directly into that headwind. As a result, this can be an uncomfortably cold place to spend a night.

Continuing northwest, the N-P Trail barely clings to dry land as it passes the east end of South Lake—really, this is just a sand bar with vegetation. A long, pier-like bridge spans the outlet channel, from which you can see Pillsbury Mountain over five miles to the east. Your car is parked on the opposite side of that mountain.

The north end of the bridge deposits you in another muddy spot, but you soon climb to higher ground. After cresting a small hill, you descend toward West Lake, with yet another side trail leading left to yet another lean-to at 9.5 miles. This site is similar to South in that the shelter is very close to the shoreline and is just as apt to be breezy and cold. It is a little more wooded, though, and rocks on the shoreline make it possible to step out from the woods and enjoy the view of this large, remote lake. Everything that you see is wilderness. A lonely foot trail traces a course along the foot of those nameless mountains to the north, but the nearest roads are miles away.

The N-P Trail reaches a major intersection at 9.6 miles, at the edge of a large clearing. Looking west toward the lake, you can see the lump of stone that is French Louie's uncompleted fireplace. You have to wade through the goldenrod to get there, although there is not much to see. The oblong stone that Louie selected for his mantel is now broken, and a thick stand of trees blocks the view of the water. The nearby foundation is all that remains of the former ranger station.

From the trail junction, continue following the N-P Trail eastward. It makes a crossing of the rocky outlet of West Lake, and then it traces an awkward route, rife with mud and hemmed in by thick stands of conifers. You pass near the northern shore of Mud Lake aptly named, considering its shallowness—and reach the bridge over Mud Creek at 11.7 miles. A series of minor climbs and descents leads you past tiny Kings Pond at 12.7 miles, and then to a side trail on the right at 13.3 miles. This one leads in 0.4 mile to the southernmost of the three lean-tos on Cedar Lakes. It is also the most solitary lean-to, and some people who value that solitude seem to ensure that the sign pointing out its location occasionally goes missing.

Your first good view of Cedar Lakes comes at 13.5 miles, where a small campsite to the right of the trail sits on the side of a small bay. Cedar Lakes is one of the larger waterbodies on this loop, but its

EARLY OCTOBER AT WEST LAKE

shape is so irregular that you can only see small pieces of it at a time from the trail. Before lumbermen dammed the outlet, the Cedars were three small ponds connected by navigable channels; what you see here is the southernmost of those ponds. Perhaps the most memorable aspect of this campsite is the metal rim of a wagon wheel that frames the fire ring.

The trail turns inland to climb around the backside of Cobble Hill, completely bypassing the second lobe of the lake. But at 15.3 miles, you descend toward the outlet channel of Beaver Pond, where a side trail leads right toward Cedar Lakes' second lean-to. This shelter stands a short distance back from the edge of a high bank, with views across the northern third of the lake toward the lumpish summit of Blue Ridge. Another side trail heading in the opposite direction, west, leads in 0.1 mile to a small spring.

From the bridge over Beaver Pond's outlet channel, you have an interesting view of the lake. If you are here in late summer or fall, the level of Cedar Lakes probably seems very low, with plenty of exposed mud and sand along the shoreline. The water in this lake rises and drops every year due to the deficiencies of the antiquated dam on the outlet. When the lake is at full capacity, Beaver Pond is nearly a continuous waterway with Cedars; but when the water drains away, the lakes return to their native configuration.

Bear right at the next intersection at 15.5 miles, following the N-P Trail to the northernmost lean-to at 16 miles. This shelter stands in a clearing at the north end of the lake, with a narrow view of the water and good swimming potential at the shoreline. The former Cedar Lakes ranger station stood nearby, but a root cellar beside the trail is all that remains today.

The lake narrows as you approach the outlet. The aging dam is hard to miss at 16.2 miles, with its concrete abutment on one end, a log crib at the other, and a rotting spillway in between. The functional problem with the dam is not a breach but an undercut created by years of erosion. Every spring as the snow melts, Cedar Lakes fills to capacity, but then through the course of the summer the water drains out through the hidden channel under the dam. Since this is a remote wilderness area with no road access, DEC plans to let nature take its course. But the lake does not depend on the dam for its existence; even if the structure fails completely, Cedar Lakes will always be here.

Just below the dam, a side trail leads right to a bridge over the nascent Cedar River. This is your return route back to the trailhead. The first thing this yellow-marked trail does is lead you back to the east end of the dam, where there is a campsite. Then it heads eastward into the woods, contouring along the foot of Noisey Ridge. At 18.3 miles you cross the aptly-named Grassy Brook, in the middle of a large grassy swale; as of 2017, the bridge here was in disrepair. Then at 18.5 miles, you cross Stony Brook, which is also descriptively named. But here's a secret: Grassy Brook and Stony Brook are the same stream, switching names as that stream leaves the mountain and enters the valley.

The trail climbs 175 feet up from the Stony Brook crossing back to the notch between Blue Ridge and Pillsbury Mountain, where at 18.9 miles you complete the loop and rejoin the French Louie Trail. This time, continue straight through the pass, following the red-marked trail back downhill toward the parking area and completing the 20.5-mile trek through the wilderness.

22

Long Pond

TOTAL DISTANCE: 7.2 miles round-trip

HIKING TIME: 1.5 hours

ELEVATION CHANGE: rolling terrain

TRAILHEAD GPS COORDINATES: N43° 36′ 04.4″ W74° 18′ 37.4″

There are thousands of lakes and ponds in the Adirondacks, and more than a few of them bear the prosaic name "Long." Whoever named this particular one in the Siamese Ponds Wilderness northeast of Speculator must have possessed an uninspired imagination, or was pressed for time, or was intentionally trying to throw people off the trail of a favorite haunt. There are a number of more descriptive names that might apply, such as Rose Pogonia Pond, Swimming Ledge Pond, or Incredibly Scenic Pond. The current name suggests this is a dime-a-dozen place, when it is most certainly not.

Long Pond possesses several features that add up to something truly unique. First are the rock ledges that line the shoreline, creating two really fine campsites and two really good swimming spots (the campsites and the swimming spots are not necessarily the same two locations). Logs floating along the shoreline support linear colonies of insectivorous plants, such as sundews, rose pogonias, and pitcher plants.

But the one element that impresses most visitors is the band of cliffs that rises to the east of the pond. This small, unnamed ridge looks as if someone sliced open a small hill and left its rocky heart exposed in cross-section; indeed, when seen from afar, the ridge resembles a wedge of fruit sitting in the landscape. If the scenic beauty of a pond can be measured by the amount of exposed rock that surrounds it, then Long Pond is off the charts.

It is a minor miracle, then, that Long Pond is not swarmed with people. In my experience, the number of visitors here is feast or famine; there have been weekends when youth groups practically take over the place, and other summer weekends when I have had it all to myself.

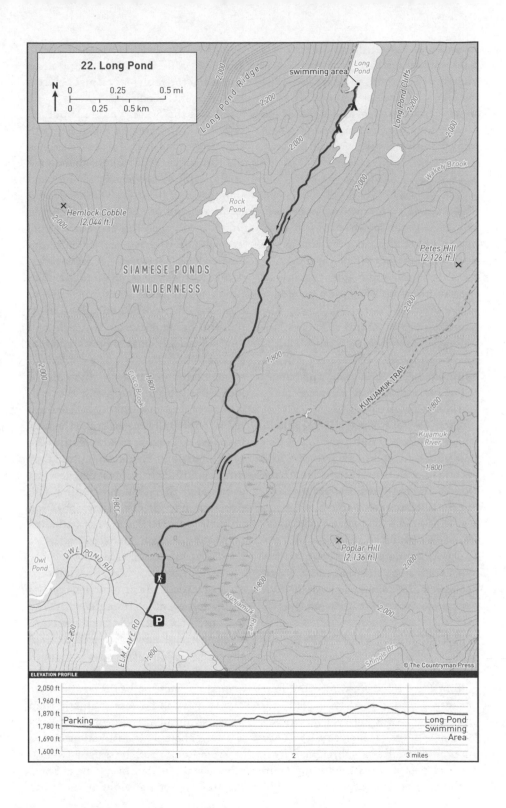

22. Long Pond

N

| 0 | 0.25 | 0.5 mi |
| 0 | 0.25 | 0.5 km |

swimming area

Long Pond

Long Pond Ridge

2,000

2,200

Long Pond Cliffs

2,200

2,000

Wakely Brook

2,000

Rock Pond

×
Hemlock Cobble
[2,044 ft.]

2,000

Petes Hill
[2,126 ft.]
×

SIAMESE PONDS
WILDERNESS

1,800

2,000

KUNJAMUK TRAIL

1,800

Cisco Brook

1,800

Kujamuk River

1,800

1,800

Owl Pond

OWL POND RD.

×
Poplar Hill
[2,136 ft.]

2,000

1,800

1,800

ELM LAKE RD.

P

Kunjamuk River

2,000

Shingle Br.

© The Countryman Press

ELEVATION PROFILE

2,050 ft			
1,960 ft			
1,870 ft	Parking		Long Pond
1,780 ft			Swimming
1,690 ft			Area
1,600 ft	1	2	3 miles

Long Pond has all the hallmarks of a backcountry destination where overuse should be expected, so we should all be thankful this has not occurred. The fact that the trailhead is located at the far end of a sketchy logging road seems to help keep visitation levels in check. So far.

GETTING THERE

The main portal for this trail network is the Cisco Brook Trailhead. It is located at the end of Elm Lake Road, near the northernmost corner of the Speculator Tree Farm, a managed timberland that abuts the southwestern boundary of the Siamese Ponds Wilderness. The primary purpose of this road is to provide access for logging trucks, but it is also open to the general public in the summer and fall. It is a long and bumpy drive, but ordinary vehicles can make the journey with care.

From the four corners in Speculator where NY 8 and NY 30 meet, follow Elm Lake Road for 8 miles northwest to a second four-way intersection deep in the woods. The trailhead is straight ahead, but the public parking area is about 100 feet to the right. Since there is no parking at the trailhead, all hikes into the backcountry necessarily begin with a short walk along the final, unimproved section of Elm Lake Road from the four corners to the state land boundary.

THE HIKE

From the parking area near the end of Elm Lake Road, return to the four corners and turn northeast. Oddly, no signs point the way until you reach state land, but the road (rough as it is) is easy enough to find. It leads through a clear-cut and past a private hunting camp to the state land boundary, where the road is barricaded and becomes a trail. Then, 0.3 mile from the parking area, you reach the register box just before a bridge over Cisco Brook.

Across the bridge you find yourself on a wide trail through a forest rich with stout white pine trees. This trail was once the Kunjamuk Road, a long-abandoned public highway between Speculator and Indian Lake. It circles wide around a large wetland on the Kunjamuk River, which most maps still show as a pond, even though the fish barrier dam that created it has been breached for decades.

At 1.2 miles you reach a fork in a plantation of red pines, where you need to bear left off the Kunjamuk Trail. Now you will be on a narrow footpath, and you will quickly exit the pine stand into a more natural hardwood forest. Except for one long muddy area where an old log bridge has rotted away, the trail is mostly dry; and although there are numerous small hills all along the way, there are no big hills of note. Nettles are a common plant in this region, and they grow plentifully here. Most people won't even notice them, but those with sensitive skin may feel a burning sensation on their legs. Nettles are not toxic like poison ivy, though, and some varieties even have medicinal value.

An hour into the hike, the trail dips to cross a small stream and then reaches a junction 2.5 miles from the start. The main trail continues right, but the left turn leads a short distance to a scenic campsite on Rock Pond. This spot is perched atop a scenic rock ledge well-suited for fishing and not too bad for swimming. The scenery is far less dramatic than what lies ahead at Long, but Rock Pond is itself a photogenic destination.

From Rock Pond, it is just a twenty-minute walk to your first view of Long. The trail is pretty straightforward, with

LONG POND AND ITS ICONIC CLIFFS

WHITE PINES AT ROCK POND

open wetlands appearing on your right just before the pond and its band of cliffs itself come into view. You reach the first of the two campsites at 3.3 miles. This spot is spacious and inviting, but the views are not quite as good as you would hope them to be, and the swimming prospects are less than enchanting.

The trail continues up along the western shoreline, through a hemlock forest with very little understory. If it weren't for the plastic trail markers, the path would be very poorly defined. But just 0.2 mile from the first campsite you arrive at the second, which is similar in size but has the added benefit of a wide rock ledge on the shoreline. In both cases the marked trail passes right through the camping area—a detail that may concern anyone seeking absolute solitude.

This is not the end of the recommended hike, though. Keep heading north along the shoreline to the prominent peninsula midway up the lake, 3.6 miles from your car. Here the trees end and a triangular rock juts out into the water. *This* is the best swimming spot on the pond, with a deep drop-off on one side of the rock, a sloping underwater ramp on the other, and good views in three directions.

Note, however, that this site is closed to camping. There may not be any signs saying so, and you may see signs of past campfires, but the smallness of the site and its proximity to water on both sides makes it substandard.

The trail continues past this spot, and indeed, if you are planning to make a weekend of your visit to Long Pond, you will want to continue exploring. No trails lead up the spectacular ridgeline, but a bushwhack from the south is always enjoyable. The biggest challenge is getting around the pond. I sometimes solve that problem by packing in my own ultralight canoe, which also allows me to explore the more distant parts of the shoreline; but absent that, the leaky rowboats often found here are good enough to get you closer to the foot of the mountain.

23

Murphy, Middle, and Bennett Lakes

TOTAL DISTANCE: 6.7 miles

HIKING TIME: 3 hours

ELEVATION CHANGE: Rolling terrain to Middle Lake; 590-foot descent from Middle Lake to Creek Road

TRAILHEAD GPS COORDINATES: N43° 22' 14.4" W74° 14' 50.9" (Pumpkin Hollow Road); N43° 18' 05.5" W74° 11' 58.4" (Creek Road)

Calling these three lakes a "chain" would be a misnomer, since each one sits at the head of its own little watershed. Nevertheless, they are all lined up in a row, with a well-used trail stringing them all together. Rock ledges on the shoreline and a mountainous backdrop conspire to make this a favorite southern Adirondack adventure.

Murphy, Middle, and Bennett lakes have long been popular hiking and backpacking destinations, sought out by veterans and families alike. There is a lean-to at Murphy Lake, and usually lean-tos are the most popular campsites in an area. But in this case, there are several choice camping spots to choose from, especially at Middle Lake, and all of them seem to be equally loved.

Two trailheads service these lakes. Most visitors park at the southern trailhead on Creek Road, hike up the mountain to the lakes, and then turn around. That is a fine way to spend a weekend, but if you can shuttle cars between the trailheads, a more enjoyable itinerary involves parking at the northern terminus on Pumpkin Hollow Road and hiking south. The two parking areas are only 8.2 miles apart by road, so it is very easy to spot vehicles at each end.

There is a little bit of history to contemplate along this route as well, since about two hundred years ago a portion of this forest was farmland. The woods have overtaken the landscape so thoroughly that you might not believe it, except that here and there—especially at Middle Lake—you may spot a cellar hole or other indication of human habitation.

GETTING THERE

Both trailheads are found by exploring the side roads that lead east from NY 30 between Northville and Wells. The

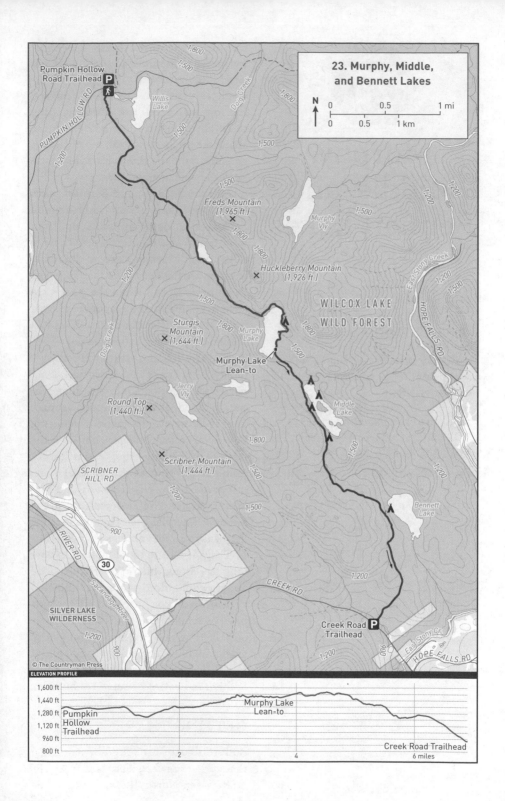

23. Murphy, Middle, and Bennett Lakes

Pumpkin Hollow
Road Trailhead

N

| 0 | | 0.5 | | 1 mi |
| 0 | 0.5 | | 1 km | |

Willis
Lake

Dog Creek

Freds Mountain
(1,965 ft.)

Murphy
Vly

WILCOX LAKE
WILD FOREST

Huckleberry Mountain
(1,926 ft.)

East Stony Creek

HOPE FALLS RD

Sturgis
Mountain
(1,644 ft.)

Murphy
Lake

Murphy Lake
Lean-to

Dog Creek

Jerry
Vly

Round Top
(1,440 ft.)

Middle
Lake

Scribner Mountain
(1,444 ft.)

SCRIBNER
HILL RD

Bennett
Lake

RIVER RD

30

Sacandaga River

900

CREEK RD

SILVER LAKE
WILDERNESS

Creek Road
Trailhead

East Stony Cr.

HOPE FALLS RD

© The Countryman Press

ELEVATION PROFILE

1,600 ft	
1,440 ft	
1,280 ft	Pumpkin
1,120 ft	Hollow
960 ft	Trailhead
800 ft	

Murphy Lake
Lean-to

Creek Road Trailhead

2   4   6 miles

southern trailhead is located on Creek Road, which turns east 6.7 miles north of Northville. Follow it up the hill for 2.3 miles, where you will find the trail on the left.

Pumpkin Hollow Road turns northeast from NY 30 just 4.3 miles north of Creek Road. Just before reaching the outlet of Willis Lake, there is a public parking area at 1.6 miles on the left. The trail to Murphy Lake starts across the road.

THE HIKE

Beginning in a forest of white pines, the trail to Murphy Lake leads southwest from Pumpkin Hollow Road to intersect an old roadbed that originates on a nearby private parcel. By "old roadbed," I mean a roadway of the ancient variety, constructed long ago for use by wagons and abandoned long before anyone ever heard of internal combustion. Today it is best suited for foot travel and the occasional snowmobile.

Turning southeast, you follow this old roadway through the valley of Doig Creek, which you cross at 1.5 miles, and then climb toward the outlet of a small, brushy vly which you pass at 2.1 miles. Freds Mountain forms the backdrop for this pretty place. The trail then falls alongside a small stream, the outlet of Murphy Lake. You climb beside it for the next 0.7 mile, eventually reaching the north end of Murphy at 3 miles.

Snowmobiles strike out across the lake, but hikers must follow a rugged shoreline trail that veers left around the

PICKERELWEED AT MURPHY LAKE

A MOMENT OF BLISS AT MIDDLE LAKE

foot of Huckleberry Mountain. Despite the popularity of these lakes, this section around the north end of Murphy always seems lightly traveled. As a consequence, the way may not always be clear.

This vague section ends at 3.5 miles, when you reach a prominent tent site located on an east shore promontory; it comes with a great view of Huckleberry to the north. Continuing south, you cut through a small beaver meadow and reach the lean-to at 3.7 miles, not far from Murphy's southernmost end. Like the campsite you just passed, the shelter has a nearby rock ledge on the shoreline with a photogenic view of Huckleberry Mountain. Pickerelweed grows in the shallows here, sprouting blue-violet spikes of flowers by mid-summer.

The snowmobile trail pulls away from Murphy Lake and cuts cross-country toward the north end of Middle Lake, which you first glimpse at 4.1 miles. If you are observant, you may notice a junction here; an unmarked, unsigned trail turns left and traces a route around Middle Lake's eastern shore. If you are able to spot that route, you will definitely find it to be a more scenic alternative than the main trail. Beginning at the site of an old farmhouse (marked by the remains of a well and a foundation), it leads past several scenic promontories, each with its own desirable campsite. The southern end of this footpath is less well defined, but with a decent sense of direction, it is not hard to find your way back up the hill to the main trail.

If you don't find that faint path, no worries. The main trail parallels Middle Lake's western shoreline, still following that old road. A side path at 4.3 miles leads to the only campsite on this side of the lake, not far from its largest island. Otherwise, the snowmobile trail stays high above the shoreline, eventually pulling away to the south.

Middle Lake, at about 1,490 feet in elevation, is the highest of the three bodies of water. From here to the Creek Road trailhead, the trail is nearly all downhill. Bennett Lake is at the end of a short side trail that bears left at 5.6 miles, leading in 400 feet to a large campsite near the northwest corner of the lake. At 1,170 feet above sea level, Bennett Lake is conspicuously low in elevation, even by southern Adirondack standards. Its shoreline is brushy, not rocky, and the one campsite seems to be enough to satisfy demand. On the other hand, this is the largest of the three lakes, as well as the most accessible.

The last part of the trail is a bit more eroded, with several detours beside the old roadway where it is too wet and rocky for easy hiking. Much of the forest consists of hemlock, one of the most common trees in the region. It takes only a half-hour to cover the 1.1 miles from Bennett Lake to the Creek Road trailhead, located at a mere 945 feet in elevation.

With so many excellent waterfront campsites to choose from on this hike, swimming might seem like an excellent idea. You'll change your mind, though, when you see leeches lurking just about everywhere.

24

Hadley Mountain

TOTAL DISTANCE: 3.2 miles

HIKING TIME: 2 hours

VERTICAL RISE: 1,530 feet

TRAILHEAD GPS COORDINATES: N43° 22′ 26.2″ W73° 57′ 00.5″

At 2,680 feet in elevation, Hadley Mountain falls well short of the Adirondacks' highest summits. Nevertheless, it towers more than 1,500 feet above the valley at its base, and the view from its summit includes a vast swath of the Adirondack landscape. For many hikers, the presence of a fire tower is an added bonus, but even without the tower, this would be a favorite hike.

For such an attractive, family-friendly hike, this trail is quite steep. Much of it is worn down to bedrock, making it seem like a paved sidewalk with an incline. You won't have to worry about mud, but on the other hand, the rock could be slippery if it is wet.

The Hadley Mountain tower has a well-documented backstory, since it was the focus of two detailed newspaper articles in the twentieth century. Those human-interest stories focused on the lives of the men who built the tower and lived on its summit every year. In 1917, Isaac Briner carted the materials for the tower and the watchman's cabin up the steep trail with a team of oxen. His father, John Briner, later served as the observer for sixteen years. Tending the tower meant more than just watching for fires all day; the observers needed to be self-sufficient, capable of making basic repairs as well as restoring the telephone line leading down the mountain in the event of a break.

The cabin in which the observer lived was (and still is) located on the summit, not far from the tower. Rather than carrying all of their staples up the steep trail, several observers tended small gardens that grew corn, beets, beans, carrots, potatoes, and cucumbers. The mountain provided raspberries in abundance, and nearby springs provided water.

Hadley's tower was last manned by

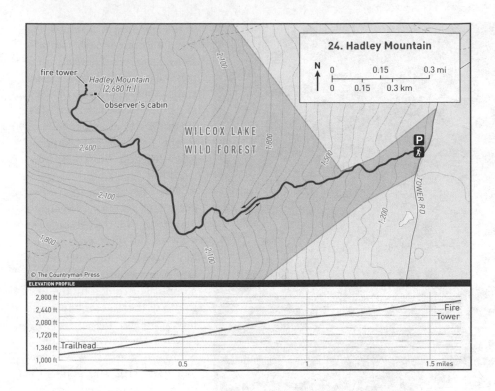

the state in 1990, but it is now staffed on an internship basis with a summit steward most weekends through July and August. The steward can help you identify the many different landmarks you will see from the top of the tower, from the Catskills to the High Peaks to Vermont. This is a favorite mountain that you will likely be drawn to climb again and again.

GETTING THERE

The mountain can be accessed via Hadley Hill Road. The easiest way to find it is to follow NY 9N to the hamlet of Hadley, across the Hudson River from Lake Luzerne. Turn north onto Stony Creek Road (CR 1) and follow it for 3.1 miles, where Hadley Hill Road bears left, west. Drive on Hadley Hill Road for 4.4 miles to Tower Road, which

bears right, north, leading in 1.4 miles to the trailhead.

THE HIKE

The hike is pretty straightforward, largely because it starts straight up the mountain and never flinches until it reaches the ridgeline. This may sound daunting, but plenty of people overcome these physical challenges every year. Curious boulders beside the trail invite rest stops for adults and exploration by children; interesting flowers such as yellow touch-me-nots, which bloom around Labor Day, invite photography.

It takes forty minutes to cover the first 0.9 mile of trail, at a significantly slower pace because of the steepness. However, you get a break at the end of that section, when the trail crests the mountain's southern ridgeline. You still

FIRE TOWER AT HADLEY MOUNTAIN

scenic opening at 1.4 miles. The main summit is still 0.2 mile away, however. The trail reenters the woods and passes a side trail leading right to the observer's cabin, located about 175 feet away. One final ledge leads up to the partially-bald summit, 1.6 miles from the Tower Road trailhead.

The mountain is open enough to permit an expansive view to the southwest; only the view to the west past Spruce Mountain is at all restricted. In late summer and early fall, the summit is rimmed by the brilliant red berries of the small mountain-ash tree.

Only the tower provides a complete view. However, not everyone will appreciate the exposed ladder leading from the topmost landing into the cab. But once inside, you will find a replica of the circular map table used by the old observers to help you identify the major landmarks. Among the highlights is Great Sacandaga Lake to the southwest, and the trio of Crane, Baldhead, and Moose mountains to the north. Beyond the latter, on the hazy horizon some fifty miles away, are portions of the Dix and Great ranges in the High Peaks.

On the descent, the biggest piece of advice is to mind your footing on the exposed bedrock on the lower half of the trail.

have plenty of climbing to cover, but for a brief distance the trail is level as it traverses the ridgeline, about 1,030 feet above the trailhead. The trail turns north to follow the narrow ridge, with slopes dropping off to your left and right.

When the climbing resumes, it is at a more moderate grade, leading to the first

25

Crane Mountain

TOTAL DISTANCE: 3.6 miles

HIKING TIME: 3 hours

VERTICAL RISE: 1,170 feet

TRAILHEAD GPS COORDINATES: N43° 32' 15.1" W73° 58' 03.8"

An apt nickname for Crane Mountain would be "High Peak of the Southern Adirondacks." This is not because Crane's summit comes anywhere close to 4,000 feet in elevation—indeed at 3,254 feet, it is surprisingly well short of that threshold—but because of its stunning profile. The mountain's rocky face dominates the valley at its foot, and even if it is not the tallest mountain in its local neighborhood, it is easily the most recognizable.

When the original Adirondack Park boundary lines were drawn in 1892, Crane was excluded by a very short distance. The original park planners must have viewed the agrarian valleys that surrounded the mountain and decided there was no wilderness here to protect. Crane was largely a local landmark, known for the berries on its summit and the commercially valuable paint pigment found in its rocks. Small family farms extended right up to its foot, some of them serving as stations on the Underground Railroad prior to the Civil War.

It was also known as a hiking destination long before the advent of the automobile; instead of grizzled guides with pipes and flannel shirts, visitors could hire one of the local children for twenty-five cents to lead the way to the summit. One such guide was Julia Oliver, who lived nearby with her uncle in the 1880s. As an adult, Julia adopted the name Jeanne Robert Foster and became an accomplished poet.

State officials placed the first fire observation station here in 1911 and later replaced it with a steel tower in 1919. That tower is now long gone, but its absence hardly impairs the view or diminishes the mountain's popularity. The views from its summit are outstanding, and the mountain is so dynamic

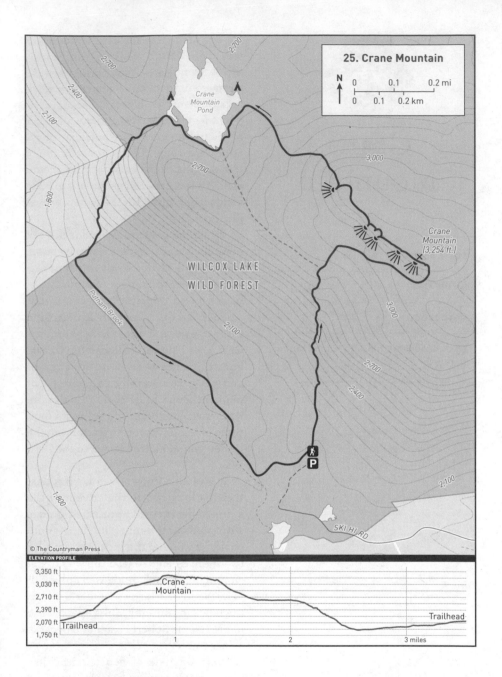

25. Crane Mountain

Crane Mountain Pond

WILCOX LAKE WILD FOREST

Putnam Brook

Crane Mountain (3,254 ft.)

SKI HI RD

© The Countryman Press

ELEVATION PROFILE

Crane Mountain

Trailhead

Trailhead

3,350 ft | 3,030 ft | 2,710 ft | 2,390 ft | 2,070 ft | 1,750 ft

1 | 2 | 3 miles

that a single visit never suffices. This is not a typical mountain, after all, but a self-contained wild area with its own summit pond, choice campsites, and several peripheral peaks with views that complement the main show.

Crane is a steep and imposing mountain, and as you drive toward the trailhead at the foot of its cliffy southern face, you may experience doubt about your desire to climb such a forbidding slope. Fret not, for although the climb is steep, the distances are short. In roughly the same one-way distance it takes to reach, say, the summit of Snowy Mountain, you can climb to the summit of Crane via the most direct trail, descend the other side to Crane Mountain Pond, and return to your car. This is an action-packed loop hike, with teaser views along most of the way, ladders to scale, the pond to explore, and a disappearing stream to investigate.

The ladders are the only thing that prevents this from being a family-friendly and pet-friendly trail, although those ladders can be avoided simply by taking the longer trail that climbs by way of the pond.

GETTING THERE

The state trailhead for Crane is located at the end of Ski Hi Road near the south end of the mountain. Follow NY 8 to Johnsburg, and then turn south onto South Johnsburg Road. At the tiny hamlet of Thurman, turn right onto Garnet Lake Road. Ski Hi Road (pronounced "Sky High") turns right at 1.3 miles and climbs 760 feet to an elevation of 2,080 feet above sea level. The parking area is located at the very end of the road.

THE HIKE

The most direct trail to the summit of Crane leads north from the Ski Hi Road parking area, straight to the foot of the mountain. Expect no more than five minutes of easy hiking before you reach the rocky slope, where the steep climb begins without much fanfare. Your view of the mountain from the road included expansive cliffs of bare rock, seemingly the last place a hiking trail should be located, but somehow the route of the trail manages to avoid the steepest parts

of the mountain and finds a reasonable way to the top.

But the steepness of the trail should not be downplayed. This is a rugged, rocky trail—and a tiring climb. On the other hand, there is no need to rush. At just about any point along this first section, you can stop to catch your breath, look over your shoulder, and catch a glimpse of the view across the valley below. Fall hikers can rejoice in the northern red oaks that predominate on these lower slopes; when other hardwoods elsewhere in the park have lost their color, these sturdy oaks might still retain some vivid ruddiness.

You pass through an area of open rock and reach a trail junction at 0.5 mile, about 780 feet above the trailhead. The route to the left is a crossover trail leading to Crane Mountain Pond; if you're not a fan of ladders in rugged places, you might want to take that detour.

The summit trail, however, bears right and continues climbing at a much gentler grade. The first of the two ladders comes 0.1 mile after the junction; this one assists you up a small ledge. The trail angles southeast here and makes a relatively gentle traverse below the cliffs on the main summit.

It is just a 0.3-mile, 10-minute hike to the second ladder. This one is much taller than the first, and a potential show-stopper for dogs—and people with a fear of heights. It is about twenty-five feet tall and leans against a craggy rock wall. At the top you need to exit to the left, stepping onto the nearest ledge for the final climb to the summit.

As trying as this trail might be, the climb is over in just 1 mile—but don't be surprised if it takes an hour to cover that distance. Just moments after stepping off the ladder, you reach the open rock that marks the main summit. The view

CRANE MOUNTAIN'S SUMMIT VIEW

ridgeline. Although it tends to favor the wooded half of the summit, there are frequent side paths to the left leading to additional ledges, each with a view similar to the one found on the main summit.

Unfortunately, the best of these peripheral views is also the easiest to miss. A narrow side path leads left off the main trail as it begins to descend toward Crane Mountain Pond, 0.4 mile and fifteen minutes past the summit. This detour is a little longer than the previous ones, but it leads to a more isolated patch of bare rock with the only summit view of the pond. Sharp-eyed hikers can also pick out Snowy Mountain on the distant horizon, with Puffer and Eleventh Mountains in the middle distance.

The descent off the summit's northwestern slopes is moderate in grade. Just 0.7 mile from the top, or 1.7 miles overall, you reach a junction near the eastern corner of Crane Mountain Pond. An unmarked trail leads right, to an excellent campsite about 400 feet away.

Bear left to follow the marked trail around the south end of the pond. Ledges along the shoreline ensure that even this interlude is on the rugged side, but there are several points where you can stop and enjoy the view across the pond. At more than 2,600 feet in elevation, Crane Mountain Pond is one of the highest ponds in the Adirondacks. It is rimmed with rock ledges and flanked with two small knobs that serve as Crane Mountain's northern and western summits. There are two good campsites on the pond, located on the eastern

is outstanding! The most obvious landmark is Garnet Lake to the southwest, even though it is only partly visible amongst the hills. With a good map of the area, you can identify some of the other features within view: Mount Blue, just beyond Garnet Lake, with a sliver of Lizard Pond visible at its foot; Hadley Mountain, to the distant south; and the rolling mountains of the Siamese Ponds Wilderness and Wilcox Lake Wild Forest, to the west and northwest.

Continue the loop hike by following the marked trail northwest along the

BREAK TIME AT CRANE MOUNTAIN POND

and western shores. Campers have also spent the night at spots along the trail around the southern shoreline, but these are poor sites with signs of degradation.

Follow the trail around the pond all the way to the outlet at 2.1 miles; another herd path can be found leading to the western campsite a short distance away. The marked trail, however, leads away from the pond at this point to begin the descent. It parallels the tiny outlet stream through a series of rocky openings before crossing it and angling more southward. The descent that follows is almost the mirror image of the first part of the ascent: steep and rocky, dropping 700 vertical feet in 0.6 mile.

There is an interesting feature at the foot of the mountain that could be easy to miss. Look for a pair of natural pits, one on each side of the trail. A stream flows out of a small wetland on your left and disappears into a slit in the rock in the first depression, and by descending into the second pit on the right you can glimpse the subterranean waterway before it disappears entirely. The stream follows a band of marble in the mountain's bedrock that has long since eroded away, leaving behind a small cave.

There is a trail junction at 2.7 miles, just past the cave. The route to the right leads into private land, so bear left to follow the state trail back to Ski Hi Road. This segment follows an old roadway, leading southeast parallel to the foot of the mountain. It climbs gently for 0.7 mile, with a left turn at the end of that section that takes you on a shortcut detour back to the main parking area. This completes the 3.6-mile loop.

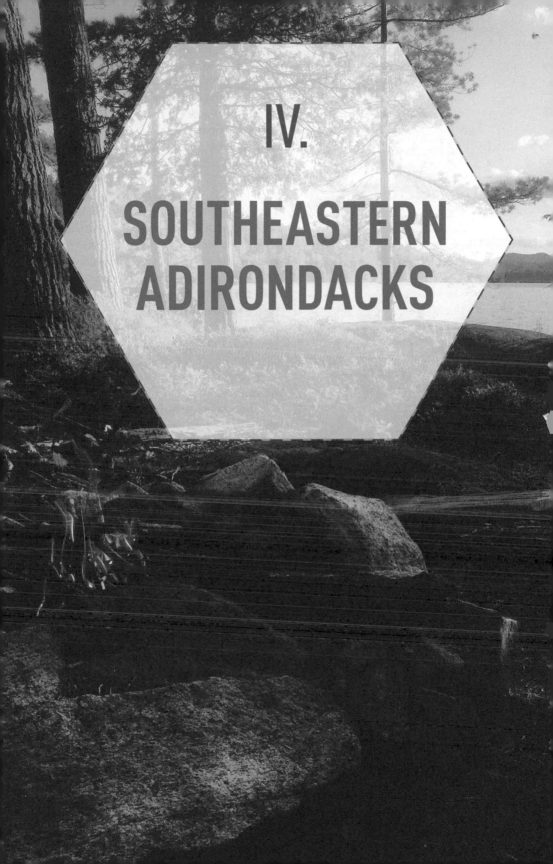

IV.

SOUTHEASTERN
ADIRONDACKS

26

Sleeping Beauty

TOTAL DISTANCE: 4.3-mile loop with optional side trips

HIKING TIME: 2 hours

VERTICAL RISE: 880 feet

TRAILHEAD GPS COORDINATES: N43° 32' 57.8" W73° 33' 21.7"

Of all the mountains that rim Lake George, none may be as attractive to families as Sleeping Beauty. Certainly, the name must play a big role in that popularity, because who could resist a small mountain named for a fairy tale? In this respect it stands out amongst the scenic destinations of the Adirondack Park.

But the novelty of the name is not the only reason why you should hike this mountain. The summit features a wide-open ledge with a view that encompasses a vast swath of wild terrain, from Lake George to the distant highlands of the southern and central Adirondacks. A well-designed trail leads over the summit and down the other side, allowing you to make a 4.3-mile loop that also includes charming little Bumps Pond.

This portion of the Lake George Wild Forest was once part of a large estate owned by a hotel owner on the eastern shore of the lake. What are now hiking, horse, and snowmobile routes were originally constructed as carriage trails in a bygone era. This explains the unusual amount of construction you will see on this loop, especially as you descend from Bumps Pond back to the trailhead.

This is a hike best enjoyed in summer and fall, when the access road is sure to be open to vehicles. It is just 1.7 miles from the parking area at Dacy Clearing to the summit and its spectacular views, and if you turned back there you would still be ensured an exceptional time on the trail. But if you have the opportunity to make a nice loop with minimal extra effort, why not take it? And for those who may be eager to extend this short hike into something more substantial, the extensive trail network can easily accommodate your desire to explore.

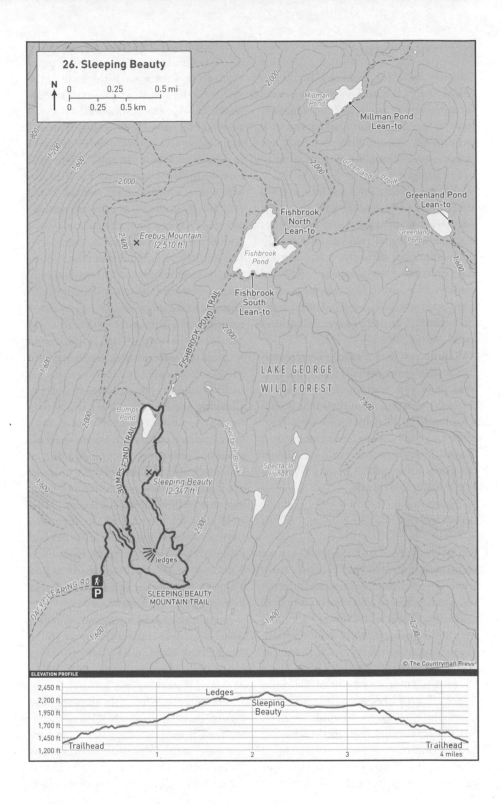

26. Sleeping Beauty

N

| 0 | 0.25 | 0.5 mi |
| 0 | 0.25 | 0.5 km |

Millman Pond

Millman Pond Lean-to

Greenland Brook

Greenland Pond Lean-to

Fishbrook North Lean-to

Erebus Mountain (2,510 ft.)

Fishbrook Pond

Greenland Pond

FISHBROOK POND TRAIL

Fishbrook South Lean-to

LAKE GEORGE WILD FOREST

Bumps Pond

Spectacle Brook

Spectacle Ponds

BUMPS POND TRAIL

Sleeping Beauty (2,347 ft.)

ledges

DACY CLEARING RD.

P

SLEEPING BEAUTY MOUNTAIN TRAIL

© The Countryman Press

ELEVATION PROFILE

Ledges

Sleeping Beauty

Trailhead

Trailhead

| 2,450 ft |
| 2,200 ft |
| 1,950 ft |
| 1,700 ft |
| 1,450 ft |
| 1,200 ft |

1 2 3 4 miles

GETTING THERE

The trailhead for Sleeping Beauty is called Dacy Clearing, in reference to a farm that once occupied the site. It is located far off the main highway, but it is generally easy to find. The final few miles to the parking area are not plowed in the winter.

To find Dacy Clearing, follow US 9 south from Lake George and turn east onto NY 149. Stay on this highway for 6 miles until you come to Buttermilk Falls Road, a left (north) turn. Buttermilk Falls Road becomes Sly Pond Road several miles later, but make no turns until you reach state land 9.6 miles later. Here you will find the Hogtown parking area.

The narrow access road to Dacy Clearing begins at the far end of the parking area. It is well graded and suitable for ordinary vehicles, but although it is only 1.6 miles long, the distance between Hogtown and Dacy Clearing may seem much longer. There is ample parking amongst the pines at the end of the road, a total of 11.2 miles from NY 149.

THE HIKE

A trail leads uphill from the parking area to intercept the nearest carriage trail, where you will find the trailhead register. Turn left here and continue uphill, following the wide trail northward on a moderate grade. It loops right through a wet area and reaches a junction at 0.6 mile, already 320 feet above Dacy Clearing. The rocky bulk of Sleeping Beauty looms above you through the trees. The carriage road swings left here, but the direct foot trail to the summit bears right.

The foot trail turns south, then southeast along the foot of the mountain on a welcome level traverse. This lasts for about ten minutes, ending at the point the trail nudges against the base of the slope. Here you will find a set of switchbacks (notice the rockwork!) to assist you up the first steep slope, with the moderately steep climb resuming above.

The trail winds through a hemlock forest on Sleeping Beauty's southeastern slope, zigging past vernal pools and zagging past outcrops of rock. At 1.6 miles, as you near the summit, your trail draws near to the continuing foot trail to Bumps Pond. Rather than intersecting each other, the two trails slowly merge with one another as they both approach Sleeping Beauty's open ledge from behind. Take note of this unusual confluence of footpaths, as you will need to pick the correct fork when you are ready to continue the hike.

The main ledge is 1.7 miles from Dacy Clearing and 880 feet above it. There is an ample amount of open, sunny rock here, and therefore plenty of room for all comers. Lake George is 3 miles away, so the views of that massive body of water are not as intimate as you will find from, say, the Tongue Mountain Range (Hike #28). But what you lack in intimacy here, you make up for in scope. Several miles of the lake are visible, from Buck Mountain to The Narrows, with Cat and Thomas Mountains (Hike #27) visible beyond Bolton Landing. Some of the more distant peaks within view in fair weather include Hadley Mountain (Hike #24), Crane Mountain (Hike #25), Gore Mountain, Moxham Mountain (Hike #12), and Mount Marcy.

Many people turn back here and return directly to Dacy Clearing, but for a really superb hike, you should continue along the ridgeline toward Bumps Pond. Return to the fork in the trail just inside the treeline, this time keeping left on the trail that leads north along the ridgeline. This route follows the edge of an old forest fire for the first 0.4 mile. To your left, on the mountain's steep western slope, is a patch of scorched woods in the process of recovery; despite the recent fire history, there are few open views here. On your right is a healthy forest, untouched by the fire. The trail follows the boundary between the two zones until it turns away from the western slope toward the east side of the ridge.

The descent down the north side of the mountain is marked by numerous tight switchbacks. You drop about 260 feet in a distance of 0.6 mile, bottoming out 2.7 miles into your hike at a wide footbridge over the outlet of Bumps Pond. Just beyond the bridge is another trail junction; right leads to Fishbrook Pond (see below) and left leads to Bumps Pond and Dacy Clearing.

Bearing left, you are first led on a detour past a wet section of trail before emerging on the north side of pretty little Bumps Pond. At 2,020 feet in elevation, this unassuming body of water is one of the highest ponds in the eastern Adirondack region. The north end of Sleeping Beauty rises beyond, but the cliffs are not visible from this angle.

The trail is briefly muddy as you circle the pond. A side trail to Erebus Mountain turns right at 0.1 mile, but you want to keep left on the shoreline route. However, if you happen to notice markers pointing inland toward a designated campsite, by all means take a look. A chimney at that site is all that remains of an old hunting lodge.

Heading south from Bumps Pond, you are once again on a wide carriage trail—almost as wide as a road. It climbs slightly to a height-of-land below Sleeping Beauty's cliffs before beginning the long descent back toward Dacy Clearing. There are two highlights along this section. First is a small overlook at the side of the trail, with a parting glimpse

LOOKING TOWARD THE TONGUE RANGE FROM SLEEPING BEAUTY

NORTHERN LEAN-TO AT FISHBROOK POND

of Lake George. Second is the elaborate set of switchbacks, which in this case are delineated by rock retaining walls. At 3.7 miles you reach the junction with the foot trail where you first veered off the carriage trail to begin the climb of the mountain. This time you need to keep right on the carriage trail, which continues descending for another 0.6 mile back to the trailhead.

SIDE TRIP: FISHBROOK POND

If you are intrigued by the trip itinerary outlined above but are eager to see more of this beautiful region, by all means explore! There are several connecting trails and endless trip possibilities, some more interesting than others. If there is one additional destination I recommend you should see, it is Fishbrook Pond, to the northeast of Sleeping Beauty.

The trail to Fishbrook begins near the outlet of Bumps Pond, as described above. It follows an old carriage trail through a narrow and rocky pass before descending over 200 feet to a large campsite at the southwestern corner of the pond, 0.9 mile away. The carriage trail ends here, but foot trails encircle the pond to create a 1.4-mile loop. There are two choice lean-tos here, with the northern one in particular standing out as a quintessential Adirondack campsite. Fishbrook Pond is hardly a secret, so don't count on finding solitude here.

If even this side trip is not enough, there are continuing trails to Greenland and Millman Ponds, each of which also boast attractive lean-tos. In fact you could continue to tack on more and more trail miles, passing Lapland Pond and the Black Mountain Ponds until you eventually wind up on the side of Lake George itself.

27

Cat and Thomas Mountains

TOTAL DISTANCE: 7.4-mile loop	
HIKING TIME: 4½ hours	
VERTICAL RISE: 750 feet to Cat Mountain, 720 feet to Thomas, rolling terrain between the summits	
TRAILHEAD GPS COORDINATES: N43° 36' 13.9" W73° 41' 34.5"	

These two little mountains to the west of Bolton Landing on Lake George can be tackled individually or as a loop. Taken one at a time, neither Cat nor Thomas is particularly difficult; in fact, both would be well suited for families. Cat Mountain, with its wide-open ledge and stunning view, is a real winner. Thomas Mountain's view is more intimate by comparison, but the trail follows an old roadway and is therefore an easy walk.

Taken together, however, the two mountains are the setting for a really fun—and slightly more challenging—loop hike. From a single trailhead located just a few miles away from I-87, you can hike up Cat Mountain to soak in the view and then work your way along a bumpy ridgeline over to Thomas. The combination of accessibility from a main highway, quality views, and a fun trail make this a popular hike.

GETTING THERE

From Exit 24 on I-87, take County Route 11 east toward Bolton Landing. In about 2 miles, turn right onto Valley Woods Road; the trailhead is just 0.1 mile from the intersection, also on the right.

THE HIKE

From the trailhead parking area, head southeast along an old gravel road, which forms the basis for the first part of the hike. Rather than diving straight into the woods, this road-trail parallels Valley Woods Road for a short distance, passing within sight of a private residence on the left. It swings southwest, contouring around the foot of Thomas Mountain's eastern shoulder and climbing at a gentle grade. With such a wide trail, you can walk side-by-side with

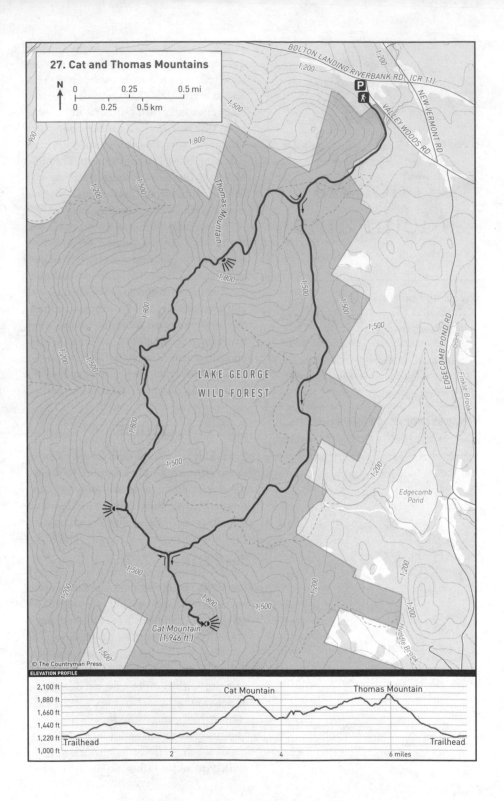

27. Cat and Thomas Mountains

N

0   0.25   0.5 mi

0   0.25   0.5 km

BOLTON LANDING RIVERBANK RD. (CR 11)

NEW VERMONT RD.

VALLEY WOODS RD.

1,200

1,200

1,200

1,500

900

1,800

1,200

1,500

Thomas Mountain

1,800

1,800

1,200

1,500

1,500

1,500

LAKE GEORGE WILD FOREST

1,500

1,500

EDGECOMB POND RD.

Finkle Brook

1,500

1,800

Edgecomb Pond

1,200

1,200

1,200

1,500

1,500

1,200

1,800

1,500

Hiddle Brook

Cat Mountain (1,946 ft.)

1,500

© The Countryman Press

ELEVATION PROFILE

2,100 ft		Cat Mountain	Thomas Mountain	
1,880 ft				
1,660 ft				
1,440 ft				
1,220 ft	Trailhead			Trailhead
1,000 ft		2	4	6 miles

your hiking partner rather than single file.

At 0.8 mile you reach a junction where the trails to Cat and Thomas go their separate ways. Either direction is correct, so it just comes down to which mountain you prefer to see first. For simplicity's sake, let's assume you're more eager to climb Cat. Bear left at the junction, staying on the main road-trail and heading south. What little bit of climbing you have achieved so far is soon lost as the trail begins to descend again, bottoming out at roughly the same elevation as the trailhead, 1,200 feet. In this area, 1.9 miles from the start, the old road passes close to the edge of a charming little beaver pond. From one corner there is even a profile view of Cat Mountain's summit.

The pond's outlet stream flows across the top of the road, requiring you to pick your steps carefully. Be alert to a right turn just a few minutes later, at 2.1 miles. Here you leave the road you have been following and turn onto a lesser logging road. This route is narrower and more trail-like, and it winds its way closer to the foot of Cat while rising and dropping over a foothill. At 2.6 miles you pass between a pair of beaver meadows, with the outlet of the upstream pond cascading over a jumble of rocks.

Shortly after this stream crossing, the hiking trail veers left off the logging road and begins the actual ascent of the mountain. The way is moderately steep, with the trail filing through the young hardwood forest. You re-cross the logging road, reaching a junction high up on the ridgeline at 3 miles. The yellow-marked trail to the right is the traverse to Thomas, so bear left to complete the climb of Cat. You still face 400 feet of vertical ascent.

The trail winds past several rock

HIKER ON CAT MOUNTAIN

outcrops and a muddy vernal pool as it climbs the mountain's northern slope. The foot trail rejoins the logging road and turns right to follow it for the final push to the summit, which you reach at 3.4 miles. You approach the ledges from behind, but once you round the corner you'll find there is no shortage of open rock—and no shortage of views. The primary feature in the landscape before you is the southern half of Lake George, from The Narrows to French Mountain, with part of Glens Falls visible on a clear day. Crane Mountain stands guard at the far right end of the vista, way to the west. Cat's summit is only 1,956 feet in elevation, and it is set 3 miles back from the shoreline, but this still ranks among the finest views of Lake George.

ABSORBING THE BEAUTY AT THOMAS MOUNTAIN

To begin the traverse to Thomas Mountain, you'll need to retrace your steps back down the blue-marked trail to the last trail junction, remembering to bear left off the logging road shortly after leaving the summit. Once you reach the start of the yellow-marked ridgeline trail, follow it northwest down to a low point, around a knoll, then up the next summit knob. Look for a side trail leading left 0.3 mile after the junction (4.1 miles overall); it takes you to a partial view about 200 feet away, with glimpses of Crane and Gore mountains.

North of this side trail, the ridgeline traverse hugs the eastern slope of an unnamed summit for about 0.3 mile. Then it intercepts a skid trail (a path carved through the forest years ago by a logging vehicle) and follows that wide path through the next col. Look for the right turn after a large muddy spot, where the marked route leaves the skid

lichen-covered rocks that grace most of the high points.

As you descend this summit, you can briefly glimpse Thomas ahead of you. The drop into the final col is gentle, but what comes next is a real adventure!

After following the winding trail through the col, it leads you directly to the foot of a large rock wall. You wouldn't be the first person to feel like the victim of a practical joke here, unwittingly led to an impossible scramble up a vertical obstacle. Upon closer inspection, however, there is a natural ramp leading up onto the ledge. Signs point you to a hairpin turn to the left, and this puts you onto the next ledge higher. So what at first appears to be a joke turns out to be a joy.

The ascent of Thomas is completed by a steep climb up a rock-studded slope. This puts you on top of the hemlock-covered shoulder of the mountain where its best view is located, 2.5 miles from Cat Mountain and 5.9 miles into the overall hike. Until 2018, a cabin stood on top of this prominent ledge, built by a prior landowner. The structure is now gone, but the view still remains. If Cat Mountain's vista was sweeping in its scope, this one is more intimate by comparison. A much smaller section of Lake George is in view here, but you can look down the ridgeline to the knobby summit of Cat.

Signs point the way northeast to the continuing trail that leads off of the mountain. You walk out of the hemlock woods and onto the old gravel road that once serviced the cabin, which you then follow down back toward the trailhead. Just 0.7 mile from the summit, you close the loop by rejoining the road-trail to Cat, so bear left and follow it for the remaining 0.8 mile back to the trailhead.

trail and becomes a rugged footpath once again.

When the trail encounters the next unnamed summit on the ridgeline, it opts to climb it rather than go around. In fact, the trail builders seemed to delight in seeking out little rock ledges for hikers to scale. Some are just small bumps, but others are noteworthy ledges where you may need to use your hands. In most cases the trail probably could have circumvented the obstacle, but then you would miss the little clearings with

28

Tongue Mountain Loop

TOTAL DISTANCE: 12.8-mile loop

HIKING TIME: 7 hours

VERTICAL RISE: 1,415 feet to Fifth Peak; very rugged terrain beyond

TRAILHEAD GPS COORDINATES: N43° 37' 45.4" W73° 36' 31.0"

This is a very tough hike, but if you are physically prepared for the challenge—and if you are fortunate enough to have fair weather—you will certainly agree that the traverse of the Tongue Mountain Range is one of the best hikes anywhere.

What is the basis for this boast? There are several, actually. The first one that will likely come to mind for many veterans of the Tongue Range is the high quality of its myriad views. As the name suggests, this string of mountains occupies a peninsula (or "tongue") that juts out into Lake George, dividing Northwest Bay from The Narrows. Thus the mountains are nearly surrounded by water—big water at that. This is not a singular peak with a singular view, but a string of peaks, each one topping the last with a stunning panorama. And when you are finished admiring the lake from above, the trail drops down to Northwest Bay so that you can appreciate the lake from its edge.

The next quality is its unusual environment, in terms of both plant and animal life. The southern parts of the range are particularly unique amongst Adirondack forest types; the trees that grow here are more commonly associated with the southerly Appalachians rather than the Northern Forest. Look for butternuts, hickories, oaks, and two varieties of juniper as you descend from First Peak toward Montcalm Point; they suggest a warmer microclimate that is the exception to the otherwise harsh Adirondack winter.

With this southern-style forest comes some sun-loving wildlife as well. The Tongue Mountain Range is one of only a few places in the Adirondack Park where timber rattlesnakes thrive. These creatures are attracted to the sun-facing ledges, where ample warmth may be

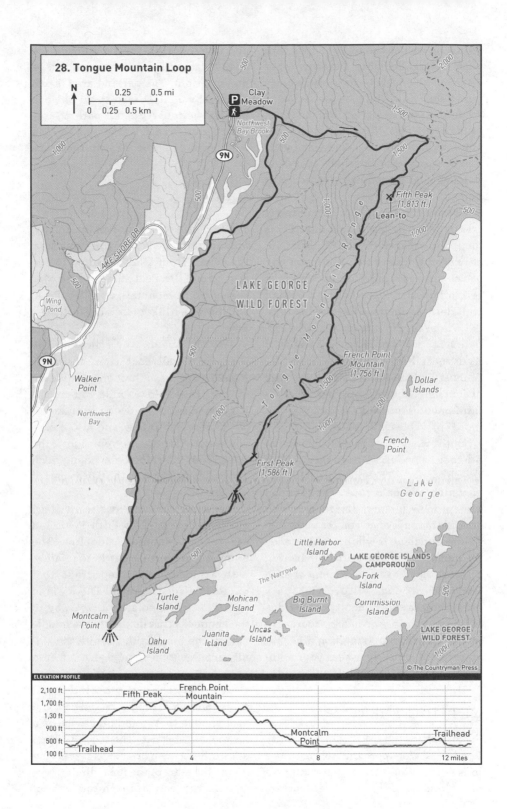

28. Tongue Mountain Loop

N

| 0 | 0.25 | 0.5 mi |
| 0 | 0.25 | 0.5 km |

Clay Meadow

Northwest Bay Brook

9N

Fifth Peak [1,813 ft.]
Lean-to

LAKE GEORGE WILD FOREST

LAKE SHORE DR.

Wing Pond

Walker Point

Northwest Bay

French Point Mountain [1,756 ft.]

Dollar Islands

First Peak [1,586 ft.]

French Point

Lake George

Little Harbor Island

LAKE GEORGE ISLANDS CAMPGROUND

The Narrows

Fork Island

Turtle Island

Mohican Island

Big Burnt Island

Commission Island

LAKE GEORGE WILD FOREST

Montcalm Point

Oahu Island

Juanita Island

Uncas Island

Tongue Mountain Range

© The Countryman Press

ELEVATION PROFILE

2,100 ft		Fifth Peak	French Point Mountain			
1,700 ft						
1,30 ft						Trailhead
900 ft				Montcalm Point		
500 ft						
100 ft	Trailhead					
			4		8	12 miles

found, as well as the rocky slopes with their natural den sites. Like any other rattlesnake species, these snakes are venomous. However, they are reclusive in nature, and lethal encounters with humans are rare. If you are planning a summer visit, always be aware of your surroundings—and perhaps it is best to leave curious canine companions at home.

Finally, the quality of the trail really stands out. The lower sections of this loop were enhanced by the Civilian Conservation Corps in the 1930s; you will see several sections built up with rock retaining walls, representing a level of trail design that goes beyond the typical wilderness foot trail. Also, the ridgeline section is noteworthy because of its dryness. Mud is an inevitable feature of most highland trails, but it is nearly absent here. The dry soils mean there is minimal erosion, thus contributing to a more enjoyable experience.

But it would be irresponsible to list all these praises without mentioning the challenges. The miles are long, the elevation change is great, the summits are apt to be hot and dry, there are no sources of water once you reach the ridgeline, and there is wildlife that intends no harm but might still be harmful. There is a lean-to on the summit of Fifth Peak, but carrying a full overnight pack only increases the difficulty of the ridge hike, and there are no nearby sources of water. This is an outstanding hike, but you should honestly assess your abilities before striking out into the woods.

GETTING THERE

From Exit 24 on I-87, follow County Road 11 east for approximately 4.7 miles to NY 9N, at an intersection just north of Bolton Landing. Turn left, north,

and follow NY 9N for 4.5 miles to the Clay Meadow Trailhead, which will be on your right. The parking area is just ahead, at 4.6 miles, next to the site of a flooded rock quarry. If this parking area is full, look for a driveway just beyond leading to a second lot just inside the woods.

THE HIKE

The 12.8-mile loop hike over the Tongue Mountain Range is a play in three acts: the climb from Clay Meadow to the lean-to on Fifth Peak, the traverse over French Point Mountain and First Peak, and the return hike alongside Northwest Bay.

Act One begins by following the wide foot trail east from the Clay Meadow Trailhead through a plantation of white pines. At 0.2 mile you cross a long wooden bridge over a tributary of Northwest Bay Brook, and at 0.4 mile you reach a junction. To your right is the return trail from Montcalm Point, which you will follow later in the day as part of Act Three.

For now, continue eastward (left) on the direct trail to Fifth Peak and the Tongue Mountain ridgeline. The climbing begins almost immediately, with a moderately steep grade that parallels a small stream. The lowland pine forest immediately gives way to the hemlocks that dominate the middle part of the mountain. Despite the significant elevation change—1,100 feet in 1.4 miles—there are only two places with switchbacks. The first, at 1.2 miles, features some CCC rockwork and gets you past a ledge that would otherwise be a formidable obstacle. The second occurs at 1.5 miles after a brief level traverse; it marks the start of the next climb.

At 1.8 miles you reach the crest of

LAKE GEORGE'S SOUTHERN BASIN FROM FIRST PEAK

AT MONTCALM POINT

Bay. As tempting a campsite as this might be, note that there is no source of water nearby.

To begin Act Two, descend back down to the main trail and turn left, continuing the ridgeline walk southwestward. About 0.5 mile later, at 3.2 miles total, you reach an open ledge with a view of the rugged terrain ahead of you. The descent from this ledge is quite steep and rugged, bottoming out in a col between two of the lesser summit knobs. You climb the next knob, traverse along its eastern slopes, and then climb yet another knob. This up-and-down hiking characterizes much of the ridgeline.

The next major highlight of the hike occurs at 4.4 miles, when you reach the summit of French Point Mountain, 1,756 feet in elevation. Here, the oak forest parts to reveal a grassy ledge with a grand view of the lake. Black Mountain is immediately opposite your location, just north of The Narrows. This summit is far enough out of alignment with the rest of the range that it affords a lengthy view of the lake, both north and south; the perspective of the southern basin beyond Shelving Rock is especially memorable.

Continuing southwest, look for a short side trail at 4.7 miles leading to another open ledge, this one at the southern tip of French Point Mountain. This is immediately followed by a 500-foot descent that winds past rocky slopes into a hardwood-forested hollow at 5.2 miles.

The next knob you encounter is First Peak. The approach is a comparatively gentle climb, gaining about 365 feet in the space of 0.5 mile. You reach the 1,586-foot summit at 5.7 miles. First Peak has always been one of the more scenic waypoints along the ridgeline, although it was not that long ago when

the ridgeline, where you will find a four-way intersection. Left leads to Fivemile Mountain, and straight leads to Five Mile Point. The trail you want turns right, although some hikers have been known to confuse this turn with the trail to Five Mile Point; be sure the trail you follow climbs to the south rather than descends to the east.

Just 0.5 mile later, a side trail veers left. This is the route to Fifth Peak, site of a lean-to and the first of the scenic summits along the ridgeline. It is 0.2 mile long and climbs 200 feet to the 1,813-foot summit, a total of 2.5 miles from Clay Meadow. The lean-to is situated between two small clearings with views of Lake George, one toward The Narrows and the other toward Northwest the summit was more wooded than what you see now. Firefighters battling a ground fire cleared many of the oaks here in 2015, greatly expanding the size of the open ledge. How much this action helped rein in the low-grade fire is uncertain, but there is no doubt that First Peak is much more exposed than it ever used to be.

An especially good view comes at 6.4 miles, after a descent from the main summit of First Peak and a short hike across some lesser knobs. This view is found on a southern foothill of First Peak, with an elevation of only 1,160 feet—just a little more than 800 feet above the lake, with Turtle Island right below you. The ledge is surrounded by junipers, including the taller variety called eastern red-cedar, which is common elsewhere in the state but very rare in the Adirondacks. These shrubs and small trees frame a highly photogenic view of Lake George's southern basin, all the way down to Lake George village, some twelve miles away.

Here begins the final descent from the ridgeline, and for all too brief a time the trail winds its way between the junipers. Mostly, though, this is a prolonged descent through open hardwood forests, with the occasional rock ledge to negotiate. It ends at 7.4 miles at a T-intersection within sight of Northwest Bay.

After several hours spent on the high, dry ridgeline, Act Three of the hike will seem like a completely different experience. Unless you are pressed for time, a side trip to Montcalm Point is mandatory before beginning your return to Clay Meadow. Turn left at the intersection and follow the trail south for 0.3 mile to the rock ledges at the tip of the peninsula. In the summer, boat activity on Lake George is very high, and you may feel as though you are in the thick of the traffic out here—even though you are still miles from your car at this remote spot on the shoreline.

Much of the remaining hike is within sight of Northwest Bay. Return to the junction and continue north along the shoreline, detouring inland around some stamp-sized private parcels. The trail is mostly level, but not entirely; there are some small knolls to climb over, streams to cross, and pockets of mud to curse. From Montcalm Point to Clay Meadow, the total distance is 5.1 miles. Towards the northern end you begin to see evidence of the CCC's trail-building activities, as the primitive footpath morphs into a graded carriage trail. As you approach the marshy mouth of Northwest Bay Brook, the trail detours inland, climbing 200 feet back up the side of the mountain before descending back toward the trail junction near Clay Meadow, where the loop began so many hours ago.

Turn left to cross the long wooden bridge again, reaching NY 9N and the Clay Meadow Trailhead at 12.8 miles.

29

Pharaoh Lake Wilderness Loop

TOTAL DISTANCE: 13.5-mile loop with optional side trips

HIKING TIME: 2 to 3 days

ELEVATION CHANGE: rolling terrain

TRAILHEAD GPS COORDINATES: N43° 50' 13.8" W73° 34' 18.3"

The Pharaoh Lake Wilderness is the easternmost of the Adirondack Park's protected motorless areas. Despite its compact size, it is topographically alive with dozens of ponds and small mountains, with Pharaoh Lake at its heart. Pick any rock ledge on just about any pond, and you are almost certain to find a scenic campsite; climb to any summit, and the odds are good you will find a bald ledge with a view.

With a network of interconnected trails and easy access from I-87, this is a very user-friendly wilderness. It should also come as no surprise that Pharaoh Lake is quite popular, with some of the management issues that come hand-in-hand with high levels of recreational use, including litter and illegal tree cutting. Currently, though, there are no special backcountry regulations or permit requirements, and most of the facilities are kept in good condition. Therefore, this remains a prime destination for weekend backpacking.

The trip possibilities for the Pharaoh Lake Wilderness may not be endless, but they are certainly numerous. This book recommends a loop of 13.8 miles beginning and ending at the Putnam Pond Campground near Ticonderoga. It passes within sight of nine lakes and ponds, with two lean-tos directly in your path as well as several choice campsites. The loop is eminently suitable for a weekend adventure any time from early spring through late fall, as winter tends to arrive later and depart earlier from these woods, compared to the rest of the Adirondacks.

This route is just a basic itinerary, however; an entire chapter could be written about all the interesting detours you could take. Did you ever want to hike around an entire "ocean"? Would you rather climb Pharaoh Mountain

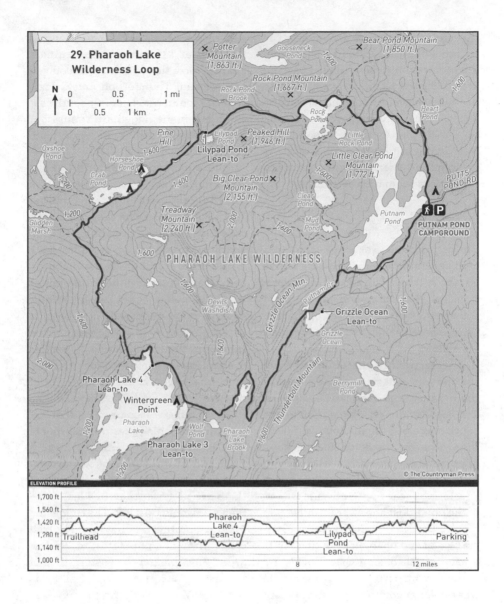

ELEVATION PROFILE

than hike past its foot? There are any number of deviations and permutations you could elect to take, depending on your inclination to explore. This is a wilderness that is ready to accommodate your adventurous spirit; it has nothing to hide, and indeed many of its best features are easy to find.

GETTING THERE

The best place to begin this loop is the Putnam Pond Campground near Ticonderoga. From Exit 28 on I-87, turn east onto NY 74 and follow it for 13.3 miles past Paradox and Eagle lakes to the tiny hamlet of Chilson. Here, bear right (south) onto Putts Pond Road, following the signs for the campground. The entrance booth is located 3.6 miles from the highway, and the trailhead parking area is located 0.5 mile beyond, near the boat launch site. An entrance fee will be charged when the campground is open, but for the rest of the year parking is free. If you are hiking with a dog, the campground attendant will want to see the rabies vaccination certificate.

THE HIKE

I have completed some version of this loop several times; in each case I have always followed it in a clockwise direction, and I have always spent one night somewhere on the north side of Pharaoh Lake. Therefore, this suggested itinerary follows the same pattern.

Several trails begin at Putnam Pond; the one you want starts at the far end of the parking area and leads southwest. The trail is generally parallel to the south shore of Putnam Pond, although there are few views of it. One good opportunity comes at 1.1 miles, where a side trail leads right for 350 feet to a scenic spot near the southernmost end of the pond. Just ahead, at 1.3 miles, you reach a junction where the trail to Grizzle Ocean and Pharaoh Lake turns left.

You climb beside Grizzle Ocean's outlet stream for 0.4 mile to a junction, where you encounter your first potential side trip. The trail to your left is a 1.1-mile loop that completely encircles this small pond and provides access to its well-used lean-to. The going is slow, but it is the best way to see this "ocean." According to lore, the name was a sarcastic response to someone's boasts about his fishing exploits here.

You can bypass Grizzle Ocean by bearing right at the junction, crossing its outlet on a long and narrow bridge,

and reconnecting with the far end of the loop at 1.9 miles. Then begins a long traverse through the secluded valley between Thunderbolt and Grizzle Ocean Mountains, heading southwest to a break in the ridgeline on your right where the trail can make its descent into Pharaoh Lake's basin.

The approach to Pharaoh Lake is anything but direct, as the extensive marshes and wetlands surrounding Wolf Pond lie in the way. The trail descends from the ridgeline and then nearly reverses course, swinging back northeast to skirt around the wetlands; one stream crossing at the northernmost tip of this detour could be a bit muddy. After making another U-turn back to the original southwesterly heading, the trail climbs over and descends a series of small knolls, some with rocky ledges, until finally you come within sight of tiny Wolf Pond.

At 4.7 miles you come to another key trail junction, this one within earshot of Wolf Pond's cascading outlet stream. If you wanted to take the long way around Pharaoh Lake's southern end—where there are no fewer than five lean-tos—then you would turn left. The suggested itinerary, however, bears right. The trail drops through a pine forest to Wintergreen Bay, the marshy eastern lobe of the lake. At 4.8 miles a side trail leads left to Wintergreen Point, a must-see chain of rocks that forms a narrow peninsula jutting out into the lake. There is a designated campsite 0.1 mile along this trail.

The loop trail, unfortunately, ventures inland as it begins its circuit around the north end of Pharaoh Lake. The forest is grand here, with a shady cover of hemlock, spruce, and birch, but the lake is only glimpsed from a distance for much of the next 0.6 mile. But

GRIZZLE OCEAN

at 5.4 miles you arrive at the Pharaoh Lake #4 Lean-to, the northernmost (and most secluded) of the lake's six shelters. A nearby rock point offers fine views of the lake.

The continuing trail is now much closer to the shoreline as it skirts around Pharaoh's northern tip. This part of the lake is called Split Rock Bay, for obvious reasons: a giant glacial erratic emerges high above the water, fractured into multiple pieces. Split Rock is visible from a variety of angles, ending with a relatively close-up look just before the trail heads inland again. There are a few sections here where the trail is not very well defined, so be sure to give as much attention to the trail markers as you do to the scenery.

The next key turn comes at 5.9 miles, where the loop turns right and begins the next leg of your journey. This section begins with a long and tiring climb, ascending nearly 300 feet in the space of 0.3 mile—always a long and difficult slog when you're carrying a full backpack. It

takes you to a height-of-land between Treadway and Pharaoh Mountains, and then begins a slow descent into the Crane Pond watershed. The trail used to pass near a large beaver meadow with intriguing views of Treadway, but it has since been rerouted onto higher ground where there is less mud to worry about.

The prolonged descent leads to the next trail junction at 7.5 miles. The continuing trail to the left leads to Crane Pond by way of Glidden Marsh, but the loop back to Putnam Pond turns right here on the Hay Marsh Trail. This is a 0.5-mile long connector trail that dips towards an open wetland, makes a rock-hop crossing of the outlet stream, and then climbs a hill to a junction at Crab Pond at 8 miles. This body of water is shallow and marshy, with lots of pond lilies and pickerelweed in the summer. Bear right at the junction, finding a good campsite near the east end of Crab Pond 0.4 mile later.

Horsehoe Pond is the next waypoint you encounter, 8.6 miles into your

WILD ROSES NEAR THE TIP OF WINTERGREEN POINT

journey. You reach its outlet after a short-but-steep climb up from Crab; a side trail leads left for 0.1 mile to a scenic little campsite. Keep right to continue the loop, following a northeasterly heading on a hilly course. The way is hardly dull because the trail seems to be constantly doing something, whether that is climbing some rocky knoll or weaving past a beaver meadow. The large mountain to the south is Treadway.

At 9.4 miles you reach a junction with the trail to Tubmill Marsh and Eagle Lake. Turn right here, coming to Lilypad Pond a moment later, at 9.5 miles. This is such a tiny pond that you might be inclined to pass it by, were it not for the attractive lean-to. Lilypad is nestled within a mountainous basin and surrounded by pines that sigh with every breeze that passes by.

The trail climbs a shoulder of Peaked Hill and descends to an open wetland on Rock Pond Brook, where you can glimpse the cliffs on Potter Mountain. You are only on the valley floor for a

Lake, this body of water is completely encircled by hiking trails. In this case the more interesting option is to turn left, even though this means you have to find a dry way to step across the noisy little outlet stream. You pass through a rocky clearing with good water views, climb steeply over a ledge on the north shore, and then descend to an intriguing campsite on a rocky point at 11.1 miles. The trail then circles around Rock Pond's northeastern bay, where you pass the site of an abandoned graphite mine on the left. A drainage tunnel, a steam boiler, and some stone foundations are all readily visible from the trail.

Continue circling around the pond, passing a side trail to Bear Pond and coming to a junction at 11.5 miles. You could turn right here, following a winding route between Rock and Little Rock ponds and their respective lean-tos, but the direct route turns left, southeast. It descends to North Pond (Putnam's northern bay) at 11.9 miles and then circles around its tip. In some spots the trail is built up with rocks to keep it dry. Then you climb back up the next hill, passing Heart Pond and reaching the final trail junction at 12.7 miles. Turn right, south.

You are in the wild backwoods only for another 0.3 mile before emerging back at the Putnam Pond Campground at 13 miles, near Campsite #38. The final 0.5 mile is a walk through the campground: briefly down one of the paved roads, then on a trail that leads past the beach and across the dam. The parking area where you started this adventure is just beyond, at 13.5 miles.

brief time, though. Look for a side trail forking left at 10.1 miles, leading to the foot of a tall waterfall on the brook. It is difficult to gauge the height of this cascade, but it is at least fifty feet tall over two drops.

The main trail seems to follow an ancient road grade as it climbs gently past the waterfall, eventually returning to the side of the stream. At 10.7 miles you arrive at its source, the rocky outlet at the east end of the appropriately named Rock Pond.

Like Grizzle Ocean and Pharaoh

30

Treadway Mountain

TOTAL DISTANCE: 7.6 miles round-trip

HIKING TIME: 4 hours

VERTICAL RISE: 920 feet

TRAILHEAD GPS COORDINATES: N43° 50' 13.8" W73° 34' 18.3"

Treadway Mountain is not the type of peak that you point to admiringly from other summits. Except for a band of cliffs on its southwestern face, its profile is long, low, and undistinguished. Its neighbor, Pharaoh Mountain, bears an unmistakable silhouette that makes it easily identifiable when seen from a distance, but Treadway blends in with its surroundings when seen from a distance.

However, the quality of the view from Treadway's summit far exceeds anything you will find on Pharaoh Mountain. This mountain is proof that you don't need high elevations for a superlative climbing experience. At 2,240 feet in elevation, there are many ponds in the central Adirondack highlands that are higher than this rocky summit. But its rocky slopes, sparse pine forests, quartz summit, and spectacular view of Pharaoh Lake conspire to make this one of the finest of all mountains—even if you would never suspect it by examining Treadway from below.

Although the round-trip hiking distance is somewhat long, the grades are moderate for the most part, and Treadway's proximity to the popular Putnam Pond Campground makes this a favorite destination for families with older children. Even the approach to the mountain can be interesting, since the shortest route passes the south side of Putnam Pond. Treadway's upper slopes, with their pine forests interspersed with rocky clearings, have always reminded me of western wilderness areas more than they do any other Adirondack mountain, thus imparting an exotic flavor to this hike.

Treadway is most commonly visited as a day hiking destination, but there are good nearby options for anyone eager to spend a full weekend in the woods. The lean-to at Clear Pond is the closest

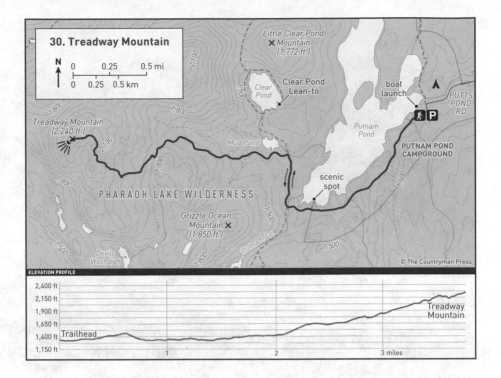

ELEVATION PROFILE

campsite, but Rock Pond and Grizzle Ocean are other nearby options.

GETTING THERE

The closest trailhead for Treadway Mountain is located within the Putnam Pond Campground near Ticonderoga. From Exit 28 on I-87, turn east onto NY 74 and follow it for 13.3 miles past Paradox and Eagle Lakes to the tiny hamlet of Chilson. Here, bear right (south) onto Putts Pond Road, following the signs for the campground. The entrance booth is located 3.6 miles from the highway, and the trailhead parking area is located 0.5 mile beyond, near the boat launch site. An entrance fee will be charged when the campground is open, but for the rest of the year parking is free. If you are hiking with a dog, the campground attendant will want to see the rabies vaccination certificate.

THE HIKE

Several trails begin at this trailhead; the one you want starts at the far end of the parking area and leads southwest. The trail is generally parallel to the south shore of Putnam Pond, although there are few views of it. One good opportunity comes at 1.1 miles, where a side trail leads right for 350 feet to a scenic spot near the southernmost end of the pond. Just ahead, at 1.3 miles, you reach a junction where the trail to Grizzle Ocean and Pharaoh Lake turns left.

Bearing right, you pass a marshy area with another glimpse of Putnam Pond, skirting around the wet area on high ground. At 1.7 miles, you reach another junction just before a bridge over the outlet of Clear Pond. The trail to Treadway turns left here, but it is worth noting that the trail straight ahead leads past Mud Pond to a pleasantly sited lean-to

PHARAOH LAKE AND PHARAOH MOUNTAIN FROM TREADWAY'S SUMMIT

at Clear Pond, just 0.6 mile away. Clear is a peaceful place, nestled between its own pine-covered mountains, and if you are looking for a place to camp this is the nearest shelter. Note, however, that some of the rock ledges on Clear's shoreline may be overgrown with poison ivy.

The red-marked trail to Treadway leads west from the junction. It is prone to muddiness at first, and at 1.9 miles the situation has the potential to get worse, because the wetlands surrounding Mud Pond sometimes come perilously close to the trail. At 2 miles you cross a tributary stream, and moments later you begin the climb.

The lower slopes of Treadway are ordinary enough. The ascent begins in an open hardwood forest, following a newer foot tread that winds onto a foothill due south of Big Clear Pond Mountain. The trail approaches another tributary stream on the right, and then the woods quickly become filled with shady hemlocks. As the terrain becomes muddy, the trail climbs over a knoll and switchbacks down the other side, passing through a small notch at 2.9 miles that marks part of the divide between the Champlain and Hudson watersheds.

You cross a small stream—a tributary of Devils Washdish—and at 3 miles you

around (it is easiest for this purpose to go to the left of the trail). For all of the openness, there are no good views yet. At 3.4 miles you reenter a denser patch of forest where hemlocks reappear. This is also the point where you arrive at the ridgeline crest.

There may be a momentary panic when you reach the foot of a large rock wall a moment later, but instead of scaling straight up this rock face the trail turns left and finds a better way around the flank. At 3.5 miles you top out on a rock knob, where you have the first view of the day. This one looks across a rocky cirque to Treadway's main summit, with Pharaoh Mountain to the left. The trail continues to climb, not quite reaching the false summits but skirting past them. There is a steep drop into the wooded notch at the head of the cirque before you climb in the open again for the final push to the summit. The cairns on this last section are stacks of quartz, because so much of the rock here consists of that mineral.

The marked trail ends 3.8 miles from the campground at the summit, which is partially bare. You do have a good view of Pharaoh Lake from here, but this view gets better if you follow herd paths southwest past the trees to a forward-pointing patch of bare rock. Here the view is truly spectacular. For photographers, the earlier you get here, the better the odds will be that you will not be fighting with the sun as you point your camera southwest toward the lake. Another nearby ledge extends the view northwest toward the High Peaks.

Allow 2 hours to hike from the Putnam Pond trailhead to the summit. The vertical climb is only about 920 feet, not counting the rolling terrain as you parallel Putnam's southern shoreline.

emerge from the woods for the first time. There are many fire-scarred mountains in the Adirondacks, and no shortage of bare slopes, but the sparseness of the woods from here to the summit is more evocative of the montane forests of the drier climates out west. The trees that you see are nothing unusual for the Adirondacks—red spruce, balsam fir, and red and white pines—but it's the arrangement that is different.

And as you pass through this area, the grade remains moderate. The one notable exception is a 5-foot-tall ledge at 3.2 miles that hikers can scramble up, but which dogs may need to detour

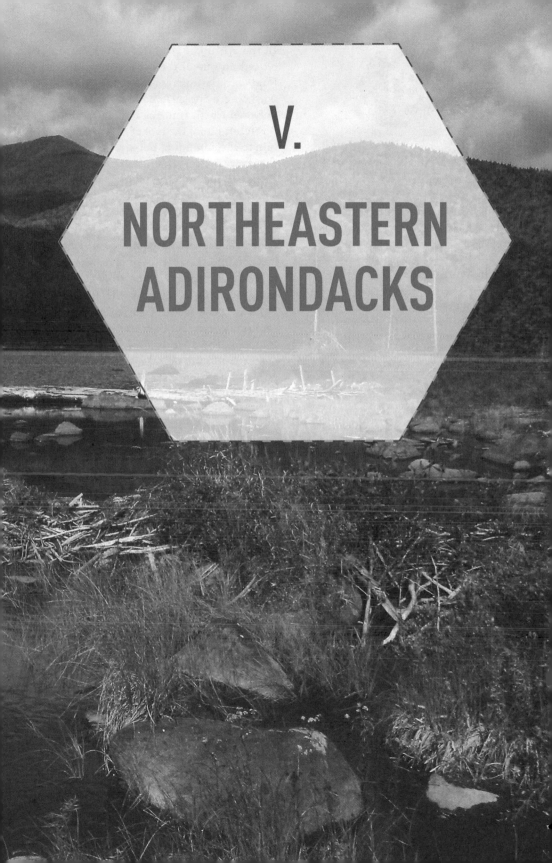

V.

NORTHEASTERN ADIRONDACKS

31

Boreas Ponds

TOTAL DISTANCE: 7 miles round-trip with optional side trips

HIKING TIME: 2.5 hours

ELEVATION CHANGE: rolling terrain

TRAILHEAD GPS COORDINATES: N43° 58' 51.8" W73° 54' 03.3"

In the spring of 2016, New York State closed on one of the most anticipated land acquisitions of our times: the 20,758-acre Boreas Ponds Tract, located between North Hudson and Newcomb. Stretching from the foot of Allen Mountain to the summit of Boreas Mountain, the entire property came into the public domain wild and uninhabited, save for a handful of temporary hunting leases. Nearly two years later, the northern half of the property was added to the High Peaks Wilderness, thus partly ensuring its protection as a refuge of remoteness.

The centerpiece of the tract is the body of water known as the Boreas Ponds. These were historically three separate ponds, but they are now united into one continuous flow by a dam, even though the plural name has been retained. The ponds are the source of the Boreas River, one of the larger tributaries of the upper Hudson River.

In any other setting, a complex of ponds, bogs, and marshes would be regarded more for its wildlife values than anything else. Indeed, the area seems especially hospitable to such charismatic species as loons and moose. However, because Boreas Ponds lie at the foot of the High Peaks, public interest in the recreational planning for this area has been very high.

At the time of this writing, state officials are planning the locations of parking areas, trails, and campsites. Currently, except for some interim parking areas, no official recreation facilities exist. However, the property is criss-crossed by a network of aging logging roads—relics of its history as a managed timberland—and so even without state-marked trails, there are already ways to get to all of the main destinations.

Obviously, most people are curious to see the main feature. An old forestry

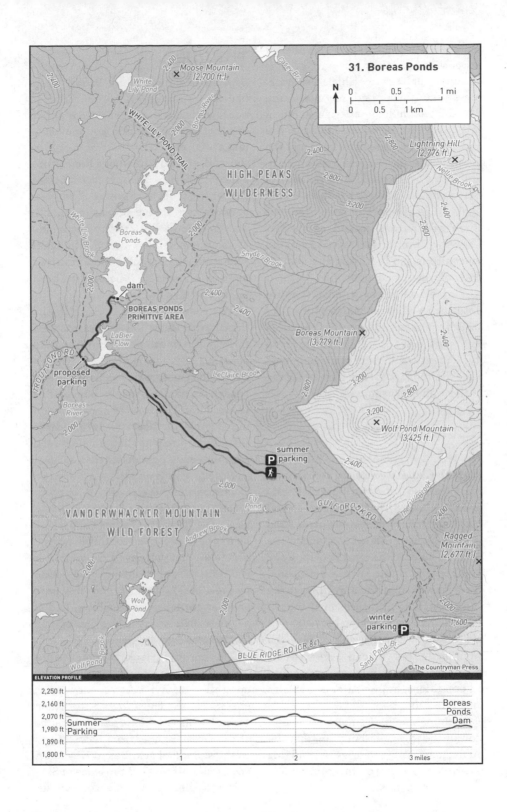

31. Boreas Ponds

N
0   0.5   1 mi
0   0.5   1 km

Moose Mountain
(2,700 ft.)

White Lily Pond

WHITE LILY POND TRAIL

Boreas River

Lightning Hill
(2,776 ft.)

Nellie Brook

HIGH PEAKS
WILDERNESS

White Lily Brook

Boreas Ponds

Snyder Brook

dam

BOREAS PONDS
PRIMITIVE AREA

Boreas Mountain
(3,779 ft.)

LaBier Flow

TROUT POND RD

proposed parking

LeClaire Brook

Boreas River

Wolf Pond Mountain
(3,425 ft.)

summer parking

P

The Gulf Brook

VANDERWHACKER MOUNTAIN
WILD FOREST

Andrew Brook

Fly Pond

GULF BROOK RD

Ragged Mountain
(2,677 ft.)

Wolf Pond

Wolf Pond Brook

winter parking

P

BLUE RIDGE RD (CR 84)

Sand Pond Br

© The Countryman Press

ELEVATION PROFILE

2,250 ft
2,160 ft
2,070 ft — Summer Parking
1,980 ft
1,890 ft
1,800 ft

1   2   3 miles

Boreas
Ponds
Dam

road leads all the way to the dam at Boreas Ponds, although part of it is closed to public motor vehicle use. Walking an old gravel road may not sound like the best hiking experience, but in this case there are two advantages: you can set a brisk pace here, covering the 3.5-mile distance in just over an hour, and if you want to paddle the ponds, it is easy to haul a canoe or kayak on a cart.

At-large camping is permitted, but there are no designated campsites. Therefore if you intend to camp, be sure your site is 150 feet from the nearest body of water, road, or trail.

Please note, however, that this entire description is provisional in nature. The state's management plan for this area was written in 2018, and DEC hopes to implement some of its trail, campsite, and lean-to proposals by the start of the 2019 summer season.

GETTING THERE

The trailhead is located on Gulf Brook Road, the name given to the main access road leading into the Boreas Ponds Tract. Follow I-87 to North Hudson and take Exit 29. Turn west onto Boreas Road (also called Blue Ridge Road) and follow it for 7.3 miles to the start of Gulf Brook Road on the right. This is a seasonal road, opened from late May through the end of the fall hunting season. In the off-season, there is a parking area 400 feet from the start of the road, but in the summer and fall you can drive 3.1 miles to an interior parking area. Depending on conditions, high-clearance vehicles may fare better here.

It is possible, pending implementation of the management plan, that the public may be able to drive beyond this interior parking area to points much closer to the ponds.

THE HIKE

Beyond the gate, Gulf Brook Road becomes a wonderful hiking route—if not a wilderness footpath, then a hiker's highway over which you may sustain a brisk pace. The area was logged in the past, yes, but the woods are mature enough to form a canopy over much of the way. You first traverse along the southwestern foot of Boreas Mountain, and then you switch to the north side of an unnamed hill. Given a little bit of time, this portion could have reverted to an excellent trail, if nature had been allowed to take its course.

You round a corner of the hill, and then the first water body comes into view through the trees to the right. The road descends to meet it at 2.5 miles, where a steel crib structure on the Boreas River backs up a shallow, mucky pond called LaBier Flow. The view of Boreas Mountain to the northeast is outstanding! Unless you are wheeling a canoe on a cart, you can be here in less than an hour.

Boreas Ponds is still a mile away. Continue along the road to a four-way junction at 2.6 miles, where you should turn right. (Note that an interior parking lot has been proposed for this location.) The cabin that you pass a moment later was once part of a lumber camp dating to the 1890s, if not earlier. You pass another corner of LaBier Flow, and at 3.5 miles you arrive at the gravel dam that creates Boreas Ponds.

The dam might lack the romance of a wilderness destination, but the view lives up to all of the hype. As you move from one end of the causeway to the other, your eye follows the tortuous ridgeline of the Great Range, from Sawteeth to Gothics, Saddleback, Basin, Haystack, and Mount Marcy. The presence of Skylight and Allen seems almost gratuitous.

ALLEN, SKYLIGHT, MARCY, AND HAYSTACK FROM THE BOREAS PONDS DAM

Canoes can easily be launched here, but land-bound explorers will need to head off-trail to seek out other vistas. I know of at least one campsite on the shores of Boreas Ponds; it is located on the southeast shore of the lobe known as Second Pond, near the end of a long peninsula. There you will find a campfire ring and some uneven ground that seems to be as good a place to camp as any. Much of the shoreline is either thickly wooded or wet and marshy, so additional camping opportunities are sure to be limited. DEC has proposed building a lean-to a short distance to the west of the dam, near the site of a former lodge.

THE TRAIL TO WHITE LILY POND PASSES NEAR CHENEY COBBLE

SIDE TRIP: WHITE LILY POND

Boreas Ponds is not the only attractive body of water on this new property. White Lily Pond, located several miles to the north, is the epitome of a remote wilderness destination, even if it is reached by a continuation of the old logging road network. There is a direct route from the Boreas Ponds dam to the outlet of Lily Pond, all of it on established roads and footpaths with no need to bushwhack. In its management plan, DEC has proposed adopting this route as a marked hiking trail—but until then, with no signs or markers to follow, it is not recommended for anyone inexperienced with backcountry navigation.

From the dam at Boreas Ponds, proceed east along the continuing logging road. This is the main route around the east side of the ponds, but because of the extensive wetlands and cedar swamps that surround them, the road is forced to maintain a quarter-mile setback the entire way. As a result there are no further views of the ponds.

At 1.9 miles, look for a prominent fork to the left. This route is less skittish about penetrating the wetlands; it leads northwest straight through them, with occasional glimpses of open marshes and nearby peaks. There is a narrow view of Third Pond (the northern tip of Boreas) at 2.7 miles, where you cross a major inlet, and then the aging road begins to climb a shoulder of Moose Mountain, gaining 260 feet in the next 0.6 mile. You have a good view of Cheney Cobble as you descend the other side of the ridge.

Most maps show a four-way intersection in this area, with one of the four directions leading to White Lily's outlet. When you reach this junction, 3.5 miles from the dam, the reality is a little less straightforward. The main road you have been following swings right, northeast, and a secondary road turns left, southwest. There is nothing but a wall of trees straight ahead. The route you want leads almost due north; it is not a road, but a narrow footpath leading through the thick brush. If you follow this for 250 feet, it will bring you to the road leading to the pond's outlet.

There is a large clearing next to the outlet stream. Look for a narrow footpath leading north back into the woods, winding around and through the foundations of a large-but-long-forgotten building. It leads within minutes to the southern shore of White Lily Pond, a total of 3.8 miles from the dam. The massive mountain rising to the north is Allen Mountain, one of the remotest High Peaks.

Dix Mountain via the Boquet River

TOTAL DISTANCE: 13.8 miles round-trip

HIKING TIME: 8 hours

VERTICAL RISE: 3,250 feet

TRAILHEAD GPS COORDINATES: N44° 07' 56.0" W73° 43' 55.4"

Dix Mountain is the highest summit in a collection of peaks known informally as the Dix Range. It is a spectacular mountain, 4,857 feet in elevation and with views in just about every direction. It is massive, it is rugged, and it is everything you could want in a wilderness peak.

It is also steep and very remote. The trip to its summit and back is an all-day affair, with a 4.4-mile hike just to reach the lean-to at the foot of the mountain. At its most grueling point, the trail climbs 1,100 feet in just 0.7 mile! If you are averse to mud and sweat, stay away from Dix Mountain at all costs.

These dire warnings aside, I selected this hike because of its beauty; the 6.9 miles from the trailhead to the summit are hardly dull. The adventure begins with a visit to Round Pond, followed by several enchanting sections beside the North Fork Boquet River. After passing the lean-to site, you climb to the foot of a long slide with views of Noonmark and Giant mountains. Only *then* do you begin the main ascent of Dix.

There has been a trail on this side of the mountain since 1870, when the proprietor of an early hotel in nearby Saint Huberts cut a route to the summit for the benefit of his guests. The forest surrounding the Dix Range largely remained untouched until 1903, when a massive forest fire swept through the region. A second fire in 1913 denuded much of the area of its forest cover and burned much of the soil away. Logging operations then moved in to salvage the remaining timber.

State acquisition of this land occurred after these events, in conjunction with the modernization of the highway through Chapel Pond Pass in the 1930s. By then the forest was characterized by charred stumps, scorched

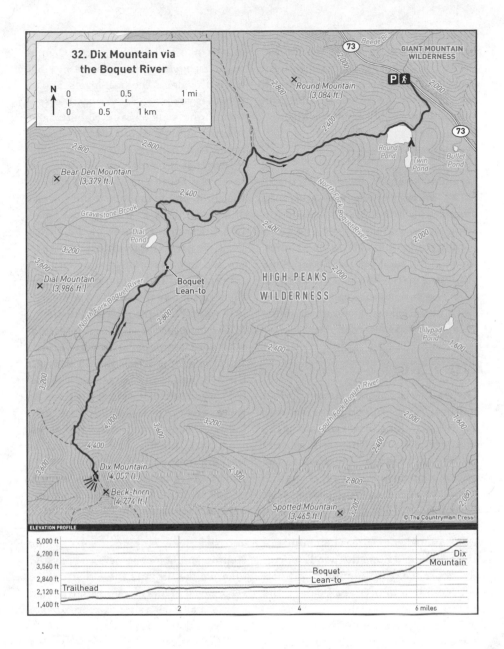

32. Dix Mountain via the Boquet River

N
0   0.5   1 mi
0   0.5   1 km

GIANT MOUNTAIN WILDERNESS

Round Mountain (3,084 ft.)

Bear Den Mountain (3,379 ft.)

Gravestone Brook

Dial Pond

Dial Mountain (3,986 ft.)

North Fork Boquet River

Boquet Lean-to

HIGH PEAKS WILDERNESS

North Fork Boquet River

Round Pond

Twin Pond

Bullet Pond

Lilypad Pond

South Fork Boquet River

Dix Mountain (4,057 ft.)

Beck-horn (4,774 ft.)

Spotted Mountain (3,465 ft.)

© The Countryman Press

ELEVATION PROFILE

5,000 ft			
4,200 ft			Dix
3,560 ft			Mountain
2,840 ft		Boquet	
2,120 ft		Lean-to	
1,400 ft	Trailhead		
	2	4	6 miles

rock, and brushy growth. Nevertheless, conservation officials cut a new trail to Dix from the recently completed highway, and this is essentially the same trail that we still hike today—except that now, the forest has come a long way in its regeneration.

Just like any place in the High Peaks Wilderness, the trail to Dix Mountain is very popular. Because the route described here leads to a single peak, it might seem a little less crowded than other High Peaks trails. Still, if you are planning to hike here on the weekend—at any time of the year—it is best to arrive early, due to the limited amount of parking at the trailhead. An early start will also ensure that you will have plenty of time for this lengthy, difficult, and thoroughly enjoyable hike.

GETTING THERE

From Exit 30 on I-87, follow US 9 north. At 2.1 miles, you reach a "spaghetti intersection" where NY 73 forks left in a somewhat confusing tangle of intersecting roads. Follow NY 73 for 3.1 miles, where signs point out the Round Pond Trailhead on the left side of the highway. The parking area can fit roughly half a dozen cars and is routinely filled to capacity on weekends.

THE HIKE

The trail to Dix begins about 100 feet southeast of the parking area, so your day begins with a brief walk along the shoulder of NY 73. Then, without any further ado, the trail climbs into the woods, topping out 200 feet above the highway. At 0.6 mile you have your first glimpse of Round Pond, where an unmarked herd path turns left toward a designated campsite. The main trail turns right and hugs the pond's northern shoreline, with glimpses of Spotted Mountain and Grace Peak in the distance.

Note how the forest here is overloaded with aspen and white birch. These are the same trees that first colonized the region after the twin 1903 and 1913 forest fires, taking advantage of all the direct sunlight created by the destruction of the original growth. While these trees were brush-sized when the trail was cut in the 1930s, they have since grown to respectable proportions.

After passing Round Pond, the trail climbs 550 feet in the next 0.8 mile to an area where conifers are notably more prevalent. The trail levels, and at 2.3 miles you reach a four-way intersection. Right leads to Saint Huberts, and the trail straight ahead leads up Noonmark. To find Dix, you must bear left.

Another 2.1 miles pass before you reach the lean-to site and the start of the climb up the mountain. But instead of a slog, this is a rather pleasant section through the valley of the North Fork Boquet (pronounced "bo-ket," not "bo-kay," as many people seem to think). There are several places where the trail follows the small river closely, with glimpses of the hills that surround it. The forest cover is more interesting, with spruce and cedar to add variety. There is a long detour inland to avoid the wetlands on Gravestone Brook before you return to side of the river. At some point you pass near tiny Dial Pond, but not close enough to see it. For the most part, this first half of the trail is well maintained, with stepping stones and other features to mitigate the mud.

You reach the lean-to site at 4.4 miles, or after 2 hours of hiking. Until recently, the shelter stood beside both the trail and the river, making it an obvious stopping point for campers and passing hikers alike. In 2017 the old structure was relocated away from the hustle and bustle, making it a slightly more private campsite than it used to be.

Hikers must ford the Boquet at this location to continue the hike. The ascent of the mountain begins here, although the grade is moderate at first. You are still parallel to the North Fork, even though at this point you are now quite high up in its headwater region, where the river is little more than a boisterous stream, hardly distinguishable from

NIPPLETOP, MARCY, AND THE GREAT RANGE ARE INCLUDED IN DIX'S GRAND VIEW

some of its tributaries. With the increase in elevation comes a corresponding increase in ruggedness, grooming you for the difficulties that lie ahead.

The next waypoint comes at 5.8 miles, where the forest opens up to reveal the massive slide extending up Dix's northern slope. This rock scar is the result of a landslide at some point in the mountain's history, where the soil came loose and swept away everything in its path. Some Adirondack slides make excellent climbing routes, but this one is too steep for most people. From its bottom, however, you can enjoy an excellent view back toward Noonmark and Giant. The trail does briefly follow the lower part of the slide; look for the cairns marking the way through the sun-lit open space, while also paying attention to the potentially slippery rock surface.

You have climbed to an elevation of 3,240 feet at this point, but you have 1,600 feet of climbing still to go! Follow the cairns across the open rock and back into the woods on the far side. Here begins the most tiring part of the ascent, where the trail shoots straight up the steep slope without flinching. Rocks, roots, and lots of mud await you, leaving little choice but to lean into your work, eating away at the elevation deficit one hard-earned step at a time. The trail angles away from the slide, and the thick forest cover ensures there are no views—so at least you won't have scenery to distract you from your efforts.

The worst of the worst is over by the time you reach a trail junction high on the mountain, 6.5 miles from the trailhead. Here, the trail through Hunters Pass climbs up from the right. The summit is to the left, still 0.4 mile away and 500 feet above you. The surrounding trees become shorter as you make this final push, until finally at 6.9 miles you reach the top of the mountain.

Dix is not a bald peak, but rather a forested summit with an array of bald ledges. It is long and narrow, and the actual high point could be easy to miss. The trail passes between two prominent ledges, one with a benchmark and a view of Grace Peak, and the other with a fine view toward Elk Lake and Mount Marcy. To the west of Nippletop you see Allen, with Santanoni on the horizon. Moving around to your right you see Skylight, Haystack almost blending in with neighboring Marcy, Basin, then Saddleback and Gothics. The summit rocks are small, but the long ridgeline contains numerous lookouts where you can find your own spot for a lunch break.

The trail continues over the summit and down toward Elk Lake, and so it would be easy to overshoot those twin ledges. The trail leading up from the Boquet River followed blue markers, and the one leading down to the south follows yellow markers. This change in colors occurs at the summit, and it may be the best clue that you have gone too far.

When you have decided it is time to begin the return journey, you may find that the descent down the steepest part of the mountain goes more quickly, if only because you are pausing less often to catch your breath, and not because it is easier. The hike off the mountain and back down the river valley toward NY 73 gives you the opportunity to see for a second time all of the scenic highlights of the morning, this time with the sun in a different position. Photographers might appreciate the afternoon lighting at the foot of the slide and alongside Round Pond.

Giant and Rocky Peak Ridge Traverse

TOTAL DISTANCE: 10.5 miles between trailheads

HIKING TIME: 9 hours

ELEVATION CHANGE: 9,400 feet

TRAILHEAD GPS COORDINATES: N44° 08' 18.1" W73° 44' 37.3" (Chapel Pond trailhead); N44° 08' 59.5" W73° 37' 35.5" (New Russia trailhead)

This is a route of extremes—as in extreme beauty and extreme difficulty. The 10.5-mile-long trail begins at Chapel Pond on NY 73 and climbs from rock to rock to the summit of Giant Mountain, one of the more popular High Peaks. After a steep descent through a col, it climbs to the neighboring summit, Rocky Peak Ridge, and from there it just keeps going. Most people turn back to Chapel Pond after summiting Rocky Peak, but those hikers are cheating themselves out of one of the best highland trails in the Adirondack Mountains.

What is the basis for that claim? Simple: there is so much open rock on this route, and so many expansive views, that after a few hours it seems futile to try to document the entire hike with pictures. On one visit, for instance, I put my camera away after Mary Louise Pond just so I could enjoy the moment. The ridgeline is not completely bare, but the open rock ledges do start to seem commonplace as you pass one after the other. Eventually you come to realize that you'll run out of daylight if you stop to savor each and every one.

But with this exceptional experience comes an exceptional physical challenge. The marked state trail that traverses the length of Rocky Peak Ridge cannot claim to be the most grueling trail in the Adirondacks, an honor that must certainly fall to the Great Range a few miles away, but it must be a close second. There are no ladders or seemingly impossible scrambles over precarious ledges, just an impressive amount of climbing and descending. By my estimate the elevation change is in the neighborhood of 9,400 feet, a figure that includes slopes both uphill and down. The fact that the day ends with a net descent of 985 feet is small

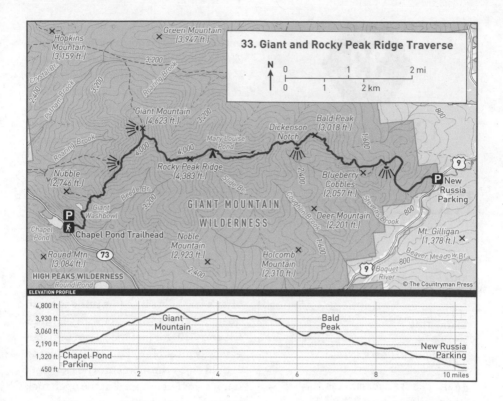

33. Giant and Rocky Peak Ridge Traverse

comfort to tired legs, because even the long descents can be grueling.

It's ironic that we now regard Rocky Peak Ridge as a place of outstanding beauty, because hikers in the early twentieth century were embarrassed by its ugliness. Commentators of that era used the words *grim* and *desolate* to describe the mountain, which had been ravaged by forest fires in 1903 and 1913. People climbed to its summit only because it was counted among the forty-six Adirondack High Peaks, and for no other reason; the mountain was held up as an example of the carelessness of humans.

Around mid-century the recovery of the mountain might have been sufficient to help a newer wave of climbers forgive the sins of the past, because by 1968 the state had marked the trail to the summit and people have been raving about this hike ever since. Once you make the journey from Chapel Pond to New Russia, you will see why. Just be sure to pick a day with good weather!

GETTING THERE

There are two trailheads for this hike, one at Chapel Pond and one near the hamlet of New Russia. First, you need to spot a car at the New Russia end. From Exit 30 on I-87, follow US 9 north. At 2.1 miles you reach a "spaghetti intersection" where NY 73 forks left and US 9 forks right in a somewhat confusing tangle of intersecting roads. The New Russia trailhead will be 4.7 miles north along US 9, located on the left under a stand of pines.

After leaving a vehicle there, return to the "spaghetti intersection" and follow NY 73 for 3.9 miles. Here, in the vicinity of Chapel Pond, the shoulder is wide enough for people to park. The start of the trail is on the right (east) side of the highway.

Note that this is an immensely popular area, so for much of the year you'll need to arrive early to find safe parking spots, especially on weekends.

THE HIKE

From the shoulder of NY 73 near Chapel Pond, follow the Giant Ridge Trail northeast into the woods. The climbing begins just minutes later, with a few switchbacks that help mitigate the initial 0.6-mile, 675-foot climb to Giant Washbowl, the first landmark of the day. This little pond is perched on a shelf high above the highway, with an open ledge overlooking Chapel Pond Pass just before you reach your first view of the water. The level of the pond tends to fluctuate; sometimes the water is pressed against the trail, and at other times it recedes to reveal a muddy shoreline. The cliffs on Giant Nubble form a scenic backdrop.

The Giant Ridge Trail cuts between a pair of campsites and resumes its climb, with more switchbacks leading up to a trail junction at 0.9 mile. Keep right, switchbacking on a rerouted section of trail for much of the next 0.4 mile, ending at an open rock ledge where the Washbowl is now 750 feet below you.

From this point upward, you will enjoy an evolving view of the surrounding landscape, because so much of the way involves hiking from one ledge to the next. Giant Washbowl recedes until it is out of sight, and the massive cliffs on Round Mountain eventually become less prominent as the sprawling Dix Range rises into view. Tiny little Twin Pond seems lost amidst a sea of forested foothills. The Green Mountains of Vermont delineate the horizon beyond Lake Champlain.

LOOKING TOWARD A FOGGY CHAMPLAIN VALLEY FROM GIANT'S RIDGE TRAIL

MARY LOUISE POND

right. For now, keep left and complete the climb of Giant, because that summit is just 0.1 mile away. There is a wide expanse of open rock here, all of it offering a panoramic view of the High Peaks Wilderness to the west. Mount Marcy and all of its neighbors can be easily identified, with the hamlet of Saint Huberts directly below you.

Now begins the traverse! Retrace your steps back to the last intersection and turn southeast toward Rocky Peak Ridge. This trail leads to a ledge from which you can see the col between the summits into which you're about to descend. It is a steep drop into that col, with several ledges and steep pitches to negotiate. Then you bottom out and begin the push toward Rocky Peak Ridge, where the slope is far more moderate. The distance between the summits is 1.2 miles.

The woods that engulf the trail come to an abrupt end as you scale the rock step that marks the perimeter of Rocky Peak's bald summit, which you reach 4 miles into your journey. The name might say "peak," but this is really a broad dome of rock with views in just about every direction. The cliffs on the back side of Giant are so impressive that you wonder how you managed not to see them until now. The array of High Peaks to the west is now so familiar that it hardly seems remarkable, except that your perspective has shifted just a touch and the mountains now seem more distant. After Giant, the Dixes are the next nearest neighbors of note.

For most peak baggers, this is the end of the road. As you relax and enjoy the view, you'll notice that party after party stands up and turns back toward Giant and Chapel Pond. That's fine, but for you the day is only just beginning. You still have 6.5 miles of the finest

The trail splits at 1.6 miles, mercifully giving you the option to climb over a rocky knob with a view or skip it and go around. This will be the last opportunity for a view until you near the summit of Giant Mountain, so choose wisely.

Much of the upper half of the trail to Giant's summit is embraced by a thick montane forest of balsam, spruce, and birch. After passing a side trail on the left at 2.1 miles, you twist along the forested shoulder of the mountain, climbing much more gently for a few minutes. Then the grade pitches upward again, with a series of ledges that seem like a stairway built for the mountain's namesake giant.

At an intersection high up on the mountain, 2.7 miles from Chapel Pond, the trail to Rocky Peak Ridge bears

alpine hiking between here and New Russia!

The ridgeline trail heads east from the summit, and within moments you have your first view of what's in store for you. Beyond the carpet of alpine vegetation is Mary Louise Pond, followed by a succession of summits, each a little lower than the last. The trail descends out of the alpine area and into the birch-filled woods that surround the tarn, reaching a bridge over a muddy corner of the pond at 4.6 miles. Mary Louise sits just a hair under 4,000 feet in elevation, and so DEC does permit camping at a designated site nearby.

A gentle climb leads up to the next summit in the chain, this one the eastward extension of Rocky Peak Ridge. You traverse this open ridgeline for a span of about 0.6 mile before making a mile-long descent to the east. Mostly you are in the trees during this descent, but every so often you come to an open rock with a view of some kind or another, either southwest toward the Dix Range, east toward Vermont, or north toward Hurricane and Jay Mountains. The descent is steep and rocky, with uneven footing that will urge you to take your time.

You lose 1,200 feet as you hike down the eastern flank of Rocky Peak Ridge into Dickenson Notch, a col notable for its stand of white birch and striped maple. After a brief respite, the trail then regains 160 feet to the western end of Bald Peak, which you reach at 6.4 miles. This begins the next summit traverse, one that will last half a mile. Bald Peak may not be completely bald, but the forest fires of the last century certainly left their mark on this summit. As you walk across bedrock and gravel, look for views in just about every direction—including back toward the imposing slopes of Rocky Peak Ridge. There is an enormous boulder perched on the edge of one ledge, right where a glacier dropped it, followed by the main summit of the mountain at 6.8 miles.

Look carefully for the scree walls—rows of rock—that define the continuing trail off the summit. It winds from rocky area to rocky area, with stands of cedar, birch, and fir defining the forest edge. There are several turns to watch for, so pay close attention to the placement of the cairns and trail markers; since much of the way is on bedrock, there is not much of a foot tread to follow.

The descent from Bald is 1.3 miles long, with one or two difficult ledges and an increasing amount of trees. After passing over one little knob, you reach a junction at 8.1 miles, where you have the option to turn right and climb steeply over the Blueberry Cobbles if you so desire. Most people skip that pleasure, bearing left and continuing the descent. The two trails reunite at 8.3 miles (8.5 miles if you chose to climb the cobbles), dropping through a layer of oak and into the hemlock-and-pine forest that predominate in the New Russia valley. But the trail just keeps going, losing elevation that you never knew you climbed. The way is no longer steep, but it does seem endless.

The downhill does not end until just before reaching the New Russia trailhead at 10.3 miles, or 10.5 miles if you followed the extension over Blueberry Cobbles. After topping out on Giant's summit at 4,626 feet, this valley at 620 feet in elevation seems to inhabit a completely different world. And that is part of the thrill of this hike: the wide variety of environments it visits, from the montane to the pseudo-alpine, and then back through bands of birch, oak, and finally pine. If this traverse didn't impress you, nothing will.

34

Pyramid and Gothics Loop

TOTAL DISTANCE: 12.7-mile loop	
HIKING TIME: 7½ hours	
VERTICAL RISE: 3,450 feet	
TRAILHEAD GPS COORDINATES: N44° 08′ 59.3″ W73° 46′ 03.0″	

Many hikers might find the route described here to be frustrating. This is a High Peaks adventure, and most people associate those mountains with peak bagging—that is, the quest to climb the forty-six Adirondack summits above 4,000 feet in elevation, first climbed by Bob Marshall, George Marshall, and Herb Clark. People who aspire to become "forty-sixers" flock to the High Peaks by the thousands every week, "bagging" as many peaks as they can. The temptation to make a short detour and summit one more mountain is often irresistible.

The route described here does lead to one of the High Peaks, but it is not a peak bagging route. This 12.7-mile loop over the summit of Gothics is one for the connoisseurs—the people who have already become forty-sixers and are now free to savor and enjoy what they might have missed the first time. The adventure begins with a visit to Rainbow Falls, then proceeds to scramble over the summit by way of its spectacular shoulder summit, Pyramid. Then, without the need to tack on additional miles and summit additional peaks, the loop descends the mountain to Beaver Meadows Falls. Return to your car and go home a very satisfied hiker.

The colorful Keene Valley guide Orson Phelps bestowed the name Gothics in the 1850s, likely inspired by the sweeping rock slides that remind some people of arches and flying buttresses. It is a mountain that is as beautiful to behold as it is to climb, easily identified from many different directions. It is also a strenuous hike, notorious for its steep ledges; but few people who have climbed Gothics regret the choice.

The mountain is located on state land, but the approach to its foot crosses a private tract called the Adirondack

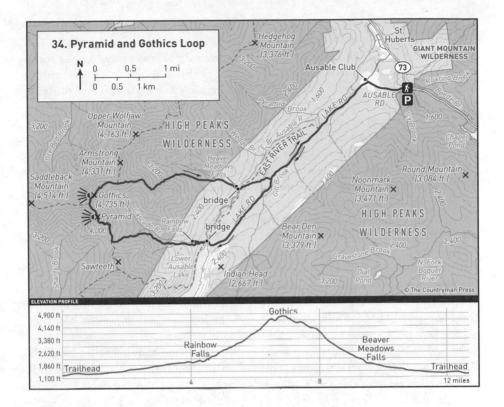

34. Pyramid and Gothics Loop

Mountain Reserve, owned by the Ausable Club in Saint Huberts. This private park was established in 1887 and originally encompassed about 25,000 acres, including the summit of Gothics and several other peaks. Two sales to the state in 1903 and 1978 reduced the size of the AMR considerably, so that today the private lands are limited to the valley between the great ranges of mountains on either side.

The privilege of crossing the private property does come with a few special restrictions. Most notably, dogs are not allowed under any circumstance, and camping is not permitted until you reach state land. (There are no campsites on Gothics, so camping is effectively prohibited here altogether.) Other rules are posted conspicuously at the entrance to the AMR.

Gothics is just one of many potential destinations available from the AMR. Because there are so many options from this one starting point, the trailhead is overwhelmingly popular. Thus, just like most other High Peaks Wilderness portals, you may need to plan an early start for this hike.

GETTING THERE

From Exit 30 on I-87, follow US 9 north. At 2.1 miles you reach a "spaghetti intersection" where NY 73 forks left. Follow that road for 5.4 miles to the intersection with Ausable Road, where there are two large parking areas on each side of the highway.

THE HIKE

This outstanding hike begins with a brisk 4.1-mile stroll down the roads leading into and through the AMR. Begin by following Ausable Road west from the twin public parking areas. It leads to a private golf course notable for its view of nearby Giant Mountain, and then to the start of Lake Road at 0.6 mile. Bear left and proceed to the elaborate wooden gate that marks the entrance to the reserve. Just before the gate is the registration booth and warden's station.

Past the gate, Lake Road is a gravel-surfaced hikers' highway. Only club members may drive on the road, and so vehicle traffic is therefore very light. For this hike you will need to follow the road all the way to its end at Lower Ausable Lake, 4.1 miles from the parking area. As you walk that distance, you pass Gill Brook and numerous side trails, all the while gaining 730 feet in elevation. If you are a veteran High Peaks hiker, you know this already, because you have probably hiked this road what must seem like a dozen times. Most people take advantage of the easy walking surface by setting a brisk pace.

Lake Road may sound dull and uneventful, but its ending is as beautiful as any national park. This is because it deposits you at the north end of Lower Ausable Lake, a fjord-like body of water pinched between the steep slopes of Colvin and Sawteeth. The public is not permitted near the club's boat launching area, but by following the last part of the road down to the footbridge over the outlet, you can enjoy a very photogenic view from locations near the dam.

Cross the long bridge over the East Branch Ausable River and look for the signs pointing the way to Pyramid and Gothics. Several trails split off in various directions, including one to Beaver Meadows and one to Sawteeth. The one detour you really should make forks right within 100 yards of the bridge, leading in 0.1 mile to the foot of Rainbow Falls. This is a 150-foot freefalling cascade that is always photogenic, no matter the water levels.

The main trail to Pyramid and Gothics begins its climb without further delay, leading to an overlook of the top of Rainbow Falls in 0.3 mile. You parallel Cascade Brook for a short distance before entering state land at 0.5 mile, and then you continue climbing at what will seem like a moderate grade compared to what lies in store for you. There is not much scenery along this portion of the loop, so just enjoy the pleasant woods walk.

This section ends 1.6 miles from the dam, or 5.7 miles overall. Here the trail reaches the saddle between Pyramid and Sawteeth, marked by a trail junction. The way left leads to Sawteeth, another of the High Peaks that is just 0.4 mile and 460 vertical feet away.

For Pyramid and Gothics you must turn right, and this is where things quickly become interesting. The mountain is unavoidably steep, and the trail has been worn to bedrock. At more than a few places, you must scramble up a steep pitch of slanted rock, including one site with a view up the valley toward Noonmark Mountain. Because of these rugged conditions, it takes an hour to cover the 0.7-mile, 920-foot climb from the col to the summit of Pyramid.

When you reach the top, look for a short side path to the left, leading to one of the most spectacular views in the entire Adirondack Park. It begins with the massive rock face of Gothics in the foreground, but extends to Saddleback, Basin, Haystack, and Marcy. Colden,

PYRAMID'S VIEW OF THE UPPER GREAT RANGE IS ONE OF THE BEST

Iroquois, Algonquin, and Wright are the more distant peaks visible beyond the summit of Saddleback. Pyramid is not a separate peak, just a shoulder of Gothics. Nevertheless, many people regard this view as better than the main summit. This spot is 6.4 miles from the parking area.

To find out for yourself how the two views compare, you must follow the long, narrow spine of rock that drops down from Pyramid and then scales the final part of Gothics. Be sure to look back to see just how narrow Pyramid's profile is when you reach the next trail junction at 6.7 miles. Bear right and file through the thick summit forest to the highest point on Gothics, 6.8 miles from the start and 4,735 feet in elevation.

The view here is more expansive and less in-your-face spectacular. Johns Brook Valley forms a great gulf between you and the next range of mountains, with Whiteface, Moose, and McKenzie on the distant horizon beyond Lake Placid. On the other hand you have Saddleback, Basin, and Marcy, which from this perspective appear to be piled on top of each other like cars in a giant train wreck. Note that there is no shelter from the elements on this exposed summit.

The continuing trail down the east side of the summit leads northeast into the woods, gently at first but soon becoming a steep affair with no shortage of precipitous rock ledges—some of them quite tall. You lose 400 feet in elevation in the 0.4 mile into the next

BEAVER MEADOWS FALLS

col, where the trail forks. Left leads to Armstrong Mountain, 0.4 mile and 430 vertical feet away. Right is the descent route to Beaver Meadows Falls, the route recommended here.

In one of the more incredible feats of Adirondack trail construction, the start of the route to the falls manages to traverse a very steep slope; if you could see it from the air, the trail would appear to be clinging to the mountainside for dear life. The trees on the downhill side of the trail keep you from feeling like you are in danger of falling into space, but it is an adventuresome section of trail nonetheless, with ladders to help you up and over some of the more difficult ledges.

This leads to a shoulder of the mountain that is far less precarious. Look for a giant rock 0.4 mile from the col (7.6 miles overall) with trees growing on top. The trail then begins to descend the mountain in earnest, alternating between steep pitches and gentle interludes. Like the climb to Pyramid through the Cascade Brook basin, this section is enshrouded by deep woods, with the trees growing taller as you lose elevation. You reenter the AMR, pass a side trail to Lost Lookout, and approach the side of the stream that creates Beaver Meadows Falls. The trail is nearly as steep as the waterfall, with a ladder to assist you on the final drop down to the valley floor, 2.2 miles and 2,330 feet below the col.

Beaver Meadows Falls, named for the nearby Beaver Meadows section of the East Branch Ausable River, is just a short walk from the ladder, and 9.4 miles into the loop hike. Unlike Rainbow Falls, this cascade is not hidden in a side canyon. It exists in full view, daring you to come in close for a photograph only to dampen you with its spray.

To complete the loop, you will need to cross the nearby bridge over the river. Turn left onto the East River Trail, then veer right at the very next intersection. This is the most direct route back to Lake Road, which you reach at 10 miles. From here, civilization is a left turn and 2.7 miles away.

35

Lower Wolf Jaw via Bennies Brook Slide

TOTAL DISTANCE: 11.1-mile loop

HIKING TIME: 7.5 hours

VERTICAL RISE: 2,665 feet

TRAILHEAD GPS COORDINATES: N44° 11' 20.5" W73° 48' 55.8" (The Garden trailhead parking); N44° 13' 06.1" W73° 47' 22.6" (Marcy Field shuttle parking)

Lower Wolf Jaw is not often regarded as one of the more spectacular Adirondack High Peaks. Although it is part of the stellar Great Range, its 4,173-foot wooded summit offers limited views, and many people have been observed saying "This is it?" upon reaching the top.

However, in 2011 the storm known as Hurricane Irene etched a superb new route to the top of Lower Wolf Jaw: a long, open slide along the course of Bennies Brook on the mountain's northwestern slopes. The extremely heavy rains deposited by that storm turned small streams into raging torrents, and it caused extensive flood damage in the communities of Keene and Keene Valley. It also created a lot of havoc in the mountains by washing out two old log dams from the 1930s, as well as several bridges. Few storms have altered the High Peaks landscape as extensively as Irene.

But for most people, the most visible reminder of the storm is the gallery of slides it created on slopes throughout the region. Although the mountains of the Adirondacks are thickly forested, the soil that supports these forests is very thin, especially on the steep upper slopes. The soils are already habitually damp just by virtue of their location amongst the clouds, but during a major rain event they can become completely saturated. The weight can pull the soil layer away from the underlying bedrock, triggering a landslide that wipes out everything in its path.

Slides have existed in the High Peaks since American settlers first penetrated the region. Some are old and starting to revegetate, some were scrubbed down to bare rock. Some are steep and inaccessible, and others have been incorporated into popular hiking trails.

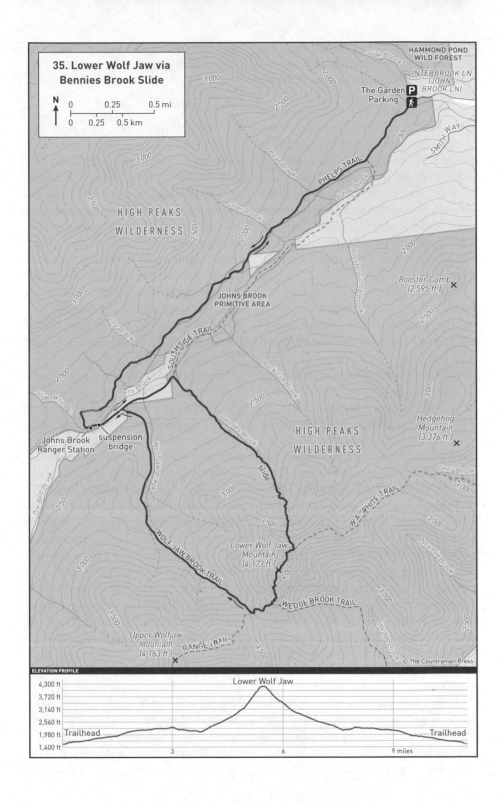

35. Lower Wolf Jaw via Bennies Brook Slide

N
0   0.25   0.5 mi
0   0.25   0.5 km

Slide Brook

HAMMOND POND
WILD FOREST

INTERBROOK LN
(JOHNS
BROOK LN)

The Garden
Parking

SMITH WAY

3,000

2,000

2,500

1,500

Bear Brook

PHELPS TRAIL

Johns Brook

HIGH PEAKS
WILDERNESS

Deer Brook

3,500

3,000

2,500

2,000

Rooster Comb Brook

Rooster Comb
(2,595 ft.)

2,500

JOHNS BROOK
PRIMITIVE AREA

Dry Brook

SOUTHSIDE TRAIL

Rock Cut Brook

3,000

Hedgehog
Mountain
(3,376 ft.)

Slide Mtn. Br.

Johns Brook

Johns Brook
Ranger Station

suspension
bridge

Bennies Brook

Slide

HIGH PEAKS
WILDERNESS

Deer Brook

3,000

2,500

Wolf Jaw Brook

WOLF JAW BROOK TRAIL

3,000

3,500

W. A. WHITE TRAIL

Pyramid Brook

3,500

2,500

Lower Wolf Jaw
Mountain
(4,173 ft.)

4,000

WEDGE BROOK TRAIL

Wedge Brook

3,000

3,500

Upper Wolfjaw
Mountain
(4,163 ft.)

RANGE TRAIL

3,500

© The Countryman Press

ELEVATION PROFILE

	Lower Wolf Jaw	
4,300 ft		
3,720 ft		
3,140 ft		
2,560 ft		
1,980 ft Trailhead		Trailhead
1,400 ft		
	3 6	9 miles

At Bennies Brook, a smaller slide that had been known mostly to backcountry skiers was greatly enlarged and converted into a route that was discovered almost immediately by hikers—the day after the storm, in fact. It extends about 1.5 miles long in total, from nearly the summit of Lower Wolf Jaw down to a point just shy of Johns Brook. When seen from a distance, it appears like a long white scar down the northwestern slope of the mountain. As a hiking route, it is a path to the summit of a High Peak where views are a constant, uninterrupted treat.

The slide itself is not a marked or maintained trail, but it extends so far up the mountain that navigation is only a minor issue. A well-used marked trail leads to its foot, and you can follow the slide with ease most of the way to the summit; a path barely 200 feet long leads from the top of the slide to a junction with the Range Trail across the summit. From there, you can follow the traditional hiking trails back down to Johns Brook to create a loop.

Some Adirondack slides are steep and slippery, but Bennies Brook Slide is a relatively gentle route. Even when the slope does become steep on the upper half of the mountain, there are plenty of ledges to serve as steps—never do you feel like you are exposed on the side of a steep precipice. There have been several man-made trails leading up Lower Wolf Jaw for generations, but in my opinion this new route—which has been gifted to us by a force of nature—is easily the most scenic.

Remember, this area falls within the High Peaks Wilderness, where high use levels have resulted in a longer set of regulations. Dogs must be leashed, campfires are banned, and if you plan to camp, your food must be stored in a bear-proof canister.

GETTING THERE

The main trailhead for this hike is a small parking area called the Garden, located near Keene Valley. Follow NY 73 into the heart of the village, and turn west onto Adirondack Street near the Ausable Inn. This narrow and winding road climbs for 1.6 miles to the Garden, where parking is limited to about sixty cars, a figure that is reached early in the morning every summer weekend. No parking is allowed anywhere along the road approaching the Garden, and illegally parked cars may be towed away. The parking fee for the Garden is $10 per vehicle per day as of 2018.

The alternate parking area is Marcy Field, located off NY 73 about 1.9 miles north of Keene Valley. Signs point the way to the public parking area, located near the south end of a former airfield. There is ample parking here, with a shuttle bus to the Garden departing approximately every thirty minutes on Saturdays, Sundays, and holidays. The round-trip cost for the shuttle is $10 per person. Remember that if you arrive back at the Garden after the last shuttle has left for the day, it's a long walk back to Marcy Field.

All parking and shuttle fees, which are charged by the Town of Keene, are subject to change. See www.town ofkeeneny.com for more information.

THE HIKE

The primary trail leading out of the Garden follows the north side of Johns Brook, one of the largest streams radiating outward from the High Peaks Wilderness. Rarely, though, will you see or hear the stream for the first 3.1 miles of your hike. The trail leads southwest from the Garden, keeping well above Johns Brook, ultimately leading to the Adirondack Mountain Club's Johns Brook Lodge, the Great Range, Mount Marcy, and several other choice destinations. This is a primary trunk trail, one that many hikers have seen over and over again on their frequent adventures. Note that it is a hilly route, with uphill slogs in both directions.

At 3.1 miles you reach an interior trail register. Turn left here toward the state's Johns Brook Ranger Station. The trail crosses the clearing beside the cabin to a suspension bridge strung high above a scenic gorge on Johns Brook. At the far end of the bridge, keep left, even though

signs warn that the continuing trail in this direction has been abandoned by the Department of Environmental Conservation. These signs refer to the Southside Trail, a private way across state land on the south side of Johns Brook. The state has ceased maintaining the trail, but the portion you need to follow is in fine shape.

Follow the Southside Trail northeast for 0.6 mile. In this distance you pass one of the marked trails to Wolf Jaw Brook (your return route for later in the day) and then the brook itself. Wolf Jaw Brook was also radically transformed by Irene, but the slide you see here only leads back to the hiking trail you just passed. Continue along the Southside Trail to the second slide, this one

NEARING THE TOP OF BENNIES BROOK SLIDE

marked by a tall cairn. This is Bennies Brook.

The slide extends 1.5 miles southeast from this point, from a bottom elevation of 2,070 feet to a headwall at about 3,870 feet. The lower stretches of the slide are narrow and gently sloped; it is an open swath through a sylvan setting, with limited views at first. You need to scramble around one small waterfall and a few other minor obstacles.

But as you gain elevation, the slide widens, and more of the surrounding landscape comes into view. The large hill across the valley is slowly revealed to be a flank of Big Slide Mountain, with Yard to the left. As you round another bend you get your first good look at the summit of Lower Wolf Jaw high above you. Porter Mountain and The Brothers appear to the right of Big Slide, and before the day is done, you will glimpse the rocky knob of Cascade's summit.

Two other slides join the main course at 1.2 miles; the one you want to follow keeps to the right, just a little east of south. It gets much steeper at this point, but the numerous ledges give the novice climber much to work with. The slide's headwall is a daunting feature, but there is a convenient exit path to the left just before you reach it. As you near the vertical wall, keep to the left of the slide and look for a small cairn, if not the path itself. From this spot, your view now includes much of the slide you just climbed.

The clear herd path leads up through ferny glades to the Range Trail, just 200 feet away. This is one of the original trails on the mountain. To reach Lower Wolf Jaw, turn right and scramble up a steep rock ledge, the steepest and most difficult part of the entire loop.

The summit is just a quarter-mile away, or 5.5 eventful miles from the Garden. There are views present, mostly just "windows" through the trees, but nothing that compares with what you have already seen.

To complete the loop, follow the marked trail south off the mountain. This is a steep descent with numerous ledges, and here and there a glimpse of neighboring Upper Wolf Jaw. Just 0.3 mile from the summit, bear right at a fork and continue dropping down into the col between the summits. Here, at 0.5 mile from the top, bear right twice more at a pair of back-to-back trail junctions.

This places you at the top of the Wolf Jaw Brook trail, which leads back into the Johns Brook valley. The forest here was mostly untouched by the hurricane, and so you have no views to distract you from your work until 0.5 mile from the col, where the trail crosses another new slide. This one was not worn down to bedrock like Bennies Brook, and so it is much grassier. Nor does it seem to be as scenic. It is interesting to look at from the edge, but in this case you will not be tempted to abandon the trail to descend the slide instead.

Just 0.3 mile later, you reach another fork where left leads to Johns Brook Lodge and right leads back to the ranger station. Keeping right, you pass a lean-to and several camping opportunities before returning to the Southside Trail, about 7.7 miles into your hike. At this point, bear left back to the suspension bridge across Johns Brook, pass the ranger outpost, and turn right back onto the trunk trail when you reach the register box. From here, it is a 3.1-mile walk back to the Garden.

36

Hurricane Mountain

TOTAL DISTANCE: 6.4 miles round-trip

HIKING TIME: 3 hours

VERTICAL RISE: 2,000 feet

TRAILHEAD GPS COORDINATES: N44° 12' 40.8" W73° 43' 21.2"

The summit of Hurricane Mountain, bared by fire, stands proudly between the hamlets of Keene and Elizabethtown. It is not one of the tallest peaks in the Adirondacks, though after making the journey to the summit you would never know it. This is a steep, rugged "little" climb, topping out at 3,678 feet in elevation; the conical summit knob resembles the alpine summits of the High Peaks even if it isn't counted among them. The climb would seem even bigger if the trailhead weren't located so high up the mountain.

Three trails lead to the summit of Hurricane, and each provides a different experience. The route from the southeast, beginning near Elizabethtown, was the route used by rangers when the summit fire tower was still in active service. Another trail approaches the mountain from the north, beginning at a trailhead high above Keene; this route has the most moderate grades, with a lean-to at the foot of the mountain for those interested in an overnight adventure.

The trail described here climbs the southwestern slopes of Hurricane Mountain, starting from a roadside trailhead on the highway between Keene and Elizabethtown. Since it is the most prominent of the three trails, it is easily the most popular.

What makes this a stand-out hike is not just the stunning 360° view from the summit, although that is certainly a key factor. In 2014 the trail was reconstructed—rerouted almost in its entirety—to eliminate the steep and eroded sections of the original trail. The new version is an excellent specimen of modern trail building, with switchbacks to minimize the steepness of the terrain as much as possible.

Adirondack trail builders used to be fond of cutting routes straight up the

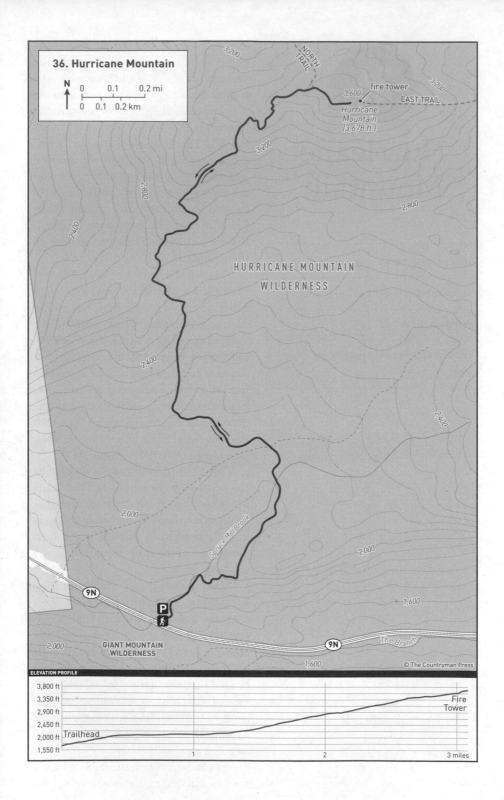

36. Hurricane Mountain

N

0   0.1   0.2 mi

0   0.1 0.2 km

NORTH TRAIL

fire tower

3,600   EAST TRAIL

Hurricane
Mountain
(3,678 ft.)

3,200

3,200

2,800

2,800

HURRICANE MOUNTAIN
WILDERNESS

2,400

2,400

2,400

2,600

2,400

2,800

2,000

Spruce Hill Brook

2,000

2,000

9N

1,600

P

1,600

GIANT MOUNTAIN
WILDERNESS

9N

The Branch

2,000

1,600

© The Countryman Press

ELEVATION PROFILE

			Fire Tower

3,800 ft
3,350 ft
2,900 ft
2,450 ft
2,000 ft   Trailhead
1,550 ft

1   2   3 miles

slopes, making the trail as short and direct as possible. Such a route is called the "fall line." Unfortunately, this is also the direction in which water flows down a mountain, and water erosion has long been the bane of trail stewards.

But this new trail avoids the fall line, leading on a tour of the mountain's most interesting features instead of just getting you from Point A to B on a steep and rocky slog. Yes, the trail is a bit longer than before, but the better design should ensure this stays an attractive hiking route for a long time.

GETTING THERE

The parking area is located along NY 9N between the hamlets of Elizabethtown and Keene, near the height-of-land as the road climbs over the mountain and down the other side. From Elizabethtown, the trailhead is 6.6 miles from downtown and located on the right. If you are coming up from Keene, look for it on the left at 3.4 miles.

THE HIKE

The trailhead is located at 1,696 feet in elevation, making it one of the higher parking areas in the vicinity. This is vertical elevation that you won't have to climb yourself. But on the downside, the climbing begins nearly as soon as you exit your car. There is no warm-up.

After signing in at the register, the rerouted trail quickly leaves the old route and ascends though a narrow valley forested with an eclectic mix of red pines and cedars. You come close to the side of Spruce Hill Brook before zigging back on a hairpin turn to the right. After several more crossings with the old trail, which has been brushed in with dead wood, you reach an open ledge on the right at 0.4 mile. This view over the highway toward the massive slopes of Tripod and Knob Lock mountains is an early treat—but you have only climbed 340 feet above the trailhead, with much, much more to go.

At this point the trail begins a long traverse of a broad shelf where there are almost no hills to speak of. Here is the "limber up" portion of the hike that you were denied at the beginning. It leads through a coniferous forest and across Spruce Hill Brook, leaving the original trail behind. At 0.9 mile you cross a long bog bridge through an open wetland with mountain views, followed a few minutes later by a second wetland where you skirt the edge.

Just after glimpsing a third, smaller wetland on the left, the trail begins climbing again. Here you are in a hardwood forest where aspens (also called poplars) are the most dominant species; these are artifacts of the fires that burned these slopes, for they primarily grow in places that have been exposed to unfiltered sunlight. The trail briefly rejoins the original route as you make your way up this slope, and the difference in the quality of the trail surface may be obvious. Rather than replace this eroded section, it was stabilized with water bars.

But before long the new trail swings left to find its own path up the mountain. The curvy trail is far more visually interesting than a straight one, as it seems to be leading you on a tour of the mountain. You climb out of the band of poplars into the standard montane forest of spruce, fir, and birch—the common forest on most Adirondack slopes—with one pause at 1.9 miles where a long strip of forest has been ravaged by wind and ice. At this spot, about 2,750 feet in elevation, there is no forest canopy at the rock knob on the shoulder of the mountain, 2.7 miles from the start. Here you will find not only your first open views west toward the High Peaks, but east to Hurricane's summit cone. The trail follows the openings on this knob before ducking back into the woods, reaching an intersection with the northern trail at 3 miles. A left turn would lead down to Gulf Brook and Crow Clearing.

Bearing right, you are in the woods for just a few more minutes before reaching the foot of a rock ledge, where the trees abruptly come to an end. Some scrambling is required to get you up this rock, but once there you are on the open summit. It is just a short walk up to the highest point, 3.2 miles from NY 9N and marked by the presence of a fire tower.

No tower is needed to enjoy the view, however. Giant Mountain is the closest of the High Peaks, but further afield the feast of mountains is almost gluttonous. Dix is scarred with slides; Marcy is a massive cone of rock; Big Slide lurks like a shark's fin. To the north, beyond Weston Mountain, are the rugged peaks in the Jay Range.

When you are ready to return to civilization, you will find that the descent is relatively easy once you clear the summit ledges. If you rushed through the wetlands the first time through, or if some of the views were obscured by clouds, here is your chance to see them a second time.

APPROACHING THE SUMMIT OF HURRICANE MOUNTAIN

moment, at least not until the trees grow back.

The upper part of the trail gets a little rockier, and this section is more prone to iciness in winter. Your route is generally northeast, but near 3,350 feet in elevation it detours south to a most scenic

37

Jay Range

TOTAL DISTANCE: 8.2 miles round-trip

HIKING TIME: 6.5 hours

VERTICAL RISE: 1,800 feet trailhead to ridgeline

TRAILHEAD GPS COORDINATES: N44° 18' 57.2" W73° 43' 14.5"

For most people, the lower reaches of the Ausable Valley seem a world apart from the rest of the Adirondacks. Here there are fewer hunting camps and more working farms, making the area seem less wild and more bucolic—perhaps in closer keeping with Vermont than the Adirondack wilderness.

But those mountains that rise above the farms and the rural communities contain some outstanding pockets of wildness. One of the most notable of these "pocket wildernesses" is Jay Mountain, which tops out at about 3,580 feet in elevation. It is the centerpiece of the 7896-acre Jay Mountain Wilderness. Although it is the smallest of the park's protected areas, it is thoroughly rugged, with almost no level terrain to speak of. Within its compact boundaries are a dozen named summits, and just about every one of them is capped with bare rock.

Fire, iron, and pulp form the story behind this scenic place. For many years the driving economic force in this area was the J & J Rogers Iron Company based in Ausable Forks, which harvested the region's forests to fuel its forges. Later the same company changed its focus to pulpwood, with lumber operations throughout the Ausable River watershed. And what J & J Rogers didn't consume, the forest fires of the early twentieth century did. Today, there are no sizeable stands of virgin forest anywhere in this region.

Commercial exploitation of this small wilderness, unfortunately, is not a thing of the past. On the east side of the mountain is an open pit mine where a multinational corporation extracts a mineral called wollastonite. A controversial referendum in 2013, which the voters of the state approved only by a narrow margin, will allow the company

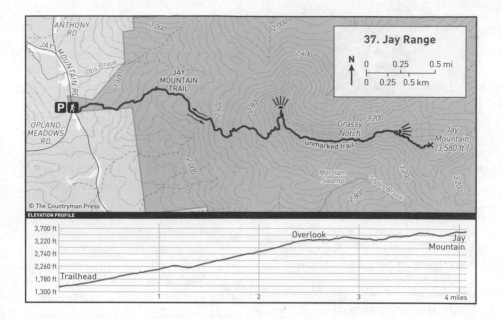

to extend its operation within the wilderness if it finds more wollastonite there.

From a hiker's perspective, the Jay Range represents a chance to hike along a ridgeline with extensive amounts of open rock, with all the big views that entails. To some people, the mountain resembles an alpine traverse, even though the views were mostly created by fire, not extreme elevation. Having visited the mountain several times, I can confirm that the hike across Jay is an exhilarating experience, on par with the Rocky Peak Ridge traverse (Hike #33) or the loop over Gothics (Hike #34).

Only a portion of this trail is marked, however. Blue markers guide you up the first 2.5 miles to the beginning of the ridgeline, where a bald rock knob allows you to orient yourself in the landscape and see what lies in store for you. The 1.6-mile trek along the ridgeline to Jay's highest point is a well-worn but unmarked footpath.

GETTING THERE

Follow NY 9N to the hamlet of Upper Jay and turn east onto Trumbulls Road just south of the bridge over the East Branch Ausable River. Follow it for 2.6 miles, where Trumbulls Road becomes Jay Mountain Road at an intersection. Keep straight, reaching the trailhead parking area at 3.4 miles at the same point that Upland Meadows Road forks right. The official parking area is big enough for only five or six cars; all latecomers will be forced to park on the shoulder. Note that much of the land in this area is private property.

THE HIKE

Following blue markers, the trail climbs a few vertical feet up from the road to the register and then delves into the woods. The grade is very gentle at first, winding through the hardwood-forested foot of the mountain and across part of an old stone fence. It makes sense that if

VIEWS OF WHITEFACE MOUNTAIN ARE EVER PRESENT ON THE JAY RANGE

farming is still an active part of life along the Ausable River today, it was probably much more prevalent long ago—and that some of those farms extended further up the slopes than they do now.

Tall red oaks characterize these lower forests, which is typical for the drier and somewhat warmer slopes of the eastern Adirondacks. It is only by ascending the mountain that you discover the northern hardwood species more typically associated with the Adirondack Mountains, and above them come the red spruce, birch, and balsam fir of the montane forest zone.

The journey through these different ecological bands is along a winding trail that is not afraid to switchback from time to time. Because of this, the way is never steep. Indeed, the trail is well constructed and a delight to hike. In the winter you can see the distinctive ski slopes on Whiteface Mountain 11 miles to the northwest; in the summer, you might have to wait until you reach one of the handful of natural openings before you can enjoy that view. But be patient, because there will be views aplenty soon enough.

The switchbacks lead up to a small notch on the ridgeline, where the unmarked ridge trail forks right. Before you turn that way, though, follow the blue markers left up a small bald knob,

CAIRNS LIKE THIS MARK THE WAY ALONG JAY'S RIDGELINE TRAIL

which is the first lookout on the mountain. An easy bit of scrambling gets you to the summit, which features a 360° view. If you missed Whiteface before, it is the easiest landmark to identify now; the massive High Peaks Wilderness occupies the entire southwestern horizon, and Lake Champlain spreads out to the east. This panoramic vista at 3,250 feet is not a bad reward for a 2.5-mile hike!

The other key element of this view is Jay Mountain itself, and from this perspective you get a good sense of the intervening ridgeline between you and the highest summit, the ultimate destination of the trail.

To begin the second phase of the hike, descend back down the knob and look for the start of the unmarked ridgeline trail to your left, which proceeds directly to the next knob. The traverse of Jay Mountain is less about a laborious climb to a single peak than it is a series of rises and drops. Many of these slopes are moderate, but a few are steep and rocky. There are pockets of forests in the low spots between the summits, but on the higher ground the trail passes through interesting meadows of goldenrod, or patches of rock covered only with mosses and lichens. The only markings for this trail are cairns, or small piles of rock.

The summit that is officially recognized on topographic maps as Jay Mountain is just 0.4 mile from the end of the marked trail. The lookout on the east end of this long knob seems to be suspended over Merriam Swamp, an open wetland that sits high up on the mountain. Looking ahead on the ridgeline,

the next two summits look like a set of not-so-identical twins: one a rocky peak, the other a partly-forested dome. The trail dips through Grassy Notch and climbs back up to another ledge with closer views of those two summits.

The second-to-last summit on the hike is the pyramidal peak that has been dominating the view so far, and this is also the steepest and rockiest part of the entire ridgeline. If the trail ended here, it would be the end of an extremely satisfying day. But it descends steeply across open rock with only the cairns to guide the way, only to climb once more from ledge to ledge toward the top of Jay's highest peak.

This last summit, 1.6 miles from the end of the marked trail and 4.1 miles from your car, is ironically the least scenic. It is not completely forested, but its patches of bald rock are interspersed with patches of balsam fir trees, so you do have to work harder to find good views here than at any other point along the ridge. That being said, the 3,580-foot summit does offer one of the mountain's best views east toward Lake Champlain and Vermont, if you are willing to hunt for it past the end of the trail.

In geographic reality, the mountain does not end here, only the trail does. The ridgeline angles south at this point toward Saddleback Mountain, the tallest summit in the Jay Mountain Wilderness. That is a very rugged place, and no trail leads there. Most people turn around at the cairn marking the top of Jay, retracing their steps along the open ridgeline and enjoying the view of Saddleback from a comfortable distance.

38

Poke-O-Moonshine Mountain

TOTAL DISTANCE: 3.6 miles round-trip	

HIKING TIME: 3.5 hours	

VERTICAL RISE: 1,250 feet	

TRAILHEAD GPS COORDINATES: N44° 24' 13.0" W73° 30' 08.2"	

Topographic maps spell the name "Poka-moonshine," but nearly everyone else spells it "Poke-O-Moonshine." Given that "poke" is an old-fashioned term for a sack, the accepted name makes far more grammatical sense if you subscribe to the theory that it refers to a stash of whiskey. This mountain, with its stunning array of cliffs, has been a landmark for passing travelers as long as there have been roads running past its foot. And since the fire tower was built on its summit in 1917, Poke-O-Moonshine has been a destination for hikers.

This is one of the easternmost fire tower summits in the park, with a view that expresses an affinity with Vermont as much as with the Adirondacks. The High Peaks may be geographically closer, but the hiker's eye is inevitably drawn across the width of Lake Champlain to the mountains that form the backbone of the Green Mountain State. The fire tower is merely an added bonus in this case, because the large open ledge on the summit of Poke-O would be just as attractive if no structures had ever been erected here.

The trail leading to the tower from the old Poke-O-Moonshine Campground may be as steep as they come, but it has been the subject of much work. Trail crews have poured hours of work into installing rock steps on the lower half of the trail, as well as rerouting the upper half as far as the lean-to. Interpretive brochures at the trailhead register make this an opportunity to explore the natural and human history of the climb. Therefore despite the forbidding profile—especially when seen from I-87—this is a climb that many people enjoy.

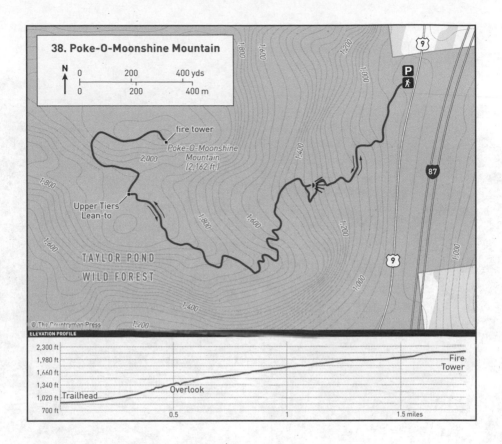

38. Poke-O-Moonshine Mountain

N

| 0 | 200 | 400 yds |
| 0 | 200 | 400 m |

fire tower

Poke-O-Moonshine
Mountain
(2,162 ft.)

2,000

1,800

Upper Tiers
Lean-to

1,800

1,600

TAYLOR POND

WILD FOREST

1,400

1,200

© The Countryman Press

ELEVATION PROFILE

2,300 ft	
1,980 ft	Fire
1,660 ft	Tower
1,340 ft	
1,020 ft	Trailhead
700 ft	

Overlook

0.5   1   1.5 miles

GETTING THERE

The main trailhead for Poke-O-Moonshine Mountain is at the entrance to the former state campground of the same name at the foot of the cliffs. From Exit 33 on I-87, turn south on US 9 and follow it for 2.9 miles. The campground entrance is on the right, with parking available just as you pull in from the highway. The facilities still remain but have not been maintained since the site closed in 2009.

THE HIKE

From the improvised trailhead parking area at the old campground entrance, the red-marked foot trail leads south past overgrown campsites to the trailhead register. The revamped trail is steep, but parts of it were rerouted just enough from the original trail that it now has a pleasing, winding character. Rock steps guard against erosion. It winds between giant boulders and overhanging ledges, and passes a rocky slope with an early view past the mountain's cliffs north along I-87. A narrow alcove in a rock wall on your right invites exploration.

A steep pitch at 0.5 mile leads to a partially bald ledge with so-so views over the valley, limited in scope by the unnamed mountain across the highway. This is worth a short break, but there are much better vistas ahead of you.

The grade is notably less steep from this point forward. This is not to say

TAKING IN POKE-O-MOONSHINE'S BIG VISTA

that the climbing is over, but rather that the grade is far more moderate for much of the next mile. At 0.7 mile a newly constructed detour veers left off the old route, which climbed directly and steeply toward the foot of the main summit. This new trail leads southwest, switchbacking up the ridgeline south of the summit. The route choice might seem puzzling, especially since you might at times spot the fire tower over your shoulder. It seems as though you're going in the wrong direction, but after ascending a set of wooden steps, the new trail sniffs out a pair of decent views from clearings of bare rock. Each view looks south along the Interstate corridor.

The rerouted trail then coursecorrects and leads back northeast,

moment later to a stone chimney in the woods; this is all that remains of the observer's cabin. The modern trail work ends at this point, and the final 0.4-mile climb to the summit is a taste of what of what the legacy trail used to be like: steep and a bit eroded. One quick scramble brings you up to the first level, and after passing some open views on the left, you reach another, taller ledge. This climb puts you on the summit proper.

From here the trail turns east and leads through a forest damaged by a 1998 ice storm to the foot of the fire tower at 1.8 miles. The only 360° views you will find are from the cab at the top of that structure, and in the summer there may even be a steward on duty to help you interpret the view.

But the wide-open ledge at ground level is more than adequate compensation for your troubles. It extends for over 100 feet with nothing to obstruct the southerly panorama. In one direction, past Long Pond and the wide expanse of Lake Champlain, lie the Green Mountains. In the other direction the horizon line is even more jagged, with Giant, Hurricane, and the Jay Range all in a row. The summit of Whiteface anchors the far right corner of the vista. When you climb to the top of the tower, you'll find additional views to the north.

Returning to the campground requires significantly less time than the ascent. When you reach the steep portion of the mountain on the final drop into the valley, the rock steps make the descent a less anxious experience than on most other steep mountains, since your footing is hardly ever in doubt.

guiding you through a piney forest toward a lean-to at 1.4 miles. The shelter stands guard over a key trail junction, with a wide trail leading left back down the mountain, and the summit trail leading right.

Taking that right turn, you come a

39

Silver Lake Mountains

TOTAL DISTANCE: 1.8 miles round-trip	
HIKING TIME: 1.25 hours	
VERTICAL RISE: 900 feet	
TRAILHEAD GPS COORDINATES: N44° 30' 38.6" W73° 50' 59.7"	

It might seem odd that a small mountain would have a plural name—that is, until you drive towards the Silver Lake Mountains from the south and see the multiple rock-scarred summits. This is not a one-off peak, but an extended family of little summits. The range is as handsome to look at as it is to climb.

Only the western end of the range falls on Forest Preserve land, though, and the state hiking trail ends at the first summit it encounters. But Silver Lake is an example of a short hike that pays big dividends. For less than a mile's worth of climbing you are rewarded with a very fine view across Taylor Pond and Silver Lake, the two side-by-side lakes that lie between you and lofty Whiteface Mountain. This is a highly enjoyable little outing, and one of the finest family hikes in the northern Adirondacks.

This area is somewhat isolated from other popular hiking areas in the Adirondacks, but not by a great distance. The nearby state campground at Taylor Pond is a convenient place to stay if you wish to explore this area further. Hiking trails encircle that lake, and the nearby nature trail at The Nature Conservancy's Silver Lake Bog Preserve is suitable for every age. For the more adventurous, Catamount Mountain is almost a mandatory climb. From the perch at the top of the western Silver Lake Mountain, you can see all of these spots and plan an extended weekend of hiking.

GETTING THERE

The key to finding this trail is, appropriately enough, Silver Lake Road. From NY 9N in Ausable Forks, turn onto North Main Street at the blinking light, then turn left onto Silver Lake Road. Follow it through the hamlet of Black Brook and past the Taylor Pond Campground

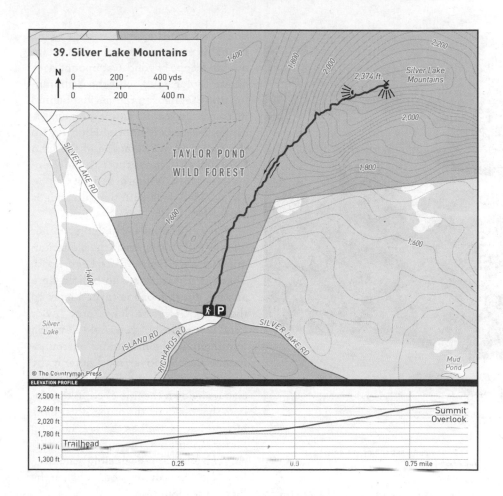

TAYLOR POND
WILD FOREST

2,374 ft.

Silver Lake
Mountains

2,200

2,000

1,800

1,600

1,400

2,000

1,800

1,600

Silver
Lake

ISLAND RD

RICHARDS RD

SILVER LAKE RD

Mud
Pond

© The Countryman Press

ELEVATION PROFILE

2,500 ft			
2,260 ft			Summit
2,020 ft			Overlook
1,780 ft			
1,540 ft	Trailhead		
1,300 ft	0.25	0.5	0.75 mile

entrance. The trailhead for Silver Lake Mountain will be on the right, 11 miles from Ausable Forks.

Alternatively, you can approach the mountain from NY 3 to the north. At Clayburg, turn south onto Silver Lake Road and follow it past Silver Lake at the small resort community of Hawkeye. There will be no views of the cliffs from this direction, but the trailhead will be on the left at 6.8 miles.

THE HIKE

Short trails such as this are almost self-explanatory. The hike begins on an old logging road leading northeast from the parking area, but it soon veers left to begin the climb. The first phase of the hike is through a hardwood forest on a wide, somewhat eroded track. There is a shoulder of the mountain rising above you on your left, and you seem to be heading for the saddle that divides it from the main part of the mountain.

Then the trail narrows and veers right, bringing you to a patch of open rock that teases at the possibility of a view without delivering on that potential. The character of the forest changes quickly here, though. The summit of Silver Lake is notable for its extensive stand of red pines, which start to appear at this point. The grade is gentle for a

SILVER LAKE FROM THE TOP OF ITS NAMESAKE MOUNTAIN

bodies of water appear as near twins from this perspective, with a mountainous landscape beyond. Catamount rises above Taylor Pond, with the Wilmington and Stephenson ranges just behind it. You can trace the zigzagging course of the Veterans Memorial Highway up the slopes of Whiteface, and the long ridgeline that constitutes the McKenzie Mountain Wilderness to its right. The wooded peak with the thin slide is Moose Mountain.

The trail continues climbing another 0.1 mile to its terminus on the main summit, 0.9 mile from Silver Lake Road. There is a wide vista to behold here as well, but this one is turned more to the south. Of the two lakes, only Taylor Pond is visible, but your field of vision now includes the mountains surrounding the Ausable River, most notably the Jay Range. From the summit you can also look down the line of clifflike summits that make up the other Silver Lake Mountains, as well as the neighboring Potter Mountains. The only things marring this view are the unsightly human-made clearings directly below you at the foot of the mountain.

If your intent is to photograph the view of the two lakes, then the best time to climb Silver Lake is in the morning. Otherwise take your time on this hike and enjoy each of the two main vistas, both of which are filled with sunshine on any clear day. Some people might find it tempting to continue along the ridgeline to see what else the Silver Lake Mountains have to offer, but for the average hiker the main summit where the trail ends is a perfectly good place to turn back toward the trailhead.

short distance as it hugs the northern side of the ridgeline. Again, there are some teasing views in this section, but nothing that opens up upon an unobstructed vista.

That describes the first half of the climb. The second half of the trail is very steep, with a few sections of rock steps and a few places where you are just climbing on exposed bedrock. The red pines part to reveal the first view, located just below the main summit. This one is the probably the most crowd-pleasing, as it reveals Silver Lake and Taylor Pond simultaneously. Both

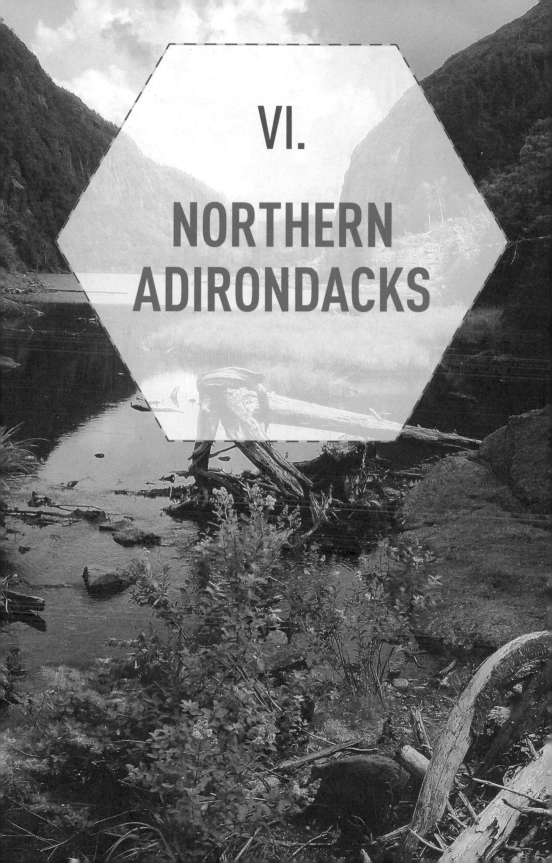

VI.

NORTHERN ADIRONDACKS

40

Avalanche Pass and the MacIntyre Range

TOTAL DISTANCE: 11.7-mile loop with 2 miles in side trips

HIKING TIME: 9 hours

VERTICAL RISE: 2,985 feet, not including side trips

TRAILHEAD GPS COORDINATES: N44° 10' 59.0" W73° 57' 49.5"

Algonquin Peak is the second tallest mountain in the Adirondacks, just 230 feet shy of its nearest competitor, Mount Marcy, but in many respects the two mountains are twins. Both exceed 5,000 feet in elevation (Algonquin's summit is 5,115 feet above sea level) and both are capped with acres of open rock and fragile alpine vegetation. The mountains are just a few miles apart from each other, and each forms the centerpiece of the other's view.

Both mountains stand in the central portion of the High Peaks Wilderness, a region as thrilling for hikers to explore as any national park. It is a grand environment, filled with soaring cliffs, rock-filled passes, and lakes pinched in the narrow spaces between mountains. This is also the most highly used area in the Adirondack Park, with thousands of people on any given day. Trailhead parking spaces disappear early, all dogs must be leashed, and campers must store all food and toiletries in bear-proof plastic canisters. Trails are very well worn, and summit stewards stand guard on the summit to educate people about the fragile alpine environment.

In a way, the High Peaks have fallen victim to their own success. For decades, this was the one part of the Adirondacks that was touted above all others as a destination for hiking, beginning in 1878, when Henry Van Hoevenberg built the original Adirondack Lodge on Heart Lake. This was billed as a base camp from which guests could venture forth onto the mountain trails, many of which had been cut by Van Hoevenberg and his crew. The innovation of these trails was that they were maintained well enough that a wider number of people could follow them—in contrast with the primitive tracks that only the experienced guides could follow.

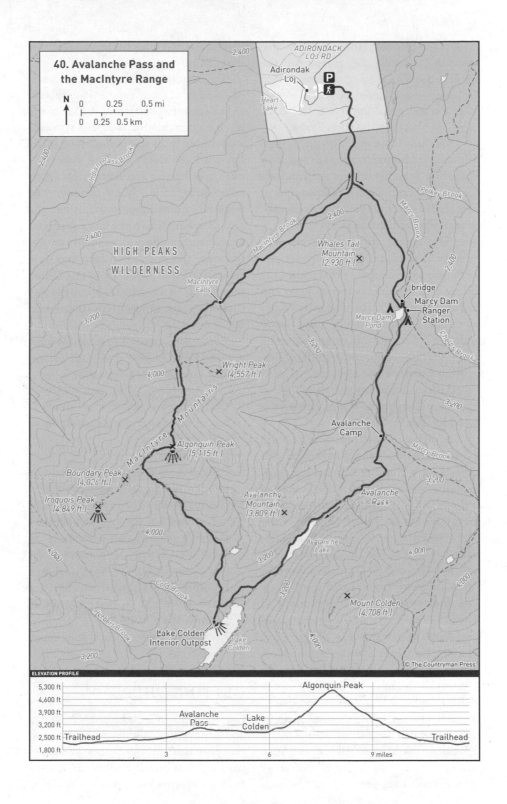

40. Avalanche Pass and the MacIntyre Range

N
0   0.25   0.5 mi
0   0.25   0.5 km

ADIRONDACK LOJ RD

Adirondak Loj

Heart Lake

HIGH PEAKS WILDERNESS

Indian Pass Brook

MacIntyre Brook

MacIntyre Falls

Whales Tail Mountain (2,930 ft.) ✕

bridge
Marcy Dam Ranger Station

Marcy Dam Pond

Pelkey Brook

Marcy Brook

Phelps Brook

Wright Peak (4,557 ft.) ✕

Avalanche Camp

Algonquin Peak (5,115 ft.)

MacIntyre Mountains

Boundary Peak (4,026 ft.) ✕

Iroquois Peak (4,849 ft.) ✕

Avalanche Mountain (3,809 ft.) ✕

Avalanche Pass

Avalanche Lake

Mount Colden (4,708 ft.) ✕

Cold Brook

Herbert Brook

Lake Colden Interior Outpost

Lake Colden

© The Countryman Press

ELEVATION PROFILE

5,300 ft
4,600 ft
3,900 ft
3,200 ft
2,500 ft
1,800 ft

Trailhead
Avalanche Pass
Lake Colden
Algonquin Peak
Trailhead

3   6   9 miles

A major fire swept through the mountains in June 1903, destroying Adirondack Lodge. The logging operations that followed erased most of Van Hoevenberg's trails, resulting in a brief "Dark Age" for hiking in the High Peaks.

This came to an end, though, in 1911, when Van Hoevenberg returned as a founding member of the Adirondack Camp and Trail Club, which sought to restore the old trail system and enhance it with the installation of the first lean-tos. The intent was to promote the greater Lake Placid region for tourism, bringing more people to the mountains by making wilderness travel easier and more convenient. When the state began to target the High Peaks for land acquisition in 1921, they further improved upon Van Hoevenberg's trail design by adding standardized signs and colored metal disks so that any tourist could find their way through the woods without the need for a guide.

The advent of the Adirondack Mountain Club (ADK for short) coincided with this new era of self-reliant hiking. ADK began as a small organization, less than a thousand strong, and at first its members were merely the consumers of the High Peaks scenery. When a new lodge at Heart Lake opened in 1927—this time spelled Adirondak Loj as a tribute to Melvil Dewey, inventor of the Dewey Decimal System and a proponent of simplified spelling—ADK members were the primary patrons. The club did not acquire the property until the late 1950s.

Now, ADK is a minor fiefdom in control of the busiest trailhead in the Adirondacks, with a year-round campground adjacent to the rebuilt Loj, and a visitor information center located in the spacious parking area. All of its facilities are open to the public, and the former Van Hoevenberg property remains an ideal base camp for hiking adventures in the mountains.

The hiking opportunities are numerous, and all of them are excellent insofar as the scenery is concerned. One of the most memorable hikes is this 11.7-mile loop, which leads up through Avalanche Pass to Lake Colden before venturing over the MacIntyre Range, of which Algonquin is the highest member. The terrain is exceedingly difficult and the miles are long. The route has you scrambling over boulders and ladders as you navigate the pass, then laboring up a steep slope that seems to go on forever. But there is so much to see along the way that one of the biggest risks is running out of daylight.

Remember, this is an extremely busy area, and with crowds come regulations. The most important rules are as follows:

- Dogs must be leashed at all times.
- Camping is permitted at designated sites only.
- No campfires.
- Backpackers must store all food and toiletries in portable bear-proof canisters, which can be rented from ADK at the trailhead information center.
- Day-use parties can consist of no more than fifteen people; overnight groups are limited to eight people.
- Snowshoes are required wherever there are eight or more inches of snow on the ground.
- Everything that you carry in must be carried out.

GETTING THERE

From downtown Lake Placid, take NY 73 south past the Olympic ski jumping complex to Adirondack Loj Road and turn right, south. It begins in an open field with tremendous mountain views, including your first glimpse of Algonquin Peak. Follow this road all the way to its end, at the Adirondack Mountain Club's entrance booth, 4.6 miles from the main highway. The parking area is to the left of the booth. The club does charge a fee for parking; if there is no attendant on hand, you can pay at the hikers' information center at the corner of the lot. See ADK's website at www.adk.org for more information on rates and services.

THE HIKE

By venturing down these trails, you are entering a place that has been trodden by many thousands of boots, going back well over a century. This hike is less about discovering a hidden beauty that few have seen and more of a tour of all the famous sights. Pick a day in early summer when daylight is longest, eat a good breakfast, and arrive as early as you can. Then plan for a full day on the trail.

Because Avalanche Lake is such a wonderful distraction, I recommend executing this loop in a clockwise circuit, beginning with the trek through the pass. This does entail a very steep climb up the mountain, though, and so not everyone may agree with me. But it does take time to get through Avalanche Pass, and for daylight budgeting purposes it is better if you do that part of the hike first.

The trail begins at the far east end of the hiker's parking lot on the ADK property, marked by a registration booth. It ventures into the woods and turns south, passing several club trails and crossing a stream on a long boardwalk at 0.4 mile. You remain on ADK land for most of the first mile, where a sign marks the boundary of the High Peaks

Wilderness. A moment later, at 1 mile, the direct trail to Algonquin turns right. That is the way you will be returning many hours from now.

Bear left at the junction, slowly climbing around the foot of the mountains to the site of Marcy Dam at 2.2 miles. Until 2011 this was the location of an overbuilt dam that impounded a small reflecting pool, with entrancing views of Mount Colden and Wright Peak. The structure was severely damaged by Hurricane Irene, and DEC has been slowly dismantling it ever since so that all the sediment from the pond does not flush all at once into the Ausable River.

The trail now detours downstream from the dam site to a footbridge before returning to the east side of Marcy Dam, where at 2.4 miles you find a ranger station and a major trail junction. Keep right on the trail to Avalanche Lake, which continues south alongside Marcy Brook past a sequence of lean-tos. The last trailside shelter is at a former logging shanty site called Avalanche Camp at 3.4 miles, with the modern lean-to located back in the woods at the end of a short side trail.

From the Avalanche Camp junction, the trail to Avalanche Lake begins the first real climb of the day, with an ascent of 400 feet in the next 0.5 mile. The trail tops out at Avalanche Pass, notable for its view of an impressive slide on the lower slopes of Mount Colden, where a 1999 landslide deposited a layer of stacked dead trees that is still decomposing beside the trail. You then begin to descend a little toward Avalanche Lake, with the trail squeezed between cliffs and boulders that harbor pockets of cool air.

You reach the north end of the lake at 4.5 miles, where you may be puzzled by what you see. There is no doubting

Avalanche Lake's scenic beauty, but the sheer cliffs that hem in both shorelines seem to leave no place for a hiking trail. Not to worry, because the solution to this is a series of ladders and catwalks along the lake's western shoreline. The going is slow but exceedingly fun, sort of like a jungle gym for grownups. The wooden catwalks bolted into the side of the cliff are often called "Hitch-up-Matildas" in reference to a popular story from the nineteenth century. At the time, hikers navigated their way around the lake by walking on a ledge that was partly underwater. As a woman named Matilda got a piggyback ride from her guide, she began to slip downward toward the water. Her loved ones urged her to hitch further up the guide's back to remain dry, thus inspiring the name that persists to this day.

The hike around Avalanche Lake is therefore slow but fun—and the view is nothing to sneeze at either. The titanic cliffs on Mount Colden tower above the water like a midtown skyscraper, slashed by the massive trench known as the Colden Trap Dike. About three-quarters of the way down the lake, you have a dead-on view of the trap dike, which appears like a vertical canyon rising up the mountainside. Nearly all of the mountain to its right is bare rock. The long gap in the cliff once encased a softer mineral that has long since eroded away, and today it is used as the most challenging climbing route to the summit of Colden.

Avalanche Lake is only 0.4 mile long, and eventually you reach the far end. At 5.3 miles you reach a junction near the north end of Lake Colden, where you need to bear right, and 0.4 mile later (5.7 miles total) you reach the beginning of the trail to Algonquin. Before you begin the climb you should see Lake Colden, so bear left and follow the signs to the Lake Colden Interior Outpost (the official name of a DEC ranger station) to find the nearest view of this beautiful lake.

The trail to the summit of Algonquin from the lake is one of the steepest trails you'll find. But it is also quite pretty, beginning with an attractive climb alongside a small stream with several cascades. The trail is not confined to just one side of the brook; there are multiple crossings, including a pool with stepping stones along the edge. There is a log ladder, and then a brief stint on a bare rock slide with views of Mount Colden.

Eventually a set of rock steps leads

COLDEN TRAP DIKE

MOUNT COLDEN AND LAKE COLDEN FROM IROQUOIS PEAK

you away from the brook, marking the start of the steepest part of the climb. The steps only lead so far, though; above them the trail is very rocky, with numerous ledges. This unevenness becomes smooth bedrock, and at 7.3 miles—after two hours of climbing—the grade finally eases and you reach a large cairn indicating the start of the unmarked trail to Iroquois Peak, described below.

Bear right at the cairn for the final 0.4-mile, 350-foot push to Algonquin's summit. The trees part almost immediately, leaving you exposed on this enormous rocky cone. The trail is marked by a combination of cairns, scree walls, and yellow paint daubs. It is extremely important that you stay on the trail because you are now in an alpine environment that exists in only a few small patches in New York State. What appear to be simple grasses are actually communities of dwarf plants that have adapted to this harsh environment. They are very fragile and damage easily when trampled. When you reach the summit at 7.7 miles a steward will likely be on duty to help you identify the alpine flora—or to at least remind you to watch where you step.

Only one other mountain in the entire summit panorama is higher than Algonquin. There are mountains everywhere, including several that looked quite imposing when you began the day but which now seem diminutive. Mount Colden, with its zebra stripes of rock slides, fits into this category. Mount Marcy is the tall, conical summit just behind it. Other intriguing views include the massive cliffs at Indian Pass (Hike #41) and the distant village of Lake Placid. Because there are no trees of any kind, Algonquin's summit is very exposed. Be prepared for just about any weather condition, from cold winds to withering heat.

The continuing trail back to Adirondack Loj leads northerly off the summit, still through the alpine environment for about 0.3 mile. Even when you reenter the woods, the way is still steep, with the trail worn to bedrock. At 8.5 miles you reach the side trail to Wright Peak, one of the optional detours described below, but the main trail bears left and continues its long plunge off the mountain.

You pass a small rock knob a short distance off the trail, then step gingerly down a steep ledge. At 9.2 miles you pass a cascade known as MacIntyre Falls, which might just be a damp, mossy ledge in midsummer. The slope moderates after this point, though it never stops losing altitude until you reach the junction with the trail to Marcy Dam at 10.7 miles. After turning left here, it is just a 1-mile hike back to the public parking lot at Adirondack Loj.

SIDE TRIPS

1. **Iroquois Peak.** This 4,849-foot summit is Algonquin's smaller sibling, a rocky knob that suffers in stature only because of its close proximity to a 5,000-footer. A well-used unmarked trail leads out along the crest of the MacIntyre ridgeline, beginning at a prominent cairn at treeline on Algonquin's southwest side. Where the main trail immediately climbs above the treeline, this side trail to Iroquois delves deeper into the thick woods, crossing a soggy saddle to Boundary Peak, then another soggy saddle to the ledges on Iroquois. The wet areas between these summits are spanned with wooden puncheons, so even though this trail is not marked, it is not hard to find. This side trip adds a total of 1.2 miles and a full hour of hiking to the day's agenda.

2. **Wright Peak.** By the time you reach the beginning of the side trail to Wright you may have long concluded you'll never climb another mountain again, especially after the long slog up Algonquin. But Algonquin, Iroquois, and Wright are often hiked as a trifecta, and so you may change your mind and decide you want to visit one more summit after all. This side trail to Wright Peak is marked and signed, beginning at a junction just 0.8 mile northeast of Algonquin's summit. It is 0.4 mile long and climbs 585 feet, the upper half of that being on the steep and exposed summit cone. Wright is frequently windy. Its view is quite photogenic, limited in scope only by the looming presence of Algonquin. This side trip adds 0.8 mile and an hour to the overall hike.

41

Indian Pass

TOTAL DISTANCE: 10 miles end-to-end

HIKING TIME: 6 hours

ELEVATION CHANGE: 1,825 feet

TRAILHEAD GPS COORDINATES: N44° 10' 59.0" W73° 57' 49.5" (northern trailhead at Heart Lake); N44° 05' 19.1" W74° 03' 21.5" (southern trailhead at Upper Works)

The first surveyors and explorers to penetrate the Adirondack Mountains in the 1830s weren't here to catalogue the highest peaks so they could proceed to climb each and every one. They were drawn by the Romantic notion of sublime beauty—that in rugged and wild landscapes could be sensed the hand of God. Scientists, poets, artists, and woodsmen all came not just to reach the loftiest summits, but to explore the chasms between the mountains.

In the nineteenth century, one of the most famous features was Indian Pass, a nearly impassible notch at the foot of the tallest cliffs in the Adirondacks. It was the subject of paintings and books (and maybe one or two tall tales). Perhaps more than any other location in the park, it epitomized the idea of sublimity: a place so inhospitable and immense that it dwarfed the travelers who dared pass through it, making them feel just a little anxious about their place in the universe.

Then, 100 years later, the notion of peak bagging began to take hold of the public imagination, and places like Indian Pass—located amidst the High Peaks, but not on a direct route to any of the summits—became landmarks that were more often admired from afar rather than visited in person.

Thus the pass remains a well-known landmark today, even though a large portion of the people who throng to the High Peaks have probably never been there. If there is a place where you can be at the heart of the largest wilderness in the northeastern United States and actually experience some small measure of solitude, this might be one of them.

The best way to enjoy Indian Pass is to hike through it, starting from ADK's Heart Lake property near Lake Placid and ending at the Upper Works

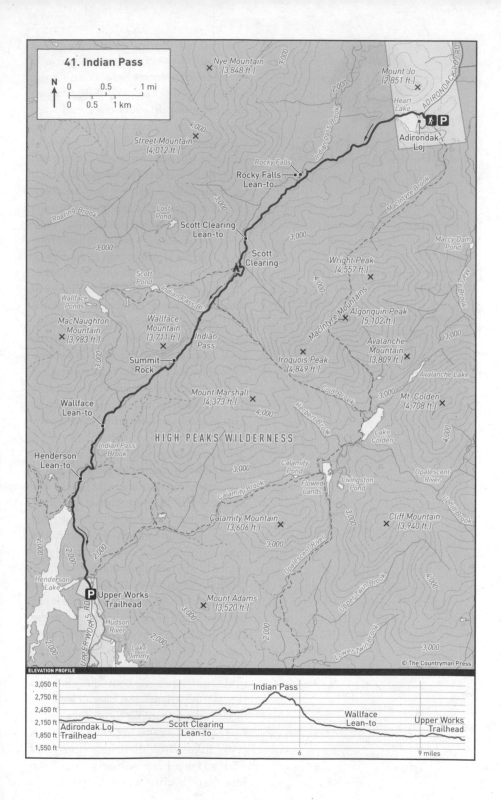

41. Indian Pass

N

| 0 | 0.5 | 1 mi |
| 0 | 0.5 | 1 km |

Nye Mountain
(3,848 ft.)

Mount Jo
(2,851 ft.)

Street Mountain
(4,012 ft.)

Heart Lake

Adirondak Loj

Rocky Falls

Rocky Falls Lean-to

Lost Pond

Scott Clearing Lean-to

Roaring Brook

Scott Clearing

Wright Peak
(4,557 ft.)

Marcy Dam Pond

Scott Pond

Indian Pass Br.

Wallface Ponds

MacNaughton Mountain
(3,983 ft.)

Wallface Mountain
(3,711 ft.)

Indian Pass

Algonquin Peak
(5,102 ft.)

Avalanche Mountain
(3,809 ft.)

Summit Rock

Iroquois Peak
(4,849 ft.)

Avalanche Lake

Mount Marshall
(4,373 ft.)

Mt. Colden
(4,708 ft.)

Wallface Lean-to

Cold Brook

Lake Colden

HIGH PEAKS WILDERNESS

Henderson Lean-to

Indian Pass Brook

Calamity Pond

Opalescent River

Flowed Lands

Livingston Pond

Calamity Brook

Calamity Mountain
(3,606 ft.)

Cliff Mountain
(3,940 ft.)

Henderson Lake

Opalescent River

Upper Works Trailhead

Hudson River

Mount Adams
(3,520 ft.)

Lake Jimmy

© The Countryman Press

ELEVATION PROFILE

3,050 ft				Indian Pass			
2,750 ft							
2,450 ft							
2,150 ft			Scott Clearing			Wallface	Upper Works
1,850 ft	Adirondak Loj		Lean-to			Lean-to	Trailhead
1,550 ft	Trailhead						

3   6   9 miles

trailhead near Newcomb. This 10-mile transect through the High Peaks Wilderness is an adventure through both nature and history, with waypoints that include lakes, waterfalls, lumber dam sites, lean-tos, and of course the storied Indian Pass itself.

Most of the terrain is moderate in nature, and indeed for the bulk of those 10 miles the trail travels peacefully through the valleys at each end of the pass, each with its own stream called Indian Pass Brook. But the section of the trail leading through the pass is anything but tame. The climb up from the north entails stepping from one slippery rock to the next, and the descent involves steep ledges and several ladders. The pass itself is only about 0.5 mile long, so be sure to savor it while you are there.

GETTING THERE

Because this is a point-to-point hike, beginning at one trailhead and ending at another, it is necessary to spot a car at the southern terminus before proceeding to Lake Placid and the northern trailhead at Heart Lake. Although the trail distance between these two points is only 10 miles, the driving distance is closer to 68.5 miles and may take two hours.

To find the southern trailhead, take I-87 to Exit 29 in North Hudson and drive west on Blue Ridge Road (also called Boreas Road) for 17 miles. Here, make the right turn for Tahawus. Follow this road, CR 25, to a fork at 6.3 miles. Turn left and continue to the Upper Works parking area at the end of the road, 9.7 miles from Blue Ridge/Boreas Road. Leave a vehicle here for the end of your hike.

Then backtrack to I-87 and drive

north to Exit 30. Follow US 9 north, then NY 73 west through Keene Valley and Keene. Along the way you pass through Chapel Pond Pass and Cascade Pass, distant cousins of Indian Pass.

Just before you reach Lake Placid, Adirondack Loj Road turns left, south toward the mountains. It begins in an open field with tremendous views, including your first glimpse of Indian Pass. Follow this road all the way to its end, at the Adirondack Mountain Club's entrance booth 4.6 miles from the main highway. The parking area is to the left of the booth. The club does charge a fee for parking; if there is no attendant on hand, you can pay at the hikers' information center at the corner of the lot. See ADK's website at www.adk.org for more information on rates and services.

THE HIKE

As described in Hike 40, the public parking area at ADK's Heart Lake property is a bustling place. If you don't arrive early enough in the day (especially on weekends), you may not find any parking spaces left. But most of the people here will be heading in the opposite direction, toward Marcy Dam and all the mountain trails that branch out from that hub. Indian Pass is to the west, so your first task is to cross the road and find the beginning of the trail near the club's entrance booth.

The first 0.5 mile of the trail passes through the core of ADK's property on what begins as a well-manicured path. You circle around the north side of Heart Lake and pass the side trails leading up to Mount Jo. Stay on the main trail without making any turns. In less than twenty minutes, you reach the last of the club's side trails, and at 0.6 mile you enter state land.

Not much happens in the next 1.4 miles, as you are in a lowland forest on a slow approach to Indian Pass Brook. But 2 miles into the hike, a well-used side trail leads right toward Rocky Falls, an impressive ledge on Indian Pass Brook with its own nearby lean-to. The side trail creates a jug-handle loop off the main trail, meaning that you can make the detour to Rocky Falls and return without backtracking, the only penalty being the extra 0.1 mile it adds to the total hiking distance.

The main trail resumes its journey through the valley, at times rocky and at times muddy, but mostly level all the way to the Scott Clearing Lean-to at 3.6 miles. Despite the name of this shelter, it is located in a wooded area along a major tributary to Indian Pass Brook—a pleasant setting, though not as scenic as what is about to come.

The actual Scott Clearing is a major landmark just 0.2 mile further up the trail. Ford the stream in front of the lean-to and continue to a T-junction at 3.8 miles. The large rock wall ahead of you in the woods was part of a dam built by lumbermen. Indian Pass is a left turn at the junction, but it's worth taking a moment of your time to explore the dam and its environs. The structure is completely breached, but an open wetland remains above the dam site with a great profile view of Wallface Mountain and Indian Pass. A small clearing next to the wall is one of the more unusual designated campsites you'll find in the Adirondacks.

The marked trail ventures inland to detour around the former lakebed, keeping to higher ground before returning to Indian Pass Brook. The valley is now much narrower, forcing the trail and the brook to keep much closer company. At 4.6 miles you pass the side trail through Cold Brook Pass, the last junction you will encounter this side of Wallface Mountain.

A moment later, at 4.7 miles, you encounter the first of two fords on Indian Pass Brook, with the second coming just 250 feet later. The brook is quite large, and you may need to take your boots off to keep them dry as you walk through the water.

But the climb into Indian Pass begins not long after the second ford. All semblance of a foot trail disappears for a while as you make your way up the bouldery slope; rather than walking along an earthen footpath, you are choosing your footing carefully, as you step from one slippery rock to another. This risk of a slip and fall is very real. The elevation gain from the last ford of the brook all the way up to the height-of-land at 5.3 miles is only about 400 feet, but the terrain is very rough.

The highest point in Indian Pass is not its most interesting feature, but this is where you need to start slowing your pace and enjoying your surroundings. Just 200 feet into the pass, you might hear a cascade on a small stream in the woods to the left of the trail, followed by open meadows with the first close-up views of the massive cliffs on Wallface Mountain—the tallest cliffs in the Adirondacks. Giant boulders fill the valley, probably debris from avalanches that occurred centuries or millennia ago. Peregrine falcons nest on the cliffs above you, forcing seasonal closings of the rock climbing routes there.

Just as you arrive at the far end of the pass at 5.7 miles, a side trail leads right to Summit Rock. The scenic perch that has attracted artists since the Romantic era is located 130 feet away, overlooking the valley southwest beyond the foot of Wallface's cliffs.

THE CLIFFS ON WALLFACE LOOM ABOVE INDIAN PASS

TRAIL LADDER BELOW SUMMIT ROCK

The steep descent out of Indian Pass begins just 120 feet past Summit Rock, where you encounter the first of three log ladders assisting you down the steep and rocky mountainside. The footing on this side of the pass is probably less treacherous than your ascent, but some of the ledges in your way are just too tall and steep, hence the need for the ladders.

After the third ladder, the grade becomes more moderate, and the trail eventually leads back to the floor of a valley. The brook here is also called Indian Pass Brook, although it has no connection with the other brook to the north of Wallface. That one flowed north toward the Ausable River, whereas this one flows south to the Hudson.

At 6.7 miles you cross the outlet stream of the Wallface Ponds, which have their own hidden cascades about 0.2 mile upstream. The trail parallels the north bank of Indian Pass Brook, leading to a side trail at 7.2 miles to the Wallface Lean-to, about 100 feet away.

You reach another junction at 7.9 miles, just after crossing the brook on a high footbridge. Bear right, arriving at the Henderson Lean-to at 8.2 miles and the trail to Duck Hole at 8.4 miles. South of this point, the trail becomes a little less savory as you enter a section of forest acquired by the state in 2003, and therefore logged at a much more recent date. It's not the past logging that makes the trail less pleasant, but the wet and muddy road that it follows. Look closely for the detours onto the nearby hillside that save you from some of the nastiest sections. Along the way, there is only one brief glimpse of Henderson Lake to your right.

At 9.6 miles, next to a desolate wetland, you intersect the main hiking trail to Flowed Lands, and from here the rest of the hike is along an abandoned road with a surface of coarse gravel. The bridge that you cross a moment later spans a stream that may not appear that special but is actually the beginning of the mighty Hudson River. A ten-minute walk along the old road leads you to the parking area at Upper Works, where your hike ends at 10 miles.

42

Ampersand Mountain

TOTAL DISTANCE: 5.2 miles round-trip	
HIKING TIME: 4 hours	
VERTICAL RISE: 1,810 feet	
TRAILHEAD GPS COORDINATES: N44° 15' 04.3" W74° 14' 22.4"	

Ampersand Mountain is a former fire tower summit that now stands guard over the northwestern corner of the High Peaks Wilderness. No tower is needed here for a view, because the bald rock knob that constitutes the summit provides an outstanding vista in all directions. To the north is the lake country of the Saranac and Saint Regis chains, and to the south and east is the mountainous wilderness interior. Few summits provide such good views of both.

The trail to Ampersand is best described as short and steep. The route follows the course of the original trail, a route that has been used for generations. It was created at a time when no one anticipated the long-term maintenance problems of erosion, or understood the best way to build a sustainable trail. It simply follows the most direct line to the summit and never flinches. Several years ago it was "modernized" with the installation of rock steps along many of the more problematic pitches, although it is not clear that these have been sufficient to end the erosion problem. Many hikers choose to hike beside the steps, and so the issue persists.

This is an immensely popular hike, and often the number of cars parked at the trailhead exceeds the capacity of the parking area. State land stewards are mulling options to relocate and enlarge the trailhead.

GETTING THERE

The trailhead is a prominent feature on NY 3 between the villages of Tupper Lake and Saranac Lake. You will find it on the north side of the highway, 8.3 miles west of downtown Saranac, or 12.5 miles east of downtown Tupper.

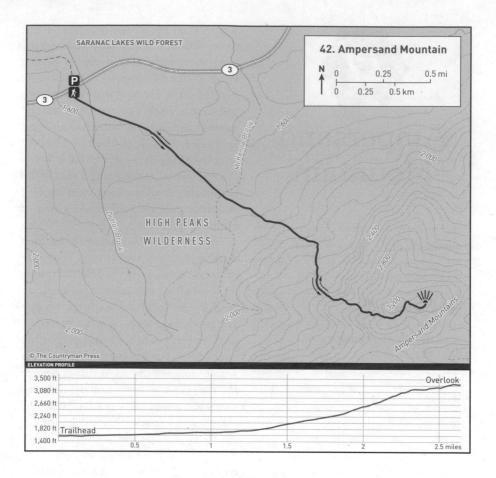

SARANAC LAKES WILD FOREST

3

3

1,600

McKenna Brook

1,600

2,000

HIGH PEAKS
WILDERNESS

Dutton Brook

2,400

2,800

3,200

2,000

2,000

2,000

© The Countryman Press

Ampersand Mountains

ELEVATION PROFILE

	0.5	1	1.5	2	2.5 miles

3,500 ft
3,080 ft
2,660 ft
2,240 ft
1,820 ft   Trailhead
1,400 ft

Overlook

A short trail to Middle Saranac Lake begins at this same location.

THE HIKE

The trail to Ampersand Mountain begins across the highway. The steep climbing does not begin right away, and in fact the first 1.6 miles of the trail are very pleasant. The route crosses Dutton Brook while you are still within earshot of the highway and then shoots southeast through a lowland forest that is tall and mature. The trail is reasonably dry despite the high traffic volumes, and it leads through several peaceful stands of hemlocks. There are small streams to step across, a patch of old blowdown where new growth shades the mossy remains of the fallen trees, and a birch tree with all of its roots standing well above the ground—left exposed when an old stump rotted away. Basically, the first part of this trail is all about the sheer joy of being in a wilderness forest.

Slowly you begin to climb, with the trail pulling near a small, unnamed stream. At 1.6 miles, or about forty minutes from the highway, you reach a tiny clearing with the remains of a metal bedframe beside the trail. This was the site of the observer's cabin from the days when Ampersand's fire tower was manned every spring, summer, and fall.

The watchman who slept here climbed the mountain every day. Other than a handful of artifacts, little remains of that cabin today.

The trail angles south here and continues climbing gently, but soon it becomes obvious that you have reached the mountain proper and have embarked on the main ascent. There is no getting around the fact that the slope is steep and relentless.

The rock steps are helpful where they are present, but they are not a perfect solution. They were constructed with the narrow dimensions of the ideal foot trail, with the hopes that the peripheral areas would recover and fill with vegetation over time. That has not occurred, though; the muddy conditions flanking the steps prove that many hikers are bypassing them and perpetuating the conditions they were intended to replace. Part of the problem is that the steps did not address the issue of stream flow down the mountain's fall line; at times, they are a lively cascade of running water.

All that aside, don't let the management issues with the trail detract too much from the hike. Your vertical progress up the mountain is marked by transitions in the forest cover, from the hemlocks and hardwoods at the foot of the mountain, which soon give way to spruce and paper birch on the mid slopes, to the balsam fir that crowns much of the summit. Along the way are a few rock ledges here and there that

MIDDLE SARANAC LAKE IS JUST PART OF THE VIEW ON AMPERSAND

may require the use of your hands to pull yourself up.

The grade does not ease until you reach the multi-knobbed summit area at 2.3 miles, having just climbed over 1,000 feet in the last 0.7 mile since the cabin site. The trail is briefly level as it swings left between two false summits, but then it climbs past an enormous rock that intrudes into the walking space and conceals a long slot that is just wide enough to walk into. You might start to think you've overshot the summit when the trail starts to lead downhill again, but it swings right and begins the final steep scramble upward.

The trees part abruptly to reveal the bald summit knob, which appears as an imposing ledge but soon becomes a scenic wonder, once you reach the top. Yellow paint daubs on the rock lead the way across one high point with the most incredible views, then down and up to the flat area where the fire tower stood. There is no shortage of room to stake out your space to sit and enjoy lunch.

The view is outstanding! In one direction is the lake-studded expanse of Middle Saranac Lake, with Mount Arab rising above the distant buildings of Tupper Lake. There are lakes everywhere in that direction, as well as the scattered mid-sized mountains that characterize the northern Adirondacks. By turning 180° you have an equally enchanting view that includes the heart of the High Peaks Wilderness. Seward and Seymour are the nearest of those summits, just across the Ampersand Lake valley, but the view extends all the way to Algonquin, some 12 miles away. Whiteface can be seen to the northeast, and a piece of Long Lake appears amidst the foothills to the southwest.

Care must be taken on the steeper portions of the descent, especially if the rocks are wet or icy. Since the trail is located on the shady north side of the mountain, ice may very well linger here well into the spring, even after it has vanished from other locations.

43

Floodwood Mountain

TOTAL DISTANCE: 3.4 miles round-trip

HIKING TIME: 2 hours

VERTICAL RISE: 675 feet

TRAILHEAD GPS COORDINATES: N44° 20' 42.8" W74° 26' 43.3"

Floodwood Mountain stands just to the west of the most popular camping area in the northern Adirondacks: the Fish Creek Ponds and Rollins Pond state campgrounds. This mixed-use area includes numerous drive-in campsites for tents and RVs, as well as dozens of backcountry campsites scattered along the shoreline of the neighboring ponds. This is a beautiful area with grand forests and miles of waterways, and so the reasons for its popularity are no mystery.

The mountain stands on the sidelines of all this hubbub, close enough to offer a fine view of the Fish Creek Ponds but far enough out of the way to not share any of the crowds. The trailhead is really tucked in a corner of the forest where it is likely to be discovered by accident, but the trail is well defined and not difficult to follow. There are two summit views at the end of the trail, including the partially bald southern summit which is Floodwood Mountain's real surprise.

GETTING THERE

The trailhead for Floodwood Mountain is the last turn at the end of Floodwood Road, just before that gravel byway enters a gated private property.

To find it, follow NY 30 for about 4.3 miles north of the entrance to the Fish Creek Ponds and Rollins Pond campgrounds. The junction for Floodwood Road is located on a curve, so the turn comes up fast and is easy to miss. Floodwood is a sharp left turn.

The road is paved at first, but at 0.4 mile, bear left at a fork. The pavement ends and Floodwood Road becomes a bumpy gravel way through the forest. If you've never been here, you're in for a treat because Floodwood is one of the more scenic drives in the

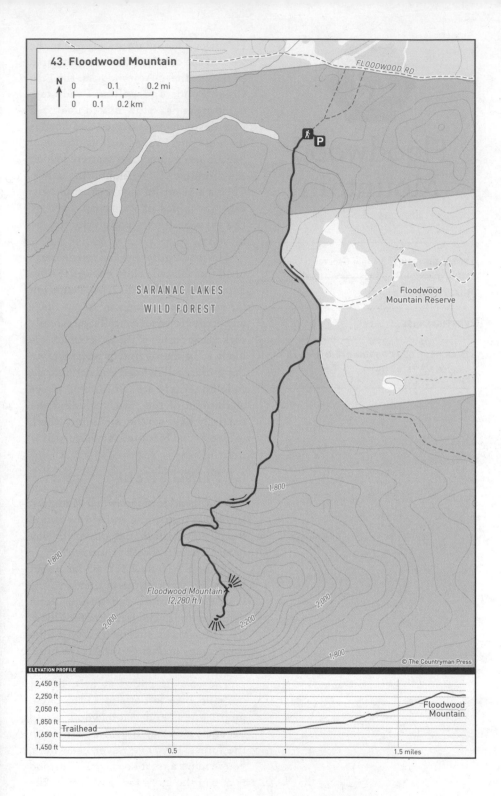

43. Floodwood Mountain

N

| 0 | 0.1 | 0.2 mi |

| 0 | 0.1 | 0.2 km |

FLOODWOOD RD

P

SARANAC LAKES
WILD FOREST

Floodwood
Mountain Reserve

1,800

1,800

Floodwood Mountain
(2,280 ft.)

2,000

2,000

2,200

1,800

© The Countryman Press

ELEVATION PROFILE

2,450 ft			
2,250 ft			Floodwood
2,050 ft			Mountain
1,850 ft			
1,650 ft	Trailhead		
1,450 ft			

| | 0.5 | 1 | 1.5 miles |

region. It passes close to five ponds, all on the south side of the road, including several with free drive-in campsites and good canoe access. Trails lead to several other ponds located just a little further into the woods.

After crossing a set of railroad tracks, you pass a canoe outfitter, two trails to Long Pond, and the access to East Pine Pond. Finally, 6.2 miles from the main highway, signs point left to the Flood-wood Mountain Reserve, just before the gate at the end of the public road. Make this left turn and follow the gravel driveway for 0.2 mile more to the public parking area, also on the left.

Note that Floodwood Road may be closed to traffic in the spring, from April through mid-May.

THE HIKE

Once you've located the parking area, the hike to Floodwood Mountain is far more straightforward. It begins by returning to the access road leading into the Floodwood Mountain Reserve, which is a Boy Scout property surrounded by state land. Heading south, the road reaches a gate and dips down to cross a stream that is subject to beaver flooding. It rises up a gentle grade and passes through a hardwood forest notable for its collection of birch trees. Three species share these woods, including yellow birch, paper birch, and gray birch; all three are common in the Adirondacks, but rarely do you see them all congregated together like this.

EARLY SPRING ON FLOODWOOD MOUNTAIN

At 0.5 mile the road forks, with the left branch leading downhill toward the private property and the right branch remaining level. Keep right, finding the start of the foot trail just 0.1 mile later on the right.

It is a welcome turn of events when you finally reach the foot trail, which leads to the west of south on a gentle grade through the hardwood forest. It is a narrow track, well-designed except for a few unfortunate muddy spots, with no indication that it is travelled as often as many other trails in the region. There are several stream crossings, each of them assisted with strategically placed stepping stones, as the trail makes its way to the foot of the mountain.

When the final ascent of the mountain begins, the trail alternates from steep to moderate. You quickly notice the pattern in which a bit of elevation is quickly gained in a tiring scramble, followed by a brief interlude where you traverse the slope for a short distance. The trail first approaches the mountain just below the steepest point of its northern slope, but as it climbs, it sidles over to the northwestern corner. Here, it locates a ramp-like spine, and the trail sharply turns left to follow this formation the remaining distance to the summit. Along the way you will find a ledge or two in your path, but on this hike even the steepest pitches are only minor obstacles.

The marked trail ends at the main summit, 1.6 miles from the public parking area. The view here is restricted but pleasant enough; it probably wouldn't exist at all if it were not for the fact that someone has been cutting trees below the ledge to preserve the opening. The view is northeast, past West Pine Pond toward the distant slopes of Long Pond Mountain and Saint Regis Mountain,

both of them in the Saint Regis Canoe Area north of Floodwood Road.

A sign points the way to the southern summit, although there are no further trail markers. Only a faint herd path spans the distance between the two summits. You really do want to make this side trip, because the southern summit is Floodwood's best feature. However, the toughest terrain features on the entire hike are found on this short, 0.1-mile-long path—perhaps explaining why the state declined to mark it as an official trail.

The herd path leads to a steep, rocky slope that pitches down into the gap between the two summits; the bedrock ramp is steep enough that your ability to maintain good footing is in doubt. Then, as soon as you scoot down that rock, you are presented with a ledge to scramble up, with a natural rock step to assist you. As soon as you reach the top of this one, you are on the southern summit.

Instead of one big bald patch with a single panorama, there are multiple openings to explore—so don't settle on the first view that you find. Walk around, seek out the various openings, and delight in the way that each one modifies and adds to the views you have already seen. (Just make sure you can find your way back to the herd path when you're done!) There are two primary elements to look for: the vista east past Rollins Pond to the mountains beyond Upper Saranac Lake, and the equally good view south past Wolf Pond to Tupper Lake. In the wedge between these two lines of sight are the High Peaks.

The herd path between the summits is faint, and finding it may be the biggest difficulty on the return hike. But once you are back on the marked state trail, it's literally all downhill back to the trailhead parking area.

44

Azure Mountain

TOTAL DISTANCE: 1.8 miles round-trip

HIKING TIME: 2 hours

VERTICAL RISE: 920 feet

TRAILHEAD GPS COORDINATES: N44° 32' 15.8" W74° 29' 04.0"

This is a short and sweet little hike in a part of the Adirondack Park that is well off the main travel corridors. Azure Mountain sits on a parcel of Forest Preserve that is virtually surrounded by private land, accessed by a long and bumpy gravel road. Despite its isolation—or perhaps because of it—this is a favorite hike, and its shortness makes it suitable for adventurous spirits of all ages.

For a small mountain (the summit is only about 2,500 feet in elevation), Azure has a remarkably sharp profile; from the perspective of the hunting camps located on the collection of beaver ponds due south of the peak, the conical silhouette must be a stunning sight. It is the largest in a band of small mountains extending westward into the industrial timberlands that dominate the landscape of the far northern Adirondacks. That string of mountains makes an intriguing sight when seen from other peaks, but Azure is the only summit in that range that is open to the public.

With no other large mountains in its way, Azure's view is far-ranging. The fire tower extends that vista in all directions, but the ground-level view from the mountain's main ledge is also quite good.

GETTING THERE

Follow NY 458 southeast from Saint Regis Falls for 4 miles, turning south onto Blue Mountain Road. The trailhead for Azure Mountain is 7.1 miles south along this bumpy byway, located at the end of a short driveway shaded by a plantation of Norway spruce. The road is plowed in the winter, but it's apt to be a bumpy experience. Note that this is a remote area, far from the nearest services.

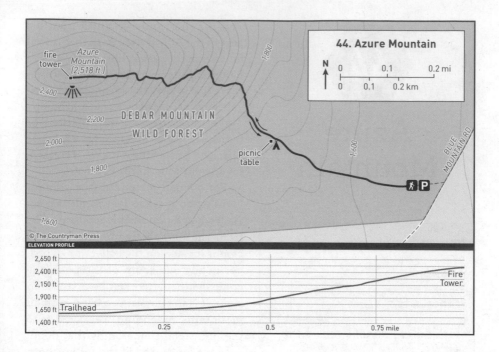

THE HIKE

This is hardly a complicated route to follow; there is only the one trail, and it leads straight up the eastern flank of the mountainside. There are no misleading junctions, no difficult scrambles, no places where the path is vague and difficult to discern. It's a straightforward climb from the bottom of the mountain to its top—moderately steep, somewhat eroded, but well-traveled and suitable for children.

Heading westward from the parking area, the hiking trail follows an old roadbed through a fen with a few scraggly balsam fir trees, and then it climbs gently through a hardwood forest. In fact, most of the mountain is covered with hardwoods, all the way up to the summit. Standard Adirondack conifers such as red spruce make only a minimal appearance on this hike.

At 0.3 mile, just ten minutes into the hike, the road grade ends at a campsite marked by a fireplace and a picnic table. Step across the small stream that flows beside this site and follow the continuing trail as it begins to climb more noticeably. At the foot of the mountain, the path cuts at an angle through an opening that is vegetated more thickly with brambles than with trees.

From here the trail is an old-fashioned climb: straight up the mountain with no real pauses. The way will seem steep to some people, but the trail has the virtue of being short. It passes near some interesting rock outcrops that may provide den sites for wildlife, and indeed, if you look closely, you may see evidence that porcupines have been busily gnawing away at the bark on tree branches all around the trail. On the uppermost slopes, paper birch begins to appear.

The summit forest is open and almost park-like, with just a scattering of the spruce trees that you would normally expect to see on a 2,500-foot summit. The grade slowly eases, and then the fire tower appears ahead of you. The hiking trail leads you directly to the foot of the tower, which is the only place where you'll get the full 360° view. However, a wide path with wooden steps leads left down to the mountain's main ledge, which overlooks a private forest with a chain of small beaver meadows. It looks like an unbroken wilderness at first, until you examine the scene more closely and spot the logging roads and scattered small camps. The more popular landmarks in the Adirondacks, including the next nearest fire tower summit, Saint Regis Mountain, all seem a long way away.

As easy and straightforward as the climb was, so too will be the descent. For the amount of effort invested in this short little gem, you are unlikely to leave Azure with any complaints.

SNOW SQUALLS APPROACHING AZURE MOUNTAIN

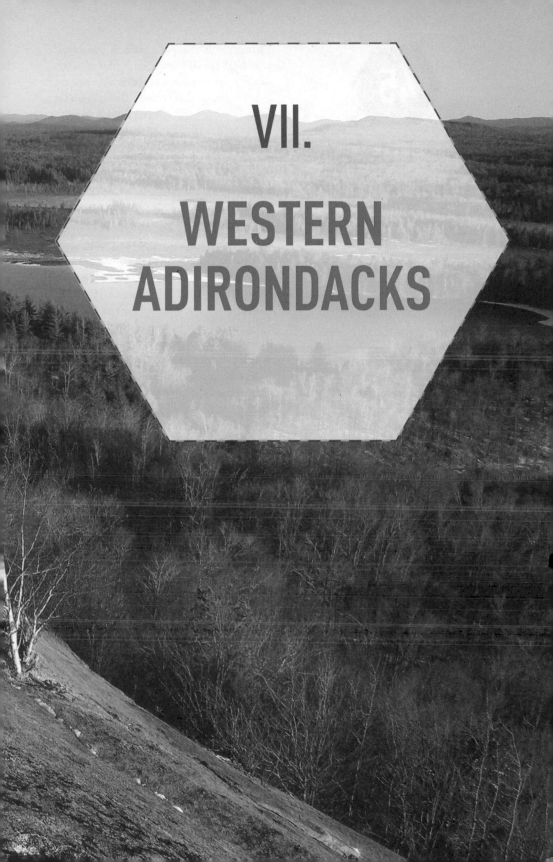

VII.

WESTERN ADIRONDACKS

Lake Lila and Frederica Mountain

TOTAL DISTANCE: 9.2 miles round-trip

HIKING TIME: 3 hours

VERTICAL RISE: 460 feet

TRAILHEAD GPS COORDINATES: N44° 01' 06.8" W74° 43' 48.3"

Throughout the Adirondack Park you will find small mountains paired with nearby lakes with exceptionally scenic results. Several of those pairings can be found in this book: Castle Rock and Blue Mountain Lake, Peaked Mountain and its namesake pond, Bald Mountain and Fourth Lake, to name a few.

No such list would be complete without mentioning Lake Lila and Frederica Mountain, located at the headwaters of the Beaver River. For about six months every year, this is one of the most popular destinations in the Adirondacks. The main star is Lake Lila, a 1409-acre gem of a canoe camping destination, and the largest lake entirely within the Forest Preserve. It is home to wind-swept pines, remote sand beaches, and two dozen popular campsites.

Frederica Mountain rises 460 feet above the lake's western shore, with a bald summit ledge that provides a panoramic vista of stunning beauty. For paddlers on the lake, Frederica is an easy diversion, suitable for anyone with a desire to climb a mountain. Not only is the entire lake spread out before you, but a wide selection of distant peaks from throughout the central Adirondack highlands can be identified.

Then the snow and ice come, and the paddlers go home. The month of November is a cold and lonely time at Lake Lila and Frederica Mountain, with only a handful of hunters for visitors. After the gate to the access road closes in early December, the only way to easily penetrate this remote area is by snowshoe, ski, or snowmobile.

For despite the popularity of Lila in the summer, it can only be accessed by driving a very long and bumpy road, way off the main highway. Most visitors come to paddle the waters of the lake, with the climb of Frederica being a pleasing side

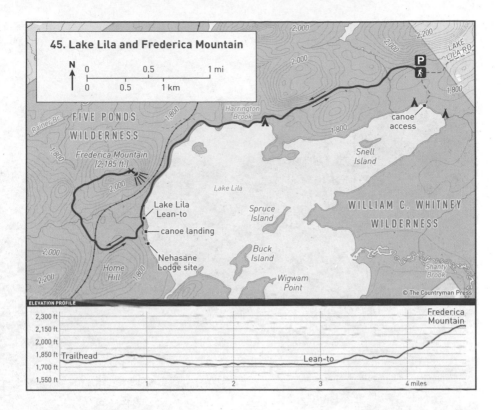

45. Lake Lila and Frederica Mountain

N
0   0.5   1 mi
0   0.5   1 km

FIVE PONDS
WILDERNESS

Rainer Br

Frederica Mountain
(2,185 ft.)

Harrington
Brook

Lake Lila

Snell
Island

canoe
access

Lake Lila
Lean-to

Spruce
Island

WILLIAM C. WHITNEY
WILDERNESS

canoe landing

Buck
Island

Nehasane
Lodge site

Home
Hill

Wigwam
Point

Shanty
Brook

© The Countryman Press

LAKE
LILA RD.

ELEVATION PROFILE

2,300 ft
2,150 ft
2,000 ft
1,850 ft   Trailhead
1,700 ft
1,550 ft

Frederica
Mountain

Lean-to

1   2   3   4 miles

trip. Certainly, a paddling adventure on Lake Lila is an outstanding adventure.

But walking the private road that circles part of the lake is not a horrible experience either, and so this recommended hike is described as a hybrid adventure: canoe to the start of the Frederica Mountain trail if you prefer, or hike the road if the water is too choppy for canoes (a frequent occurrence on this big lake). You are sure to have a memorable day either way.

Prior to state acquisition, Lake Lila was the centerpiece of Nehasane Park, established in the 1890s by Dr. William Seward Webb. This private park included 115,000 acres of forest, including numerous other lakes and small mountains. Webb's claim to fame in the Adirondacks was his Mohawk and Malone Railroad, completed in 1892.

The tracks squeezed between Frederica and Lila, where he built his own private station. Nehasane Lodge on Lila's western shoreline became his rustic getaway.

The lodge was razed years ago, and the train station is in severe disrepair. Lila is now managed as a wilderness resource, except for the train tracks and a road along the shoreline that is still required for private access to other private lands. As you drive the long and bumpy road to the public parking area, you may convince yourself that you've discovered a place no one else knows about. That illusion will evaporate when you see the crowded parking area, which often fills to capacity on summer weekends. If you can arrange a midweek visit, you'll enjoy one of the finest hikes ever.

EARLY SNOW AT FREDERICA MOUNTAIN AND LAKE LILA

GETTING THERE

Follow NY 30 for 7.1 miles north of Long Lake, or 11.5 miles south of Tupper Lake. Turn west onto Sabattis Road, also known as County Road 10. At 2.9 miles, bear left at an intersection beside Little Tupper Lake and continue for another 4.5 miles. The surface turns to gravel and you reach the start of the Lake Lila Access Road at 7.4 miles. Turn left and follow this narrow, winding, bumpy lane for 5.6 miles through private land to the public parking area. The road is suitable for ordinary vehicles, but this would be an inconvenient place to suffer a breakdown.

The Lake Lila Access Road is closed

shoreline. For this hike, follow the second option. The road, which is closed to public motor vehicles and is only used by rangers and members of private hunting clubs, leads westward to a wetland at 0.3 mile. It climbs gently to a notch between two hills before descending gradually to Lake Lila's northern shoreline. Just thirty minutes into the hike, you start enjoying views of the enormous lake, but it's not until the road passes a small beach at 1.7 miles that you can approach the water and formally introduce yourself. Frederica Mountain is the small knob a mile southwest.

From this point forward, the road never strays too far from the water. It leads you past Harrington Brook, one of the lake's larger inlets, and then curves southwest toward the foot of the mountain. The woods are thick enough that you may or may not notice the railroad corridor to your right, at Frederica's base. A path leads to a sandy spot on the shoreline at 2.9 miles, and at 3 miles another spur trail leads left to the lake's only lean-to. It is not Lila's most scenic campsite, but it is a convenient spot to stop and enjoy the watery landscape before beginning the climb.

Just past the lean-to, at 3.1 miles, the road splits. Left leads in just 0.2 mile to the site of the old Nehasane Lodge, which was razed in 1984; now there is a sign to mark its location, but not much else. The right fork is the continuing trail to the mountain. It leads southwest at first, but then swings west to a railroad crossing at 3.6 miles. The railroad may be Webb's most enduring impact on this wild landscape, but it is rarely used by trains anymore.

Beyond the tracks, the private access road becomes a little more primitive, with a few wet spots you'll need to step around. But you are not on this road for

to automobiles every year from early December through mid-May. Only foot access is allowed in the winter.

THE HIKE

Two trails begin at the parking area: the ever-popular canoe carry path to the nearest beach on the shoreline, and the private road around the northern

long. After passing a small, open wetland, the access road begins to climb, and this is where you need to pay attention to the start of the foot trail to the summit on the right. There is a sign, and the turn is usually easy to spot.

Now, for the final 0.5 mile to the summit of Frederica, you are on a wide footpath, which climbs gently to the east. The trail approaches the summit from behind, and the view at first may not seem as open and stunning as I have advertised. There are ledges on each side where the view is better, but the one that is further down to the left is by far the best. Here the entire lake and all of its islands are revealed, with a horizon line made jagged by all of the distant mountains. Several distinctive profiles stand out, including Blue Mountain near the center of the park, and Algonquin in the High Peaks.

SIDE TRIP: FREDERICA MOUNTAIN BY CANOE

The water-based alternative to the route described above involves carrying a canoe or kayak down the 0.3-mile carry trail leading south from the parking area, and then paddling a minimum of 2.5 miles to a landing on the western shore just south of the lean-to. Trail signs mark the spot where you can park your vessel while you climb the mountain. From here it is 1.2 miles to the summit, along a route that is very family-friendly. Follow the short trail up from the canoe landing, turn right onto the private access road, and continue for 0.2 mile to the point where the roads fork. A hairpin turn to the left begins your journey to the mountain, following the same trail described above.

46

Winding Falls Loop

TOTAL DISTANCE: 6.6-mile loop with side trips
HIKING TIME: 3 to 6 hours
ELEVATION CHANGE: rolling terrain
TRAILHEAD GPS COORDINATES: N44° 07′ 18.9″ W74° 32′ 28.1″

Mankind has allowed the Bog River to be a wild and free-flowing stream for only 6 miles, from Hitchins Pond to its mouth on Tupper Lake; above this point, a pair of large dams has converted the river into a continuous stretch of impounded water. However, within the 6 miles below Lows Lower Dam, the Bog is a beautiful little river. It is half rapid and half stillwater, winding through a secluded valley out of sight of the nearest road.

Within this valley lies Winding Falls. For years this 20-foot-tall cascade was a little-known site, as none of the footpaths or logging roads converging here were marked or signed for the benefit of the general public. That status is poised to change, however, since the state is currently (as of 2018) constructing a trail loop around a section of the lower Bog River that is sure to become a favorite spring hike, once it becomes discovered.

What is now a wilderness valley, split between the Round Lake Wilderness to the south and the Horseshoe Lake Wild Forest to the north, was pieced together over the decades through multiple acquisitions. This has resulted in a checkerboard pattern in terms of forest quality, from patches that have been part of the Forest Preserve for about a century to others that were purchased by the state much more recently. As you follow the loop, you will walk along narrow footpaths winding through primeval forests, as well as abandoned gravel roads in varying states of natural reclamation.

But what an outstanding spring adventure! The base loop is 6.6 miles in length, with glimpses of the Bog and its main tributary, Round Lake Stream. The highlight is Winding Falls, which is the river's tallest cascade, but there are several very memorable sections of

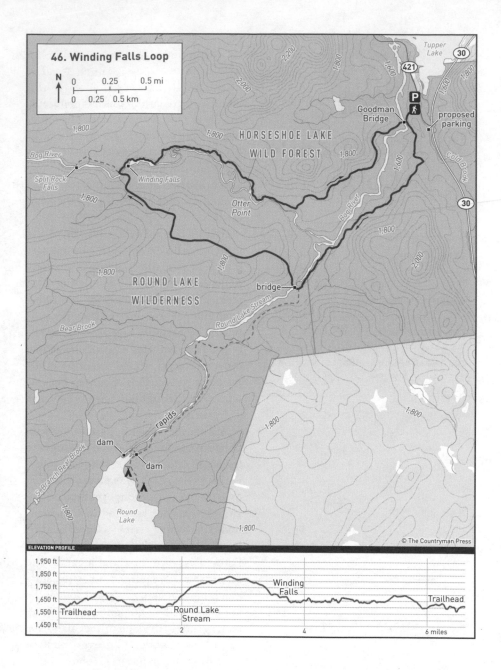

46. Winding Falls Loop

the loop where the trail simply follows closely beside one stream or the other. It is a land-based celebration of rivers.

However, there are two side trips that can be tacked onto this loop that turn this into an unparalleled spring hike, with enough cascading water to satisfy anyone. The longest is the 2.2-mile-long footpath along Round Lake Stream to the eponymous lake at its source; a mile-long section of this creek is a nearly continuous run of fast-moving water, and hiking here never gets old, even after many repeat visits. There are no signs or markers along this trail, but it has not exactly been a secret. Plenty of people have found this trail and enjoyed its charms.

The second optional side trip leads to Split Rock Falls on the Bog River, just 0.3 mile upstream from Winding Falls. The footpath to this site is very crude and is recommended only for expert pathfinders.

As of this writing, the main trail is marked for the benefit of the hiking public, but signage is limited. By the time you read this the new trailhead parking should be completed and all of the bog bridging should be installed. I predict that within a few years, as people learn of the trail's existence, this will become one of the most beloved waterfall hikes in the Adirondacks.

GETTING THERE

Follow NY 30 south from Tupper Lake to the intersection with NY 421. Turn west onto NY 421 and follow it for no more than 0.1 mile, where a gated side road leads left into state land. This is the traditional start of the trail, with room to park along the shoulder.

Note that a new parking area is planned nearby, closer to the highway intersection, and this might result in a slight adjustment to the start of the trail.

THE HIKE

This loop is best enjoyed in a clockwise circuit, following the southern half of the trail first and returning via the northern half. Beginning at the gate marking the traditional start of the trail, follow a wide old road southwest for 0.1 mile to an enormous concrete bridge over a placid section of the Bog River. This is Goodman Bridge, named for the family who once owned and logged this land. The bridge is now one of the largest pedestrian bridges you could ever hope to encounter in the Adirondacks. A handicapped-accessible picnic area is proposed for this location.

The new trail splits immediately before the bridge, and to begin the loop you should turn left (south) onto the yellow-marked trail. It files through a corridor lined with spruce and fir to an open hardwood forest, where the trail intercepts an old logging road at 0.5 mile. Turn right and follow this gentle grade through a forest with an unusually high number of yellow birch trees.

The old road begins high on a hill so far from the river you can barely see it. However, it slowly descends to approach the river just in time to offer a view of the confluence with Round Lake Stream. For a distance of about 0.3 mile, you are quite close to that tributary, a restless stream that offers a steady diet of rolling water. This section leads up to the junction with an overgrown gravel road at 1.8 miles. Although no sign may say as much, the way left is the beginning of the side trip to Round Lake described below.

To reach Winding Falls, bear right onto the old road. This section was added to the Forest Preserve in 2006, completing the state's ownership of the valley. However, the tract was logged extensively by the prior owner, and the forest still has much growing to do before it matches the other parts of the loop. As a result, this next section will probably be the least admired section of the trail for a while, at least until nature has had a chance to cover over the hand of humans.

It begins by crossing a bridge over Round Lake Stream right at the head of the sequence of rapids along which you just hiked. The bridge was originally constructed for log trucks but has since been retrofitted for pedestrians. It begins to climb away from the stream to the northwest, rising through a hardwood forest that, for the moment, is too short to provide much shade. Grasses and other vegetation have already colonized the gravel surface, however, in a demonstration of what natural forces can accomplish if given the chance. There are no markers here, but none are really needed; if you stay on the main road and make no turns, you will be on the trail to Winding Falls.

After an ascent of about 200 feet from the Round Lake Stream bridge, the old road begins to descend slightly. It narrows considerably and turns north, reaching a boundary with an older parcel of state land at 3 miles. The route bears left here and for a brief time becomes an excellent trail again, cutting a corner through a stand of large sugar maples. Within moments, though, you reach another parcel with signs of extensive logging, but by this point you should be able to hear Winding Falls off in the distance.

At 3.6 miles you reach another old bridge, this one spanning the Bog River. Upstream, the river is placid and still, but downstream the water is starting its run toward the top of the falls. The wood portion of this bridge rotted away years ago, revealing a set of steel I-beams across which DEC has constructed a narrow footbridge. Turtles seem to return every year to deposit eggs in the gravel surface at each end of the bridge, although that might change if human foot traffic increases with the opening of the trail.

At the far end of the bridge, the blue-marked trail along the north side of the river bears right off the road. It passes through a small clearing that was previously an outstanding campsite, both solitary and scenic, but is now undesirable since it literally straddles the new trail. (The rugged path to Split Rock Falls, described below, can be found by continuing straight at the junction.)

The marked trail doesn't quite lead to Winding Falls, but a side path leads along the riverbank to its top. A narrow ridge of rock provides an open view of the upper half of the waterfall and an overlook of the bottom half. The waterfall is an impressive sight at any time of the year due to its size and configuration, but it is especially so in early spring when the combined snowmelt of an entire watershed is funneled through the rock gorge that gives the falls its name. The river makes an S-turn through this gorge, exiting with a distinct offset from its upstream course, hence the name. A trio of memorial stones nearby pays tribute to three fathers who once maintained a hunting camp nearby, and some commercial maps have taken the liberty of calling this "Pa's Falls." Don't believe it for a second; the name Winding Falls has the weight of history behind it, in use since at least 1858, when a travel writer named Joel T. Headley passed this way.

The new hiking trail swings briefly away from the falls before circling around the wide pool at its foot. Because of the winding nature of the cataract, there is no one place where you can see the entire drop at once, although from the farthest point on the pool you can glimpse part of the upper waterfall above and behind the lower ramp-like portion.

Most of the next 1.3 miles of trail is new construction—or rather, the improvement of what was previously a very primitive footpath. It follows the north bank of the Bog River quite closely,

BOG RIVER AT OTTER POINT

WINDING FALLS

long stillwater at a point known locally as Otter Point. The valley narrows considerably here, and the river becomes a noisy stream over a rocky bed. The trail begins to pull away from the river at this point, sidling up a hill to intersect the end of another old logging road at 5.3 miles. This old road was not constructed with gravel, and its surface is riddled with pockets of mud. For this reason, the hiking trail veers off of it at several points to avoid the wettest mires. It contours a hillside high above the river—and so far removed from it that you have no views of the water for quite a while. On the other hand, the woods are filled in early May with a glorious display of tiny wildflowers called Carolina spring beauties. You might find entire acres of them, more than I've seen anywhere else.

When you do glimpse the river again on your right, it is a sign that your loop is almost complete. A moment later, at 6.5 miles, you reach Goodman Bridge. Cross this wide span to the far side of the river, where you should recognize the trail junction where the loop began. Bearing left, you will be back at NY 421 in just five minutes.

SIDE TRIPS

1. **Round Lake Stream.** The first of the two recommended side trips begins 1.8 miles from NY 421 and leads an additional 2.2 miles to Round Lake, adding a total of 4.4 miles to the day's itinerary. The route is not desirable just because it ends at a large, undeveloped lake—although that is a good justification—but because it passes so close to the wild and scenic outlet stream, a place where cascades abound. The downside is that this trail is not marked, and novice hikers

passing through an older parcel of state land where the woods are quite tall and handsome. The river here is placid, not tumultuous, and it winds between alder beds and banks lined with tall red spruce. The trail veers inland only where wetlands and other obstacles force it to do so.

I hope this part of the trail weathers well, but I fear that it might not. As a faint footpath, it held up well against the minimal traffic it saw from year to year. As a potentially popular state hiking trail, it might be vulnerable to erosion, especially where it ventures onto the soft and moist soils near the river's edge. The installation of new bridges may help, but the route may not be sustainable in the long term. I'd love to be proven wrong, because this really is a pretty route, one that I would like to savor time and again.

At 4.9 miles you reach the foot of a

will have trouble navigating the mile-long approach to the stream.

Upon reaching the junction with the overgrown logging road near Round Lake Stream as described above, bear left and follow the old road southwest for 0.5 mile. Watch closely for the side trail that bears right, continuing the southwesterly course at a point where the road swings southeast. The next 0.5-mile section follows what used to be a primitive tote road but is now a wide trail through a young forest. It skirts a swampy area and approaches the foot of the rapids on Round Lake Stream, opposite the mouth of Bear Brook.

The fun part of the hike begins here. The trail cuts a corner through the thick coniferous forest and comes out beside the first of the cascades, where rock ledges invite you out for a closer look. The narrow footpath is now fairly easy to follow; the thick woods make it unlikely you will venture in the wrong direction. At any rate, you merely have to keep the stream close by on your right, enjoying each new cascade as you encounter them. This, too, was part of the 2006 land acquisition, but here the prior landowner preserved a buffer of mature forest alongside the stream. The sense of wilderness is quite strong.

Further upstream, the sight of long rock walls in the streambed will catch your attention. These were created by lumbermen interested in straightening the river's course during their spring log drive to Tupper Lake, and the ones here are among the longest such structures in the Adirondacks.

At 2.1 miles you pass one half of the concrete dam that enlarges Round Lake (the other half is on the far side of a rocky island) as the trail becomes more road-like again. You should continue at least as far as the first shoreline campsite at 2.2 miles, although the trail does continue another 0.2 mile to another camp-site—this one larger, with its own nearby sand beach. Either way, you'll need to turn back around and revisit the cascades on the outlet stream to continue the Winding Falls Loop.

2. **Split Rock Falls.** This small waterfall on the Bog River is a worthy compan-ion to Winding Falls, but it is not part of the new state hiking trail. The herd path that leads to it is actually quite rough, with a key turn that may be so hard to find that this side trip cannot be recommended for people who are not comfortable navigating off-trail.

After crossing the old logging bridge immediately upstream from Winding Falls, keep on the aban-doned logging road as it leads north-west. Just 0.1 mile from the bridge bear left at a prominent fork, follow-ing a rough tote road that is being crowded by a growth of young spruce trees. Just after dipping through a wet area, this road starts to climb to the northwest. This is your clue to look for a flagged path leading left. It is incredibly faint—so much so that many people might not even register it as a path, although it is occasionally used as an improvised canoe carry.

This faint trail leads to the foot of a stillwater on the Bog River at 0.3 mile. Split Rock Falls is a few yards downstream. It is only about six or eight feet tall, but given the size of the river, this is still a worthy destination.

Hitchins Pond Overlook

TOTAL DISTANCE: 6.8 miles round-trip

HIKING TIME: 2.5 hours

VERTICAL RISE: 450 feet

TRAILHEAD GPS COORDINATES: N44° 08' 02.7" W74° 38' 46.2"

Hitchins Pond Overlook is a spine of rock rising out of a landscape better known for its bogs and lakes—and indeed, bogs and lakes form a significant part of the view from its top. In a region where most people come to paddle, the overlook provides a sweeping vista of a landscape that is nearly impassable to humans outside the established travel corridors.

This ridge, which is not named on most topographic maps, stands sentry above not just Hitchins Pond, but above the beginning of Lows Lake as well. Technically, it anchors the easternmost end of the Five Ponds Wilderness, although seventy percent of the hike is anything but wilderness. That's because it follows a service road from Horseshoe Lake to Lows Upper Dam, a large concrete structure that impounds the Bog River to create Lows Lake. Much of the foot traffic through this area is in the form of paddlers, as they carry canoes and kayaks around the dam from the pond to the lake.

The original dams on this part of the Bog River were created by Abbot Augustus Low in 1903 and 1907 to supply power to his various commercial operations. Low maintained a lodge on the shores of Hitchins Pond, but rustic pleasure was not his only interest in this forest retreat; from here he exported lumber, spring water, maple syrup, and berry preserves to distant cities, taking advantage of the fact that William Seward Webb's Mohawk and Malone Railroad cut right through his estate.

The dams you see now are modern reconstructions that serve no other purpose than to sustain the two lakes for recreation; otherwise, all that remains of Low's estate is a handful of ruins near the Upper Dam. The state acquired this region in 1985 and has been managing

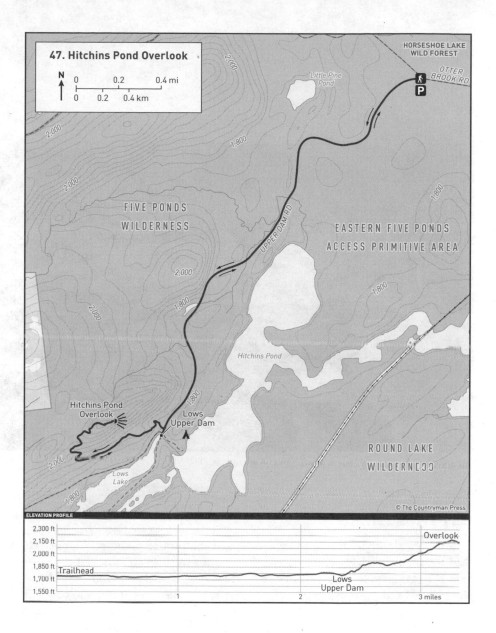

© The Countryman Press

ELEVATION PROFILE

it as a paddling destination ever since. Despite its artificial origins, Lows Lake is one of the most favored canoe camping areas in the Adirondacks.

The overlook above Hitchins Pond is a notable exception to this paddle-centric focus. This short hiking trail might be most commonly climbed by passing canoers and kayakers, but it can also be reached entirely by land. Although this approach adds significant distance to the hike, it is all on easy grades through an intriguing array of open wetlands. The road-based portion is a nature walk through unusual habitats with birding opportunities, and the climb is a reasonably easy hike to one of the finest perches in the western Adirondacks.

HITCHINS POND AS SEEN FROM THE TOP OF ITS OVERLOOK

GETTING THERE

Follow NY 30 south from Tupper Lake to the intersection with NY 421. Turn west onto NY 421 and follow it for 4.6 miles to Horseshoe Lake, 5.7 miles to the end of the pavement, 6.6 miles to the railroad tracks, and 7.4 miles to the start of the service road to Lows Upper Dam on the left. Parking is available on the shoulder of the road. Note that plowing ends well short of this trailhead in the winter.

THE HIKE

The service road to Lows Upper Dam is 2.4 miles long. It is wide enough to walk two abreast, it features no hills of note, and it is easy to sustain a brisk hiking pace that entire distance. The attraction lies in the wetlands that it passes through—areas that you would not otherwise have access to, such as fens filled with black spruce and marshes interrupted with small beaver ponds. You may notice a large rocky mountain in the distance; this is Silver Lake Mountain, an impressive landmark that lies mostly on private land to the west.

The road passes the foot of one rocky hillside that appears to be the twin to the Hitchins Pond Overlook, at least from below, but it continues southwest another 0.7 mile past this point before

downstream for 0.2 mile. Along the way, this carry trail passes the remains of Low's main lodge, marked only by its stone foundations today. There is a designated campsite about 300 feet north of the carry trail on Hitchins Pond, frequented mostly by paddlers but equally attractive to backpackers as well.

A sign near the Upper Dam marks the beginning of the foot trail to Hitchins Pond Overlook. It leads northwest into a small glen, but almost immediately swings sharp left onto a bit of high ground. The mountainside is steep, but the trail ventures well out of its way to find a gentler approach to the summit. The result is a moderate grade with a mile-long ascent and just a little over 400 vertical feet of climbing. Aside from a small ledge or two, nothing about this climb prevents it from being suitable for families, other than the longish approach from the road.

The trail approaches the open rock ledge from behind, with an initial view eastward across Hitchins Pond and its winding outlet to the distant High Peaks. You can follow the spine of rock for about 300 feet to a plaque commemorating Low's son, A. A. Low, a total of 3.4 miles from your car. The view becomes even less obstructed, ranging from Frederica Mountain (can you pick it out among the rolling hills to the southwest?) to Algonquin and Whiteface in the east, about 34 and 42 miles away, respectively. The railroad cuts straight through the open bogs adjacent to Hitchins Pond.

you reach your actual destination. Here, 2.4 miles from where you parked, you reach the start of the trail up the mountain to your right, next to a set of crumbling foundations.

However, before you climb the ridge, it is worth exploring your immediate surroundings. Lows Upper Dam is just ahead, with the slender outlet arm of Lows Lake extending southwest behind it. A private access road crosses the top of the dam and bends around the northern side of the lake, and the canoe carry trail to Hitchins Pond follows the river

When you've had your fill of this view, the return route is a simple matter of retracing your steps back down to the dam and out through the bogs along the service road.

48

Mount Arab

TOTAL DISTANCE: 2 miles round-trip	
HIKING TIME: 1.5 hours	
VERTICAL RISE: 730 feet	
TRAILHEAD GPS COORDINATES: N44° 12' 48.1" W74° 35' 45.0"	

Mount Arab is a short-and-simple climb to a fire tower with a sweet view of the Tupper Lake region. If you are looking for a straightforward climb suitable for just about any member of your family, then you will be very pleased with this mountain. There are no frills, no long approaches, no long drives far from the nearest population center. You can be up and down in just a couple hours—back in Tupper Lake in time for lunch.

When seen from a distance, the mountain's profile is broad and flat-topped, like a fugitive from the Catskills laying low here in the Adirondacks. It stands apart from other mountains, allowing its views to be far-ranging in nature while at the same time making Arab seem isolated. But this sense of isolation is also one of the things making the view unique, because no other summit can provide the perspective that Arab offers.

The fire tower is staffed by a summit steward in the summer, and it is an excellent snowshoe hike in the winter. If you happen to find the steward on duty, he or she will be happy to help you identify all of the mountains in view. Brochures found in the trailhead registration box provide keys to all of the numbered waypoints along the trail, helping you understand the nature of the mountain in addition to its scenic pleasures.

There is one question that the brochure doesn't resolve, though, and that is the mountain's proper name. Topographic maps label this 2,539-foot summit as Arab Mountain, while just about everyone else calls it Mount Arab. The latter style is also repeated in the names of a nearby road, hamlet, and lake, and therefore that is the name used in this book as well.

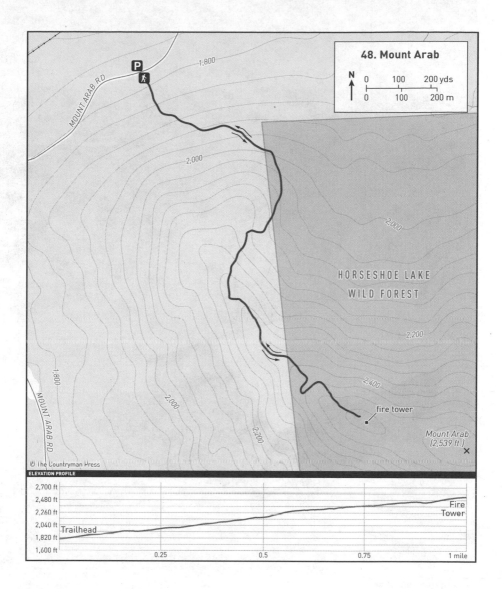

GETTING THERE

Follow NY 3 west from downtown Tupper Lake, passing the dam at Piercefield Flow on the Raquette River. Just after the side road leading into the hamlet of Piercefield, turn left (west) onto County Road 62, and then left again onto Mount Arab Road at 1.8 miles. You cross the tracks of the Adirondack Railroad and reach the trailhead at 2.6 miles. The trail starts on the left, with parking on the right.

THE HIKE

One of the striking things about this hike is how so much of the forest consists of hardwoods, with only a few conifers on the summit—despite the fact that

THE SUMMIT OF MOUNT ARAB

a nearby hamlet is called Conifer. Beginning across the road from the parking area, the red-marked trail begins to climb immediately. The first 0.4 mile of the trail is on private land protected by a public conservation easement—meaning that hiking access is unrestricted, but that logging might occur nearby. As if to illustrate this point, the trail briefly sidles up to a strip of forest that has been thinned in a recent timber harvest.

Then the trail swings southeast, circling around a lower portion of the mountain to reach state land at 0.4 mile. If you picked up one of the interpretive pamphlets at the register, it will help you identify some of the trees that grow

placed at some of the sections most ~~sus~~ceptible to erosion.

The worst of the climbing is over at about 0.6 mile, when the trail reaches the top of the ridgeline. Then it becomes a pleasant traverse interrupted only by the presence of a wide rock wall. The trail swings right to flank that wall, making one brief-but-steep scramble to the summit at 1 mile.

The top of Mount Arab is hardly a wilderness setting. It is the home of a well-preserved cabin (still used by the summer summit stewards), a few small benches, and of course the fire tower. There are a few open ledges on the south side of the summit that offer views southwest across Mount Arab Lake and Eagle Crag Lake, with the rolling hills of the Conifer-Emporium Easement and Five Ponds Wilderness beyond.

The full view, however, can only be found by climbing the tower. There you can look north along the timberlands that flank the Raquette River, or you can look east past Tupper Lake toward the High Peaks. Of those distant mountains, Whiteface is the most prominent, due to its near-perfect alignment with Tupper's former Oval Wood Dish plant. Panels mounted in the tower's cab will help you pick out the Seward Range, Mount Matumbla, and other landmarks even if no steward is on duty.

Oddly, the tower was not placed on the mountain's highest point, and therefore the view is not as unobstructed as it could be. But for the amount of effort invested in this hike, there can no cause for complaint.

beside the trail, most notably the tall specimens of sugar maple and white ash. The climb alternates between moderately steep and gentle, with rock steps

49

Grass River Waterfalls

TOTAL DISTANCE: 4.8 miles round-trip in eight separate walks

HIKING TIME: 5 minutes to 1 hour per hike

ELEVATION CHANGE: rolling terrain

TRAILHEAD GPS COORDINATES: N44° 13' 10.6" W74° 51' 07.0" (southern end of Tooley Pond Road)

The format of this outing to the Grass River and its various branches differs from the forty-nine other trips in this book. Rather than a single trail leading to a single destination, the trip described here is as much a driving tour as it is a walking tour. This chapter describes an entire string of short hikes, each leading to a truly remarkable cascade. The theme of your day spent exploring the Grass River waterfalls might best be described as "drive, park, hike, repeat." Each individual walk ranges from only 200 feet to 0.6 mile in length; and while this may not sound like much, you can easily fill an entire day with these half-mile hikes!

To be more specific, there are eight waterfalls on this tour, none of them more than a few minutes' walk from the nearest parking area. The Grass River's three branches drain the northwestern corner of the Adirondack Park and converge at two points just outside the park boundaries. The South Branch is the largest of the three and features the most waterfalls, but there are additional sites on the North Branch as well as the river's main stem.

The only downside to these hikes is that only two have marked trails (three, if you count the canoe carry at Copper Rock Falls). However, all of them have trails of some kind, and even if markers and signs aren't present the routes are easy to find, with one or two exceptions. None of the hikes are strenuous, and they attract explorers of all ages and abilities.

Tooley Pond Road parallels the South Branch and provides access to all of its waterfall trails. It is a winding town road maintained all year round, paved for most of its length. This road leads to Clare Road (County Road 27) in Degrasse, which leads to the trailhead

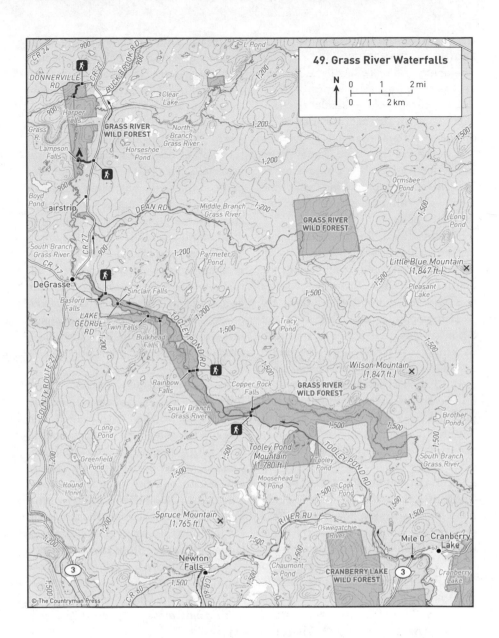

49. Grass River Waterfalls

N
0   1   2 mi
0   1   2 km

for Lampson Falls, the largest and most famous of all the cascades. In turn, CR 27 connects with Donnerville Road, whereupon you'll find the trailhead for Harper Falls on the North Branch Grass River.

The only way to visit all eight sites in one day—and what better way to spend a sunny day in April!—is to tackle them systematically. What I recommend is starting at the hamlet of Cranberry Lake, where Tooley Pond Road begins, and setting the trip odometer in your car to 0.0. The easiest way to find most of the trailheads is by marking the miles as you go. Thus each trail description here begins with an odometer reading.

MILE 0.0: TOOLEY POND ROAD BEGINS IN CRANBERRY LAKE

The south end of Tooley Pond Road is very easy to find, as it begins on NY 3 just to the west of the hamlet of Cranberry Lake, and immediately beside the bridge over the Oswegatchie River. As you make the turn onto Tooley Pond Road, set your car's trip odometer to 0.0. The starting points for each of the eight walks will be measured from this reference point.

Tooley Pond Road parallels the Oswegatchie briefly before cutting across the watershed divide toward the South Branch Grass River. At 5.8 miles you pass Tooley Pond, where there are paddling opportunities. Then at 5.9 and 6.3 miles you pass a pair of trailhead parking areas for Tooley Pond Mountain, a small hill that once hosted a fire tower. Two marked trails now converge on the 1,780-foot summit, which has minimal views. The combined length of both trails is only 1.4 miles, with only about a 250-foot vertical rise.

MILE 8.1: COPPER ROCK FALLS

Continuing northwest past Tooley Pond Mountain, slow down as you near the 8-mile mark from Cranberry Lake. Here the road descends a quarter-mile-long hill, and the unmarked path to the first waterfall begins at its bottom, at 8.1 miles. Look for a paint daub on a tree, as well as one or two small signs marking the start of the path. There is a bit of space to park on the shoulder on the right side of the road.

Once you identify the start of the path, the rest is quite easy, as there is nothing faint about this route. It leads north from the road straight to the river in a span of just 0.1 mile, then it turns right to follow the South Branch upstream. Your first look at the lower portion of Copper Rock Falls occurs right away. Rather than a single cataract, Copper Rock is a prolonged cascade over a series of ledges.

This is not all there is to see, however. The path continues upstream for another 0.4 mile to visit two other waterfalls. This part of the trail appears to be unmarked, but when you turn around, you should notice yellow canoe carry markers, placed for the benefit of downstream paddlers. Above the lower, gentler portion of Copper Rock Falls the river emerges from a small gorge. You'll find one small cataract midway up this gorge and its twin at the head of the gorge. The canoe carry continues past this site to a pool well above the falls, a total of 0.5 mile from your car.

MILE 10.8: RAINBOW FALLS

Rainbow Falls has always been my favorite site on the South Branch. The river is funneled into a narrow gorge here, with a thunderous drop at its head. The raw power of nature is on display at this site, and the river seems like a wild beast resisting its captivity within the rocky cage. Adding to the tension is the fact that the best overlooks are rock ledges with sheer drops into the gorge.

The unmarked trail to Rainbow begins at the 10.8-mile mark, on the left side of the road. One small sign may be all that indicates its existence. The walk is just 0.3 mile long and takes only ten minutes. It begins in what used to be a small clearing, leads west through an open hardwood forest with almost no understory, and then hugs the left edge of a second small clearing.

The river is just ahead. Reenter the woods and cross a small footbridge over a side channel, where the path veers right toward the main ledge at the top of the falls. Another side path leads to an overlook on the river just above the waterfall, and the main trail ends at a perch partway down the gorge. This last viewpoint may be the most photogenic.

The waterfall is about twenty-five feet high and quite powerful, especially in spring. It sends up a cloud of mist that dampens the entire gorge.

MILE 13.3: BULKHEAD FALLS

This may be the hardest of the eight waterfalls to find, partly because the path is so seldom used. About 2 miles from Rainbow Falls, Tooley Pond Road makes a broad bend parallel with a corresponding bend on the South Branch. Just after this curve, the road starts to pull away from the river once more, but just as it does so, at 13.3 miles, look for a small NO MOTORIZED VEHICLES sign on the left side of the road. This marks the start of an old trail that almost nobody uses; if it weren't for the sign, the path would be invisible.

The walking distance to the river is only 450 feet. The faint path leads through a stand of pines to an enormous pool, with Bulkhead Falls a short distance to the left. You'll need to follow the rocks along the riverbank to find a closer view, but this waterfall is worth the effort. The river forces its way through a gap in a rock ledge, with a total drop of at least twelve feet. Bulkhead is just as impressive as any of its neighbors, so the absence of visitors is inexplicable.

MILE 13.6: TWIN FALLS

This is the most frustrating of the eight sites. Twin Falls is exactly what the name says: a pair of waterfalls on the South Branch separated by a small island. The eastern cascade is visible from the road,

BULKHEAD FALLS

but the best place from which to view the western cascade is a parcel of private land off-limits to the general public.

What makes this frustrating is the absence of a bridge to the island. The channel that separates it from the road was once a millrace, and you can still see the man-made rock wall that lines the waterway. In low water you may be able to safely cross the stream to get to the island, where you will find an old kiln in the woods. Both structures are all that remain of a small blast furnace operation, where iron ore was smelted for a brief period in the 1860s. At the downstream end of the island, you will find a beach made of slag, a glassy byproduct.

Without a bridge, the island is inaccessible for much of the year, at which time you can merely enjoy the eastern cascade from the road. You might not even need to get out of your car for that.

MILE 14.7: SINCLAIR FALLS

About 1.1 miles past Twin Falls, Tooley Pond Road reaches an intersection with Lake George Road, 14.7 miles from Cranberry Lake. There is a large parking area at this intersection. Sinclair Falls is 400 feet away through the trees, but the best way to get there is to walk down Lake George Road. Just before the bridge over the river, a well-used path leads downstream beside the sinuous cascade, formed by a ledge of rock with a gentle slope. The path leads to the pool at the bottom of the cascade and then fades away in the woods less than 300 feet from the road.

MILE 15.3: BASFORD FALLS

This waterfall offers a pleasing combination of seclusion and accessibility. The hemlock and pine forest beside the river has no understory, and rock ledges make it easy to explore the waterfall from top to bottom, ensuring this site has nothing to hide. The path is just the right length for a short hike, suitable for any age.

The unmarked trail begins just 0.6 mile past the Lake George Road intersection; look for an old logging road with a pair of metal posts on the left side of the road. Walk between the posts, following the trail along one hilltop, then down and up to the next knoll, and finally down a 100-foot grade to the river, about 0.3 mile from the road. Basford Falls is a gentle giant, impressive in size but easy to explore.

MILE 16.7: DEGRASSE

Tooley Pond Road comes to an end 16.7 miles from Cranberry Lake, at an intersection with Clare Road (also known as County Road 27) in the hamlet of Degrasse. Turn right (north) here to reach the remaining two Grass River waterfalls.

MILE 20.7: LAMPSON FALLS

This is the largest of all the waterfalls on the Grass River, and the most popular. Lampson Falls is so far removed from the major population centers in the Adirondack Park that it is easy to forget that this is one of the park's most famous sites. The 0.5-mile trail to the top of the falls is designed for universal access, including access by people in wheelchairs. An extension of the trail leads down to a rocky point below the falls, and this part is much more rugged. On some weekends there may be dozens of people gathered here at any given time, by contrast with the other waterfalls in this chapter.

Follow CR 27 north for 4 miles beyond the end of Tooley Pond Road, past a rural airstrip to the marked trailhead with parking on both sides of the road. The trail, which begins to the left of the highway, is a gated road that leads west toward the river. One fork leads to a sunny rock at the end of the stillwater above the falls, and the wheelchair trail leads to an overlook beside the cascade. The rugged foot trail to the base of the falls forks right off the wheelchair trail, descending to an open area where people have obviously been camping, and then up onto the rock ledge that juts out like an arrow into the river. Here you will find the most photogenic viewing points, no more than 0.6 mile from your car.

Lampson Falls is about 20 to 30 feet high, but the rock ledge over which the water spills is about five times as wide. The river is much larger here; this section represents the combined output of the north and middle branches.

However, as the summer progresses and the river level drops, more and more of that rock becomes exposed.

MILE 23.4: DONNERVILLE ROAD AND HARPER FALLS

Donnerville Road is a left turn from CR 27 about 6.7 miles north of Degrasse, or 23.4 miles from Cranberry Lake. This is a seasonal gravel road that leads in 0.6 mile to the trailhead for Harper Falls, the lone cascade on the North Branch Grass River. The marked trail follows an old road southwest for 0.6 mile to the river. A side trail leads downstream beside the North Branch, but the waterfalls (there are actually two cascades here) are to the left. This was also a mill site, with stone foundations and a millrace to enjoy.

LAMPSON FALLS

50

High Falls Loop

TOTAL DISTANCE: 15.8-mile loop, with 0.5 mile of road between trailheads

HIKING TIME: 7 hours

ELEVATION CHANGE: rolling terrain

TRAILHEAD GPS COORDINATES: N44° 07′ 59.2″ W74° 54′ 55.1″

The Five Ponds Wilderness is the largest of the protected areas in the western Adirondacks, accessible by a combination of canoe routes and hiking trails. Of the latter, the 15.8-mile High Falls Loop is one of the finer options. This trail begins and ends at the hamlet of Wanakena, leading to several of the same landmarks enjoyed by paddlers on the Oswegatchie River.

This is a route with almost no major hills, but lots of wetness. The Oswegatchie headwater region is known for its extensive network of wetlands, with populations of beavers just about everywhere. Their impromptu ponds can spring up at nearly any point along the trail, forcing hikers to either make a detour or walk through the water. Interspersed throughout these meadows, ponds, and bogs are stands of black cherry, white pine, and the occasional black spruce. There are several places where you can view the river, including High Rock and Ross Rapids, as well as Dead Creek Flow on Cranberry Lake.

Of course, the focal point of the loop is High Falls on the Oswegatchie. "High" in this case is a relative term, since the 15-foot-tall waterfall is hardly superlative, but it is a distinctive landmark as well as a traditional campsite. There are two lean-tos (only one of which is accessible by trail) and several campsites at High Falls, so although the entire loop can be completed in one long day's outing, most people prefer to carry an overnight pack and split the loop up into two or more days.

No one disputes the wildness of this area today, but the story of the High Falls Loop's origin is hardly limited to hiking and wilderness preservation. In 1901, the Rich Lumber Company purchased this entire area and established the hamlet of Wanakena as its company

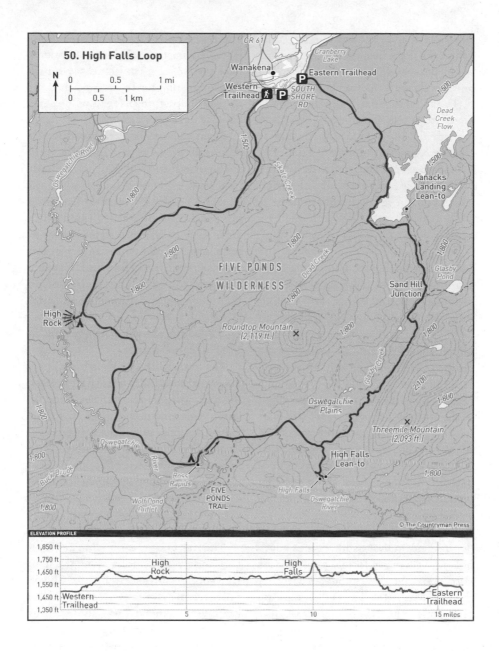

50. High Falls Loop

ELEVATION PROFILE

town. It extended two branch railroads into what is now the Five Ponds Wilderness, choosing to haul out its loads of lumber by mechanical means rather than by floating them down the river. The company was active for only a decade, however, before vacating the area and moving to Vermont.

The state acquired the land in 1919, after a forest fire had devastated much of the area. The two logging railroad corridors became truck trails, managed for emergency access to the interior but also used by the public for recreation. The eastern railroad ended at Dead Creek Flow, but the western railroad extended most of the way to High Falls. When the state designated the area as wilderness in the 1970s, both routes became closed to motor vehicles.

Today, the High Falls Loop is a key part of the Cranberry Lake 50, a long-distance backpacking trail that circumnavigates Cranberry Lake. For those who are not prepared to devote the better part of a week to a hike, the High Falls Loop is a very good alternative.

GETTING THERE

The trailheads for the High Falls Loop are located in Wanakena, near Cranberry Lake. To find them, follow County Road 61 south from NY 3, bearing right at two intersections onto South Shore Road. At 1.2 miles you cross the bridge over the Oswegatchie River, and at 1.3 miles you should look for a road turning off to the right. The western half of the trail begins here, but you cannot park here because a nearby residence requires it for access to a driveway. Parking has traditionally been accommodated at a small turnoff about 100 feet farther along South Shore Road, near a tennis court.

The eastern leg begins another 0.4 mile down the road, 1.7 miles south of NY 3. There is a formal parking area here, which can hold about ten cars. For the purposes of this loop, either parking area works equally well.

THE HIKE

The two halves of this loop are not equal in length, in terms of the distance between Wanakena and High Falls. The western route is 8.9 miles long, whereas the eastern leg is 6.7 miles. Although it is longer, the western side of the loop is nearly all level; the east side is shorter

but contains the most hills (none of which are particularly large). I prefer to hike the western trail first, saving the shorter section for the second day, and so this chapter describes the loop in a counterclockwise direction.

From the western trailhead (a 0.5-mile walk from the parking area at the eastern trailhead) the trail heads southwest past a wetland that occupies the site of an old Rich Lumber Company millpond. Part of this trail is used by Wanakena to access a water source on state land, but otherwise the former railroad has aged into a fine trail. It swings west and passes an enormous wetland, then it continues southwest to a junction at 3.8 miles. The way is so flat and easy that it should take about ninety minutes to cover this distance.

The trail to the right is a must-see detour. It leads in 0.1 mile to High Rock, the first designated campsite along the loop. The name derives from the giant ledge that rises out of the Oswegatchie River, providing one of the best overlooks of the river's vast floodplain. Even if no one is camped here, most paddlers on the river cannot resist the urge to stop at High Rock for a break as they pass by.

The risk of beaver flooding begins to appear as you continue along the main trail southeast from High Rock. The old rail corridor detours away from the river, skirting the extensive wetlands that surround the Oswegatchie. At the time the lumber company constructed this grade circa 1903, beavers had been extirpated from the Adirondacks and were not a consideration, and therefore the railroad was not built that high above the surrounding waterways. But now that beavers have long since resettled the region, they have become quite good at flooding certain low-lying sections of the trail. Sometimes you can skirt around the ponds or cross on top of the dam itself, and at other times the beaver flows turn out not to be an issue. However, anyone hiking this area should come prepared for wet conditions.

Your next good look at the Oswegatchie comes at 6.9 miles, where the old railroad grade draws near a straight section of the river. At the head of this run is a spot called Ross Rapids, where the water flows swiftly past a few protruding rocks, just below a small designated campsite (#28 in the river's numbering system). You glimpse one more bend in the river before veering inland to meet a junction with the Five Ponds Trail at 7.5 miles. That route heads south across the river into the heart of the wilderness.

From the junction it is just a 45-minute walk to High Falls, with another look at the river at a site known historically as Carter Landing. The trail cuts through the wetlands surrounding Glasby Creek at this point, where some amount of wetness is almost guaranteed. The trail itself has a firm surface, but there is no way to defend it against the potential for beaver flooding—and if the trail is underwater, there is no high ground for a detour. The only way to keep your boots dry in that case is to take them off.

After crossing a bridge over Glasby Creek, the trail climbs just a few feet and leaves the wetland behind. It passes through a pine-filled forest, with glimpses of the Oswegatchie Plains to the north. The plains are a heath-filled area where trees have struggled to take hold, except for pockets of tamarack

AT THE TOP OF HIGH FALLS

VIEW OF THE OSWEGATCHIE RIVER FROM HIGH ROCK

and black spruce. An older version of the High Falls Loop once cut a corner through the plains, but that was abandoned decades ago and is now overgrown.

At 8.7 miles, just a short distance beyond the Oswegatchie Plains, you reach a junction with the eastern half of the loop trail, which leads northeast (left). High Falls is located 0.4 mile away on the trail to the right. This last section was not part of the railroad grade, and so the way is less flat. You pass the rusted

frame of an old log skidder on the right before emerging at a well-used campsite at High Falls, 9.1 miles from Wanakena.

A canoe carry trail leads left and right. The way right leads to the part of the river below the falls. There is a clearing beside the carry trail where people have been camping illegally for years; the state has tried to close the site by posting signs and planting seedlings, but the signs turn up missing and the small trees get trampled. Nevertheless, rocks on the riverbank nearby offer

the best views of High Falls, which in the grand scheme of the Adirondack Park are not that tall, but are definitely noteworthy as a landmark on the otherwise-placid Oswegatchie.

The top half of the canoe carry trail provides easy access to the massive rock ledges that make up the waterfall, with a side trail leading into the woods to one of the two lean-tos at High Falls. The concrete piers that stand incongruously above the falls were once pylons for a footbridge that led to the second lean-to on the other side of the river; in one of its weirder management actions,

the state removed the bridge for wilderness aesthetic reasons but left the pylons—the least appealing parts of the structure—where they stood. Now, without the bridge, the second lean-to is primarily used by paddlers.

To begin the return journey to Wanakena, you will first need to backtrack to the junction near the Oswegatchie Plains. This time take the right fork, which leads northeast. The trail makes a serpentine course through a blowdown area, winding sharply between broken logs and upturned root masses as it rises over a knoll and descends on the other side. Compared to what you have seen so far, this is a very rugged area! The blowdown was caused by a July 1995 windstorm that flattened thousands of acres throughout the Five Ponds Wilderness. Imagine what trails like this must have looked like in the immediate aftermath of that storm; it took several years for trail crews to reopen all of the impacted routes.

You pass out of the blowdown area and enter a pine forest dotted by the occasional beaver pond. The trail meanders to the base of Threemile Mountain, where three small waterfalls at various points tumble down from the mountain's shoulder on the right, their streams disappearing westward toward Glasby Creek.

Relatively new bridges simplify what used to be a tricky crossing of Glasby Creek, and then you ascend slightly to an intersection called Sand Hill Junction at 12.2 miles; it may take you two hours to cover the 2.7 miles from the Oswegatchie Plains. Right leads to Glasby Pond, Cat Mountain, and other points along the Cranberry Lake 50. Cat Mountain is a small eminence 1.4 miles to the east, and it offers the only mountain views of the region. If you have time and interest for a short side adventure, this is one of the best options available.

What follows is an enjoyable descent along an old roadway as the High Falls Loop continues north toward Dead Creek Flow. At 13 miles you reach the side trail to Janacks Landing, a lean-to about 0.2 mile away on the shoreline of the flow, which is actually a long bay on the southwest side of Cranberry Lake. The main trail veers west to begin a 0.9-mile-long detour around the tip of the flow, a section that includes one more stream crossing where beaver flooding has been an on-gain-off-again issue for years. This section leads to a nice camping area at 13.9 miles where the Rich Lumber Company's eastern railroad once ended beside the flow.

The final 1.9 miles of the loop are very similar in character to the entire western half, in that it follows a level railroad corridor. There are a few more views of Dead Creek Flow at first before pulling inland, where there are pockets of blowdown from the 1995 storm and at least three spots where the potential for beaver flooding is very real. It takes only about forty minutes to cover this distance, bringing you back to Wanakena and closing the loop after 15.8 miles in the backcountry.